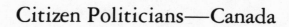

Citizen Politicians—Canada

Citizen Politicians—Canada:
Party Officials in a Democratic Society

Allan Kornberg

Joel Smith

Harold D. Clarke

Carolina Academic Press, Durham, North Carolina

1979

© 1979 by Allan Kornberg, Joel Smith, and Harold D. Clarke
All rights reserved.
L.C.C. card no. 78-74108
I.S.B.N. 0-89089-099-4
Printed in the United States of America

For Linda, Barbara and Marianne

Contents

Preface

POLITICAL parties have been developing in Western democracies since the 18th century and currently play a central role in their political systems even though most such states make no formal provisions for their organization, operation, or maintenance.[1] Consequently, the continued survival of most parties depends in great part on the unpaid labors of a relatively minute portion of their populations, individuals who occupy formal positions in party hierarchies and carry out many of their organizational activities both during and between elections. This book is about the men and women officials in the party organizations of two metropolitan areas in one of the world's oldest liberal democracies, Canada.

We focus on two relatively simple questions. What induces these people to accept and retain responsible official positions in their respective party organizations? Under what conditions will a few members of this already small group[3] become contenders for elective and appointive public offices or the powers behind those who hold them? Although the questions seem straightforward, social scientists have had difficulty answering them. For one thing, attempts at answers almost always result in disputes over nominal and operational definitions of key concepts such as "political elite," "recruitment," and "power and influence." Investigators also differ over the most appropriate research strategies to employ, the kinds of data to collect, the methods for analysis and the interpretation of results.

We have relied primarily on two major theoretical orientations to guide this investigation of participation in party organizations in a Western democracy: the *social structural* and *political socialization* perspectives. The former emphasizes the explanatory importance of impersonal social forces rooted in social structure and organization. The latter gives precedence to individual experiences accumulated continuously in the course of personal development. The socialization perspective appears more pertinent for explaining why people *join* parties, whereas the social structural orientation helps explain both joining and *careers* within parties.

The data brought to bear on these questions derive from structured personal interviews of some two hours in length that were conducted with three groups of people in metropolitan Vancouver and Winnipeg: 625 officials in the organizations of the four parties of the two cities; nearby residents similar in age,

Devides them into 4 categories

sex, and current social status, but who were not official members of any party, whom we term *nigh-dwellers;* and a cross-section of more than 1100 members of the general population.[4] We introduce these people to the reader by presenting vignettes about four of them at the beginning of the first chapter. "Susan Spillman," "Samuel Neilsen," and "Gus Hammerling" exemplify the three types of officials who may be found in each of the party organizations. "Pat Robertson" is illustrative of the kinds of people who well might be but are not in parties. Mrs. Spillman (although atypical for parties because she is a woman) possesses many of the attributes of/people who attain their parties' highest offices and become their candidates for public office. We term them *Elites.* Mr. Neilsen's attributes and experiences illustrate the/party careers of those people who actually maintain them as organizations. We term such people *Insiders.* Gus Hammerling exemplifies those who form the base of the party officialdom, party *Stalwarts.* Mrs. Robertson and the other members of the two nonparty groups are included in this study because detailed information about their lives, when compared with similar information about the lives of party officials, facilitates our understanding of why the latter but not the former are willing to engage in a relatively exotic form of political behavior.

The subjects of these vignettes and the hundreds of other people whom they are intended to represent have a story to tell. We have tried to tell that story in this book. It is organized into four sections. The first (Chapters 1 and 2) suggests how social structural and socialization factors help explain why only a small segment of the population of a democratic society become party officials and/or rise to prominence within party hierarchies. Analysis indicates that there is considerable support for our expectation that formal positions in party organizations in democratic societies, even those at the local level, are disproportionately the preserves of a small, rather strongly politicized segment of the middle and upper middle classes.

Section two (Chapters 3–5) is concerned with the political recruitment of: the two nonparty groups for temporary campaign work (Chapter 3); and the officials themselves (Chapters 4 and 5). An examination of the social and political characteristics of people in the two nonparty samples whose assistance in performing campaign-related activities has been solicited by party officials indicates that parties seem to be quite selective about whom they turn to for assistance. Those whose help they seek are distinguished by a variety of attributes, not the least of which is the considerable number of political stimuli they have been exposed to during the course of their lifetimes. Comparisons of the reasons given by people who have and have not or who would or would not work for a party suggest that many individuals who have attributes that characterize party officials do not become involved in organizational work because they have negative images of political parties, the parties' officials, or politics as a process.

In Chapters 4 and 5 we turn our attention to the officials themselves. In the fourth chapter the experience of joining is analyzed from the perspective of the party leaders whereas in the next chapter the process is analyzed systematically with multivariate analytic techniques that enable us, as social scientists, to deal in a simplified and manageable way with the many discrete details associated with the joining experience.

• The third section of the book is concerned with careers within these party organizations. Chapter 6 explains and clarifies the considerations and assumptions that underlie the choice of criteria used to classify party functionaries as Stalwarts, Insiders, and Elites. Essentially the classification is grounded in perceptions of key features of parties as organizations, their private and public dimensions, and the patterns of influence within them.

Relationships among these key features are examined and the distribution of the three types of officials within each of the four parties is compared. The finding that each party contains relatively similar proportions of Elites, Insiders, and Stalwarts suggests that regardless of any other differences that may exist among them, the four parties primarily are public office-seeking organizations • which share basic structural commonalities.

The prejoining, recruitment, and career patterns of the three types of officials are compared in the next chapter (Chapter 7). "Who you are" factors are important in determining membership in Elite and Insider groups but so also are "what you do" factors. However, the seeming rationality of political parties (i.e., allocating highest level organizational positions and public office candidacies according to performance) rarely extends to women officials. Women are dramatically underrepresented in the Elites. Both social structural and socialization theories help explain why this is the case and, more generally, why political party organizations historically have been the preserve of the male (Chapter 8).

In the concluding section (Chapter 9) we return to the two questions that prompted this study. After reviewing significant findings, we try to indicate how both the level and nature of societal politicization affect the structure and function of political party organizations. Although, admittedly, our conclusions rest upon data that were derived from two metropolitan communities in a single country, their generality, nevertheless, transcends particular place or time. They enable us to comprehend a critical dimension of human activity in institutions that historically have facilitated the democratization of societies such as Canada.[5]

NOTES

1. On the importance of political parties in Western democracies see, for example, Leon D. Epstein, *Political Parties in Western Democracies* (New York: Praeger, 1967); Sigmund Neumann, ed., *Modern Political Parties* (Chicago: University of Chicago Press, 1956); Austin Ranney and Wilmoore Kendall, *Democracy and the American Party System* (New York: Harcourt, Brace and World, 1965); Roy C. Macridis, ed., *Political Parties: Contemporary Trends and Ideas* (New York: Harper and Row, 1967); Andrew J. Milnor, *Elections and Political Stability* (Boston: Little, Brown, 1969). For recent discussions of political parties in Canada see Frederick C. Engelmann and Mildred A. Schwartz, *Canadian Political Parties: Origin, Character, Impact* (Scarborough, Ontario: Prentice-Hall, 1975); and Conrad Winn and John McMenemy, *Political Parties in Canada* (Toronto: McGraw-Hill Ryerson, 1976).

2. The term "amateur" has been applied to such people by James Q. Wilson, writing in another context. See Wilson, *The Amateur Democrat* (Chicago: University of Chicago Press, 1962). Also see John W. Soule and James W. Clarke, "Amateurs and Professionals: A Study of Delegates to the 1968 Democratic National Convention," *American Political Science Review*, 64 (1970):888-898; David Nexon, "Asymmetry in the Political System: Occasional Activists in the Republican and Democratic Parties, 1956-1964," *American Political Science Review*, 65 (1971):716-730; Henry Jacek, John McDonough, Ronald Shimizu, and Patrick Smith, "The Congruence of Federal-Provincial Campaign Activity in Party Organizations: The Influence of Recruitment Patterns in Three Hamilton Ridings," *Canadian Journal of Political Science*, 5 (1972): 190-205; Harold D. Clarke, Richard G. Price, Marianne C. Stewart, and Robert Krause, "Motivational Patterns and Differential Participation in a Canadian Party: The Ontario Liberals," *American Journal of Political Science*, 22 (1978):130-151.

3. Lester Milbrath estimates that at any particular point in time about 4% of the populations of most Western democracies are actively involved in party organizations. See Lester Milbrath, *Political Participation* (Chicago: Rand McNally, 1965), p. 16. For data suggesting that the total number of individuals who at *some point in their lives* have done some type of party or related campaign work is considerably larger than the 4% cited by Milbrath see Norman H. Nie and Sidney Verba, "Political Participation," in Fred I. Greenstein and Nelson W. Polsby, eds., *Handbook of Political Science* v. 4 (Reading, Mass.: Addison Wesley, 1975), pp. 24-25. For data on political participation in Canada see Rick Van Loon, "Political Participation in Canada: The 1965 Election," *Canadian Journal of Political Science*, 3 (1970):384, n.14; Susan Welch, "Dimensions of Political Participation in a Canadian Sample," *Canadian Journal of Political Science* 8 (1975):554; Mike Burke, Harold D. Clarke and Lawrence L. LeDuc, "Federal and Provincial Participation in Canada: Some Methodological and Substantive Considerations," *Canadian Review of Sociology and Anthropology*, 15 (1978): 61-75.

4. The selection of Canada and the metropolitan areas of Vancouver and Winnipeg as research sites was indicated by certain advantages of data available to us. These will be explained in detail below.

5. Documentation in the first chapter will support this assertion of greater generality.

Acknowledgements

A N endeavor as long and complex as this required the contribution and support of many individuals and organizations. The primary sources of support for this study were the National Science Foundation (GS-1134) and The Canada Council (68-0434, 69-1415, and 70-0527). We also are pleased to acknowledge the assistance and financial support of the Commonwealth Studies Center, The Canadian Studies Program, the Comparative Legislative Studies Program, and the Research Council, all of Duke University. Generous allotments of computer time were provided by Duke University and the University of Windsor. Athough we are grateful for their support and encouragement, any errors of fact or interpretation are our responsibility.

A number of people contributed significantly to this study. At different times Lenora Chambers, David Falcone, Donna Giles, Pat Hahn, William Mishler, Marilyn Petersen, Kay Shaw, Herbert Smith, Larry Suter, George Watson, and John Zipp were heavily involved in the preparation and processing of the data. Professors Taylor Cole, William Form, Robert Jackson, Seymour Martin Lipset, Robert Presthus, and Lester Seligman read the manuscript in draft form and made many helpful suggestions.

For other help too diverse to catalogue in detail, we thank Charlene Anderson, Gail Boyarsky, Catherine Eason, Grant Kornberg, Douglas Nord, Doris Ralston, Stephen Scotten, Lawrence Silverman, Eric Stallard and Marianne Stewart. Dorothy Weathers was a tower of strength and typed with skill and unfailing good humor the many versions through which each chapter passed. Finally, without the generous co-operation of the hundreds of people who agreed to be interviewed there would be no book. We are indeed grateful to them for their collaboration.

Allan Kornberg
Joel Smith
Harold D. Clarke

Durham, N.C.
January, 1979

Chapter One

Perspectives on
Party Work

> Most adults are skeptical, to say the least, of involvement in party
> activity.
>
> Samuel J. Eldersveld, *Political Parties: A Behavioral Analysis*, p. 440.

A Tale of Two Women

For "Susan Spillman" it was the best of times and the worst of times. It
was the best of times because she had begun overseeing the construction of her
large new home in Winnipeg's best residential area. She had purchased a
condominium in Fort Lauderdale for her mother and father, a recently retired
farmer. She had been appointed to the Senate of the University of Manitoba
from which she graduated with honors in Political Science and History. She
also had been appointed to the boards of both the city's new zoo and theatre
center and she had concluded preliminary negotiations with an American firm
of campaign specialists who had been recommended to her by some well-placed
Republican friends in the Northeast. Assuming a satisfactory conclusion of the
preliminary negotiations, the firm would be engaged to run her husband Ted's
prospective campaign for the leadership of the provincial Progressive Conservative party. If the campaign was successful and the Conservatives remained in
office, Ted, a cabinet minister in the Conservative government of Manitoba,
would become Premier. It was the worst of times because she could not direct
Ted's campaign for the party's leadership, keep up with the house and her
board work, remain active in the University Women's Club, look after her
three children, 8, 6, and 3, and also run for a seat on the Metropolitan Council
of Winnipeg—an office she wants and for which she feels qualified.

Her perception that she is qualified for public office is widely shared by a
number of other Conservative party officials in Winnipeg. She is credited by
them with being the architect of and "real power" behind three of her

husband's four successful campaigns for a provincial legislative seat. She not only holds a high level position in the Conservative organization of the constituency her husband represents, but she also is one of only a handful of women who receives more than ten nominations from party colleagues for being one of the most important people in the party. The adjectives "terrific," "fantastic," "capable," "ambitious," "dynamic," and "intelligent" are frequently invoked (even by people who are not especially fond of either her or her husband) to describe her administrative ability and political acumen. As one remarked, only partly in jest, "If Susan were in the government and Ted were home looking after the kids, the party and probably the people of Manitoba would be better off."

Interestingly, in view of Mrs. Spillman's prominence in the Conservative party, at the time of her marriage she considered herself a socialist. Her vote in the first election for which she was eligible had been cast for a CCF (NDP) candidate. Moreover, she had not been born in Canada but had been brought from Holland, together with her parents and an older brother, by an uncle living in Winnipeg. "We got out a couple of steps ahead of the Nazis," she related. "My dad was a tailor there but I guess he had always wanted to be a farmer. Anyway, I've been told that when we got here he somehow managed to borrow $1,200, bought a farm . . . and prospered."

Mrs. Spillman's first recollections of politics and public affairs are grounded in World War II experiences. "My dad was a constant listener to the CBC 9 o'clock news during the war. He never let us say a word when it was on. During elementary school we all had to help the war effort by buying War Savings Stamps and knitting horrible little six inch squares that were sewn together and used as afghans—for the troops, we were told. The teacher who taught the junior high grades was the principal of the school and always made patriotic speeches when he came to collect our quarters for the stamps. I think I still may have some of them [the stamps]."

Although she became aware of public affairs rather early in life and although her father was actively involved in the cooperative movement in Southern Manitoba, Mrs. Spillman did not become interested in political parties until she was 16 and a student in a Winnipeg high school. "My dad bought a house for us in Winnipeg so that my brother, Mark, and I could go to a good high school. One of my history teachers was marvelous. He also was a real CCF stalwart. That's what the NDP was called then. I can remember him talking about the CCF, about socialism, the Regina Manifesto, and about the party's founder, J.S. Woodsworth. As far as I can remember he was the only teacher I ever had who talked about politics, not just about government."

Mrs. Spillman continued to think of herself as a CCFer throughout her undergraduate years at the University of Manitoba and, in fact, twice represented the CCF in the University's student parliament. She did not begin to identify with the Conservative party until the second year of her marriage, largely, she confessed, to avoid embarrassing her husband, Ted, already a prosperous lawyer and businessman, a member of the Conservative party's provincial executive committee, and a close friend of the leader. "Mr. _____ wanted Ted to run for the legislature. So, when an opening came . . . we worked hard for the nomination, won the election and we have been going strong ever since."

She describes herself as "a person who is interested in people because I find people in all walks of life interesting. I feel very fortunate in knowing famous people, people whom I don't think I ever would have met if it hadn't been for politics. I've loved all of Ted's campaigns." Perhaps, because of these considerations, she does not mind the fact that, despite having three children under the age of ten, she has had to devote so much of her time to party work or that "the phone rings constantly about politics" because of her husband's cabinet position. Her politically oriented self-conception also may explain the great sense of accomplishment she derives from her work in the party, an organization she regards as extremely effective and in which she intends to be active "as long as I am able."

"Pat Robertson" is the president and founder of a prosperous market research and consulting firm with offices in Winnipeg, Regina, Edmonton, and Vancouver. Unlike Susan Spillman, Pat Robertson has no childen. Her husband, a physician, was killed in a hunting accident two years after their marriage. Also, unlike Susan, Pat's family—Scottish-Presbyterians on her father's side, English-Anglicans on her mother's—is of old Canadian stock, having settled in Ontario in the late 1820's.

Mrs. Robertson's first recollection of politics and public affairs was a conversation she overheard between her parents when she was seven. Her father, a professional soldier, was extremely concerned that an expected economy measure by the then Liberal government of W.L. Mackenzie King might force his early retirement from the army. "It wasn't the money. My mother had a fairly comfortable income of her own. It was his career. Dad loved the army and couldn't imagine doing anything but soldiering." The only other reference to politics that she could recall from her childhood and adolescent years also concerned the King government—her mother's anger during World War II over its unwillingness to send conscripts to reinforce the Canadian army in Europe, an army in which her father was then a Brigadier General.

In response to a series of questions concerning her family's, her friends', and her own interest in politics during her adolescence and early adult years, Mrs. Robertson indicated that politics were *not* a matter of particular interest or concern to any of them. "We were Army. Politics, unless they were service politics, were not the kind of stuff you discussed over the dinner table. I don't know which party my dad supported. I don't know if he even voted when he was in the service, although my mother probably did." Perhaps because of this, Pat never followed or cared to follow politics when she was in high school or at the University of Toronto. Although, she now follows politics fairly closely because of her work (she has done some polling for individual Liberal and Conservative candidates for parliament in all four Western provinces), she still considers herself a political Independent. She acknowledges that officials in the Conservative and Liberal parties have asked her to become active in their respective organizations, and although she regularly contributes to the coffers of both ("call it sound business practice"), she has resisted every request to date. "Unless you want to tie yourself to a particular party in the hope that you will get something substantial and regular in the way of contracts, advertising, or consulting—after all, I am not a lawyer so I am not going to get any mortgages to handle or an appointment to Queen's Bench—you can't afford in this business to get firmly identified with anyone. If you do you'll brown off the others. . . . Look, if you have worked with them, and I have, there is no way you want to get involved with them on any permanent basis, especially if you are a woman. The things they want you to do—telephoning, committee room work, typing, holding coffee parties—are not my idea of fun and excitement. There are only so many hours in a day. I fly, I ski and sail and I have a business to build and look after. If I wanted to get involved, I couldn't. No time. But who would want to?"

These two vignettes offer some helpful clues for answering the first question we posed—why the small fraction of the public in a democratic society that becomes active in a political party does so. Obviously, Susan Spillman's experiences at home, in high school, and during her undergraduate days were considerably different from Pat Robertson's. Mrs. Spillman was interested in politics and public affairs, as was her father. Mrs. Spillman's husband has been active in party organizational politics and is a provincial cabinet minister, whereas no one in Pat Robertson's family is, or ever had been even remotely interested or involved. Mrs. Spillman obviously enjoys her involvement, has a high regard for politicians, and finds party work extremely gratifying. Mrs. Robertson has relatively low regard for party and public officials and, although she regularly contributes money to two of the parties, she does not find party organizational work attractive. Although these factors may help explain party involvement or lack of involvement, they shed no light on our second question—why a small percentage of these party workers become candidates for, or are appointed to, public offices or help others to attain such offices. However, two more vignettes suggest appropriate areas for research.

Two Other Party Officials

"Samuel Neilsen" is a Lutheran, father of three children and a grandfather of eight. Two years earlier he had retired from his job as chief foreman of one of Winnipeg's largest construction companies. Born in South Dakota of Danish immigrant parents, he had moved with his parents to the West End of Winnipeg at age four. He still lives on the street on which his father's original house stands. Mr. Neilsen managed to complete eight years of public school before economic necessity forced him, the oldest of seven children, to take a job as a construction worker.

He was 37 years old when he first became active in the CCF. Until then he had not considered himself a member or a supporter of any party. He became active during the party's formative years because "I was in the union at age 18, and the union was an influence on me in the way I thought. I guess I just followed the CCF for that reason." Since beginning working for the party Mr. Neilsen has devoted, on the average, three hours a week to it. In the two year period before he was interviewed "there were about eight weeks in which the party took up almost all of my free time." Although he is a long-term member of his provincial constituency's executive committee and has helped elect a number of CCF and NDP candidates to parliament, the provincial legislature, and the Winnipeg City Council, he never has been his party's candidate for any of these offices. Nonetheless, Mr. Neilsen enjoys party work. He likes the people who are his co-workers and feels that the CCF-NDP and the people in it have improved over the years. Illustrative of his level of satisfaction with the party is the fact that during more than thirty years of involvement in organizational affairs not once has he ever contemplated quitting. Indeed, he expects, as does Mrs. Spillman, "to continue party work as long as I am able."

"Gus Hammerling" is a 57 year old bachelor and, like Mr. Neilsen, a Lutheran, who is employed as a real estate salesman by a large land development company in Vancouver. Born in a small town in Alberta, this Social Credit party official completed elementary school and moved to Vancouver in 1946 after wartime service with the Canadian army in Europe. Until the age of 42, when he volunteered to work in the Social Credit party, Mr. Hammerling had not been interested in politics and had considered himself an Independent. In fact, until affiliating with Social Credit, he always had disliked political parties and politicians. "You could never believe a damn thing they said. They

ruined this country during the Depression. With the kind of birds we had
running this country, there would still be a depression if the war hadn't come
along."

He became a Social Credit party worker, he says, in part because Mr.
W.A.C. Bennett, the then Social Credit Premier of British Columbia, was not
really a politician. "He was a businessman and he ran this province like a
business. He made good sense the first time I heard him. I thought he was
giving us real good government here in B.C. and that as a citizen I should do
something to help him." In part, however, he was influenced by the president
of the large real estate firm for whom he worked. His employer, a Conservative
turned Social Crediter, was one of the provincial Social Credit party's strongest
financial supporters and had encouraged Mr. Hammerling and many of the
other salesmen to become active in the party organization.

On the whole, Mr. Hammerling says he has enjoyed his work for the party
and, as does Samuel Neilsen, he likes most of his co-workers. However, he says
the amount of time required has proven to be more than he bargained for.
And, although he is concerned that it may create some problems with his
employer, he is uncertain whether he can continue in the party. "Most of my
work is in the evening when the men are home, you know. It doesn't matter
how many times you show a house to a woman, she isn't going to buy it
without her husband's okay." In the year before he was interviewed he acknowl-
edged that he had not engaged in any intensive work, and, on the average, he
had given very little time a week to the party. Also, he did not expect to be in
a position to do much more in the future even during election campaigns.

We may infer from a comparison of the biographical sketches of Susan
Spillman, Samuel Neilsen, and Gus Hammerling that one reason many party
functionaries do not become candidates for elective or appointive public
offices is that they lack the proper social credentials for such positions.
Canadian parties, like those in almost every Western society, do not normally
select as candidates or give public appointments to either retired construction
workers or real estate salesmen with grade 9 educations whose efforts on their
behalf are, at best, sporadic. Nor, because of an assumed lack of political
sophistication, do such individuals usually become powers behind the scenes.
(Conversely, being politically well-connected, as Susan Spillman obviously is,
certainly does not limit opportunities for political advancement). However,
voluntary associations, political parties included, also must have certain
mundane organizational maintenance functions performed and *ceteris paribus*,
they try to allocate their high level offices to those of their members who are
willing and able to do the required work competently. Thus, political parties
tend to reserve upper echelon positions in their organizational hierarchies for
the Samuel Neilsens rather than the Gus Hammerlings of this world.

Unfortunately, the four vignettes we have presented raise as many questions as they answer. By way of illustration, research has indicated that party officials derive from higher social backgrounds than do their fellow citizens. Assuming this, one would have expected Pat Robertson to have been more likely than Susan Spillman to have become a party official, given their social backgrounds. Similarly, the Conservative party is conventionally regarded as Canada's most "Waspish" party. Susan Spillman may be many things but she is not a Wasp. One could argue that she is a special case; her importance in the party derives from her status as the wife of a provincial cabinet minister. Why, then, do not wives of the hundreds of other Conservative MLAs and MPs, even the cabinet ministers among them, have the kind of influence in party affairs Mrs. Spillman seemingly possesses?

No matter how interesting these kinds of biographical sketches are in a general descriptive way, more light can be shed on such questions if one has an explanation that can be tested and evaluated with comparable evidence derived from large numbers of cases. We have such an explanation. More precisely, we have a number of theoretical expectations that we wish to test, some grounded in previous research on parties and political participation, others in conventional wisdom and our experience. Let us briefly describe them.

An Explanation of Party Involvement

As observed earlier, political party officials in virtually every Western democracy derive largely from higher socioeconomic strata. As a group they are better educated, work at more prestigious occupations, and enjoy considerably higher incomes than do average citizens in the communities in which they reside. A variety of studies support this description.[1] Since in most Western societies one's parents' socioeconomic status strongly affects one's own chances in life,[2] it is not surprising that a number of studies also have indicated that party functionaries disproportionately have middle class and upper-middle class backgrounds. For a variety of reasons (e.g., they may be more aware of the link between individual political participation and the content of public policy decisions, they may be more sensitive to how their personal welfare is affected by governmental decisions, they may seek and be sought by peers and by adults who share this awareness and sensitivity) people from such backgrounds tend to be more interested and involved in political activities that go beyond voting than are most members of lower status groups.[3] This is not to suggest that a middle class or upper-middle class social background and current status are necessary and sufficient conditions for becoming involved in party organizations.[4] Were this the case, we would never find people such as Samuel

Neilsen and Gus Hammerling in political parties. Moreover, we could not account for the fact that so few of the group Pat Robertson represents become involved in party politics.

There is, then, another major factor. We assume that party workers come from backgrounds that are not only middle and upper-middle class but also highly politicized.[5] Being reared in such an environment can have important consequences because Canadian society is not highly politicized. Neither the schools, media, nor for that matter, political authorities, urge Canadians to do anything other than vote. Consequently, the great majority, regardless of social class, is quite content to do just that: to vote in periodic elections and leave the practice of politics to the "politicians." Socialization to participate in politics in such an environment devolves largely and almost by default upon informal agents such as the family, peer and friendship groups. Most party officials, in our view, are socialized by such agents (some members of which may be either very interested or active in politics and public affairs) to accept participation beyond mere voting as both natural and desirable. Let us elaborate.

When they are children, many future party officials live in homes where politics are a frequent and normal topic of conversation. Their parents, and other more mature members of their nuclear and extended families, as well as other significant adults (e.g., close neighbors, family friends, exceptional teachers) are greatly interested in the honesty and efficiency of government, in the conduct of political campaigns, and in the behavior of political parties and individual political leaders. Members of their families frequently are acquainted with public and political party officials, or may occupy such positions for varying periods of time. Consequently, during childhood and adolescence future party officials frequently hear strong feelings expressed about political parties, political authorities, and public policies. Since they are reared in what is almost a political hothouse by normal standards, they develop politically rather quickly. They become aware of the political world, become interested in various aspects of this world, and develop attachments to parties and to individual politicians relatively early in life. Moreover, they are attracted to peers who share such interests. In secondary schools and universities they become involved in student politics, political clubs, and paraparty organizations (cf., Susan Spillman). Some actually may become active party workers while still in their teens. The majority, however, do not become actively involved in party affairs until they are adults. Whatever the age, it is the concatenation and interaction of intensive and extensive socialization experiences, socioeconomic status, and a particularly favorable set of contextual factors that result in the launching of a party career.

Many avenues can lead to involvement in a party organization. For some, the vehicle may be a voluntary association such as a service club or a trade union (cf., Samuel Neilsen). It may be a professional organization or a good government group. And for others it may be the campaign of a friend or associate for a nonpartisan public office, or the attractiveness of a charismatic political figure (cf., Gus Hammerling). People who become party officials also have a variety of motives for beginning this work. Some may view it as the beginning of a political career or as an opportunity to expand and enhance a legal practice. Many may be motivated, at least in part, by a desire to be good citizens or improve the honesty and efficiency of government. Others may be spurred by ideological or partisan considerations, by the attraction of, or antipathy toward, a party's platform and candidates, and still others may be motivated by a desire to meet and interact regularly with congenial and like-minded people. Regarding modes of entry into party organizations, several possibilities exist. Some highly motivated individuals may volunteer their services eagerly, being willing to do any work asked of them. Others may volunteer, but only after having been subjected to a subtle process of co-option by current party officials with whom they are connected socially. In such instances, personal friendships and family relationships may be traded on by officials trying to provide their parties with needed human resources. Still other individuals possessing highly valued status attributes, skills, and resources may join only after being strenuously courted by senior officials. Inducements such as prestigious positions within the local organizations, exciting task assignments, even the promise of an immediate nomination for an elective office or subsequent consideration for appointive office may be required to entice such people to join.

Careers within party organizations also can be expected to vary substantially. For a small minority of people, party work is an escalator to political prominence. Such individuals will hold high offices in their party's organizational hierarchy. They will become the standard-bearers in elections. They will receive appointments to nonelective public offices of varying importance, or they will become kingmakers, the behind-the-scenes figures who help decide who will and will not hold public office. The majority of the officials of any party, however, will become none of these things. For these people, party activity is sporadic and decidedly avocational, geared primarily to periodic election campaigns and characterized by meagre investments of time, energy, and other resources. Without much status or influence in party affairs, and perhaps without even the psychic gratification that can derive from interacting with interesting people, a substantial number of such individuals simply will drop out of their organizations after a relatively short period of service.[6]

Organizational Features of Local Parties

In trying to determine why a small portion of an already small group moves on to more exclusive circles and prestigious attainments in a party, we must consider the role of such idiosyncratic elements and events as being in the right place at the right time, being unusually energetic, and mastering techniques of personal ingratiation. However, the effects of unique factors of this kind often are mediated by parties' distinctive organizational features and the needs generated by their functions and associated structures. Let us briefly discuss these, since they bear directly upon our notions about individual prominence in party organizations.

The first noteworthy feature of Canadian parties is that (similar to parties in other democratic systems) they have been controlled by people whose principal organizational goals have been to select and elect candidates for public office.[7] Second, in Canada this function is virtually monopolized by the constituency level party organizations,[8] either federal or provincial. Their monopolies rest upon and are a consequence of the decentralized, loosely articulated, and skeletal character[9] of the national and provincial organizations of the four parties. Third, most party work is not very glamorous. The few activities (e.g., fund raising, selecting candidates, making policy decisions and public statements on behalf of a party) to which some degree of prestige is ascribed are normally the preserve of a small number of officials and public officeholders and candidates. Consequently, only a minority (cf., Susan Spillman) can work at them.

The organizational form of local parties is the fourth noteworthy feature. It tends to be a squat, truncated pyramid.[10] The rate of decline in the number of positions as one moves higher is relatively extreme and there are few layers between the narrow top and the broad bottom of the pyramid. Further, the more elaborately organized constituency parties in metropolitan areas usually contain four levels of organization. From smallest to largest these are the poll, area, zone, and constituency. The less fully organized generally dispense with the two intermediate layers. Because there are so few layers the possibility of a systematic and relatively continuous upward movement through a hierarchy of positions, a process we usually term a career, is considerably restricted in local parties. Career positions are attractive to individuals because they give continuity to their experiences and are a means of judging their typicality and success.[11] Since careers also hold the prospect of continuous, predictable experiences and rewards, they foster a willingness to train, achieve, adopt a long-term perspective, and defer immediate gratification in hope of later reward. Local parties do have a career analogue, the prospect of working for the party and then being selected for elective or appointive office. Susan Spillman's husband, Ted, it will be recalled, had experienced this kind of career and Mrs. Spillman herself was looking forward to furthering hers by running for the Winnipeg Metropolitan Area Council.

Fifth, local organizations are made up almost entirely of "amateurs." In some areas, generally the least prosperous ones, workers are paid directly and immediately for their services. In most cases these payments are modest and are almost entirely restricted to individuals holding positions at the very bottom level of a hierarchy. An overwhelming majority of a party's functionaries are unpaid, however, and although an organization and its candidates may benefit greatly from the financial and other assistance periodically received from outsiders such as Pat Robertson, the continued organizational existence of a local party—particularly between elections—depends upon the voluntary labors of party regulars like Susan Spillman, Samuel Neilsen, and Gus Hammerling. Because they are unpaid, however, when a conflict occurs between the demands of party work and workers' primary obligations, the latter usually take precedence. In this regard even the politically ambitious and extremely energetic Susan Spillman was not an exception. The potential for conflict is heightened by the episodic nature of most party work, oriented as it is toward electoral competition. Since in Canada the periods between active campaigns are quite lengthy, often lasting two or three years, local parties experience considerable morale problems and the organizations are characterized by a high rate of turnover of personnel, especially in the lowest level of a hierarchy.

Sixth, democratic norms and customary practice, as well as party constitutions, usually prescribe openness of entry for local parties. Although they are not legally required to admit just anyone seeking entry, the need to maintain and broaden the base of support is a strong inducement for current leaders to accept and actively recruit or co-opt representative members of a broad spectrum of social groups, including those who do not traditionally support their respective parties. For this reason, party organizations have been described as "alliances of sub-coalitions."[12] Given the distinctive features of party organizational structures and functions, recruitment is by no means an easy task, and a considerable number of those recruited probably join as a convenience to leaders. If these workers rarely develop a great desire to become contenders for public offices or organizational powers, they also do not expect to devote much time or effort to party affairs, as many candidates for parliament or for provincial legislative seats have found to their sorrow. Others who might wish to work hard for the party and its candidates are often frustrated by the aforementioned demands of their primary activities. Gus Hammerling was one such person and, undoubtedly, it was the activity or, more precisely, the lack thereof of Mr. Hammerling's counterparts in Wayne County party organizations that led Samuel Eldersveld to describe local party organizations in the United States as at best "minimally efficient."[13]

Types of Leaders in Local Parties

These features of local party organization in Canada, the United States, and other Western democracies have been observed and evaluated by a number of scholars. Eldersveld, for example, argued that rather than conceptualizing them as hierarchically organized oligarchies, local United States party organizations should be viewed as stratarchies: clientele oriented, social coalitions which provide opportunites for a number of elites to interact on a basis of reciprocal deference.[14] Joseph Schlesinger viewed United States party organizations as social collectivities devoted to the winning of public offices. Organizational "nuclei," he proposed, are vehicles that politically ambitious men use to achieve public office either for themselves as public leaders, or on behalf of others, as associational leaders.[15] Samuel Barnes hypothesized alternatively that political parties are most appropriately perceived as networks that specialize in the aggregation of political communications for a polity.[16] Different patterns, of course, characterize different political systems. William E. Wright conceptualized two ideal types of party organization.[17] And Frederick Engelmann and Mildred Schwartz, although their textbook on Canadian political parties is concerned with far more than parties as organizations, acknowledge that "first and foremost" political parties are, in fact, organizations, the goal of which is to "acquire sufficient power . . . to institute a particular set of programs and policies."[18]

We view local party organizations as essentially voluntary associations whose principal organizational goals are contesting for and filling public offices with candidates bearing their respective party labels. As do most organizations, parties overrepresent certain population groups—in their case, middle and upper-middle class males. The conditions under which individuals enter a party will differ, as will their reasons for initiating and sustaining the several activities related to a party's principal goals. Nonetheless, we assume that local parties, although they may vary with respect to the proportion of their workers found in each category, will be comprised of people who fall into one of three groups: "Stalwarts," "Insiders," and "Elites."

The first of these, Stalwarts, disproportionately will occupy the bottom and middle level positions of the truncated structures of local parties. They will be men and women whose backgrounds and current social statuses are somewhat lower than those of their colleagues who are Insiders and Elites. They largely will perform what Schlesinger has termed "memory," "intelligence," and "communications" functions on behalf of their local organization and its candidates for elected offices.[19] They will engage in a variety of routine record-keeping tasks and they will apprise upper echelon position holders and candidates for public office of the distribution of partisan sentiments among voters, information they generally collect in face-to-face canvassing and other forms of social interaction with members of the public. Stalwarts also help build support for their candidates through these interactions and by means of written communications (e.g., pamphlets, brochures) that they deliver to voters' homes. Since a disproportionate number of Stalwarts will be women with families and men who are holders of blue- and low status white-collar jobs, the demands of work and home may fall more heavily upon them than upon more advantaged colleagues. Thus, they may have less leisure time to commit to party work and these activities may be interrupted more often. Since their party work normally is routine and since many Stalwarts may be neither personally ambitious for office nor especially excited by the prospect of helping others to attain it, their interruptions often may become permanent. Consequently, there is likely to be more substantial "turnover" among Stalwarts than among the two other party types.

Officials in the second group, Insiders, will be holders of high level positions in the formal party hierarchies. Their principal task will be to coordinate and supervise the work of the Stalwarts. Although they too will perform the same kinds of tasks, we assume that Insiders usually will have done them for longer periods of time and with greater efficiency than have the Stalwarts. In our view, it is precisely this willingness and ability to commit substantial portions of time over the years without losing interest during long periods of party somnolence that will have earned them their high level positions in provincial and federal constituency organizations. It also will have earned at least some of them both a reputation for being influential in party affairs and the right to be contenders for public offices, either appointive or elective.

The third category, Elites, by and large will occupy the highest level organizational positions. We expect this group to be comprised predominantly of persons of higher social status and background who were reared in especially politicized milieux. They will combine this high status with relatively long, faithful and effective service to a party. Consequently, they even more than the Insiders will have earned reputations for being influential in party affairs. Assuming such service is rewarded, they also will have earned for themselves the right to be the most seriously considered for public offices when appropriate opportunities arise. (The reader will recall Susan Spillman's comment about her husband's desire to run for the provincial legislature: "So when an opening came . . . we worked hard for the nomination, won the election, and we have been going strong ever since.")

In our view, the three types of officials constitute, albeit in varying degrees, both a positional and a kind of psychic elite. They are a positional elite due to their backgrounds and achieved socioeconomic statuses and a psychic elite in the sense that they have a longer and more intense interest and involvement in politics than have other members of their social classes. We shall have more to say about all three types in Chapters 6 and 7 of this volume where we shall stipulate the characteristics that define each of the types and test whether, in fact, they are correlated with these clusters of attributes.

For the present it should be noted that, historically, local parties in Canada and other democratic societies have varied in both their ability and their willingness to attract people from the several social strata to their ranks. Consequently, we can expect that somewhat different configurations of attributes will characterize the Stalwarts, the Insiders, and the Elites of each of the parties. Because of these expected variations, some of our comparative analyses of people within and outside the party organizations of the two communities will be structured in terms of interparty differences. Despite these expected differences, we assume that in the aggregate: 1) party officials will be distinguished from other people by differences in a variety of social characteristics and political socialization experiences; 2) people not formally affiliated with a party who nevertheless periodically are approached for assistance also will have different attribute clusters than those who are not approached; and 3) within each party, Elites and, to a lesser extent, Insiders will possess certain social and political traits that set them apart from their colleagues who are Stalwarts.

The "Chinese Box"

These assumptions are similar to those underlying the structure of Kenneth Prewitt's "Chinese Box," a model that he used to describe the recruitment of city councilmen in the San Francisco Bay area.[20] A schematic representation of how our own Chinese box would look is depicted in Figure 1.1. The largest sector represents the general population, and the second smaller sector represents the middle and upper-middle class segments of the population. The third depicts the relatively small segment of the middle and upper-middle class reared in highly politicized milieux. These kinds of backgrounds and statuses are conducive to, although not necessary conditions for, entering party organizations. It also is this segment of the population which, even if it does not become formally active in party organizations, disproportionately participates in political activities beyond periodic voting in elections. Within the fourth sector, set off with a heavy black border, is a subset of the politicized segment of the middle and upper-middle class who become party officials. Included in the party organizations are three categories of officials. The first and most

Figure 1.1
"Chinese Box" Model of the Recruitment of Canadian Party Officials

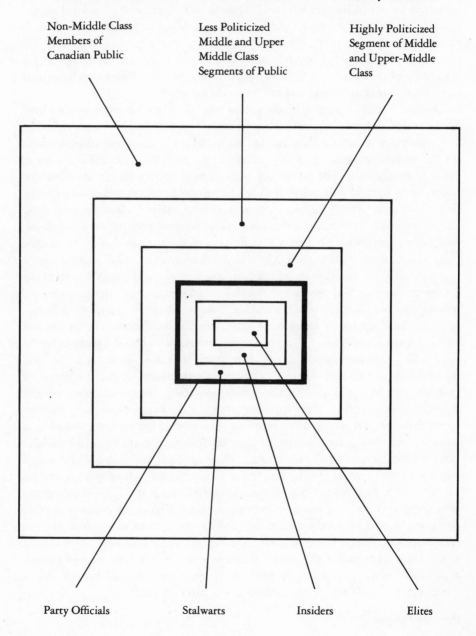

Non-Middle Class
Members of
Canadian Public

Less Politicized
Middle and Upper
Middle Class
Segments of Public

Highly Politicized
Segment of Middle
and Upper-Middle
Class

Party Officials   Stalwarts   Insiders   Elites

numerous (Sector IV) are the Stalwarts. The second (Sector V) represents the group of Insiders. The attributes that distinguish party officials in this seg-ment from their colleagues who are Stalwarts include either higher level organ-izational position holding or public office candidacy or greater than average ascribed influence in party affairs. The third and smallest category (Sector VI) is comprised of the officials who are termed Elites. They are characterized by a syndrome of occupancy of high party positions, public office candidacies and reputations for being extremely influential in party affairs.

Figure 1.2 is another schematic that represents the assumptions we have made regarding political party activity and career possibilities. Unlike Figure 1.1, however, it takes a longitudinal rather than a cross-sectional perspective on the several processes that lead to affiliation with and career differences in these organizations. The upper segment depicts factors that may affect the course of an individual's political socialization and hence the possibility that he or she may enter a party organization and become active. Included among these factors are various social institutions, public events, and personal attitudes. The bottom segment represents that portion of the middle and upper-middle class which never joins a party. On a scale representing the life span of such a person it may be seen that experiences in social institutions, together with the course of major public events and the individual's emerging values, goals, and interests do *not* combine in a facilitating fashion. Moreover, contextual factors such as a lack of time or a dislike of politics inhibit affiliation. The second and third segments of Figure 1.2 represent individuals who become party officials. For both groups experiences in social institutions, values, goals, and the like, do combine to affect political socialization experiences (e.g., awareness of politics, psychological identification with political parties, and rising interest in politics) so that they come together to encourage a career as a party worker. Contextual factors, too, tend to promote this result. However, the individuals who are Stalwarts, represented in the third segment, are assumed to have careers characterized by more frequent interruptions and limited individual commitment to party work, and by a failure to rise steadily in a party's organizational hierarchy. Party officials who are Insiders and Elites, in contrast, have longer periods of continuous service, higher levels of commitment to party work, and relatively continuous upward movement through a party to candidacies for appointive and elective offices. In the section immediately below we will acquaint the reader with the manner in which we went about acquiring the data necessary to test the extent to which and the respects in which these models fit the experiences of real party officials.

Research Design

Ideally, a longitudinal investigation to monitor the experiences of a

Figure 1.2
Variables Affecting Individuals With and Without A Party Career

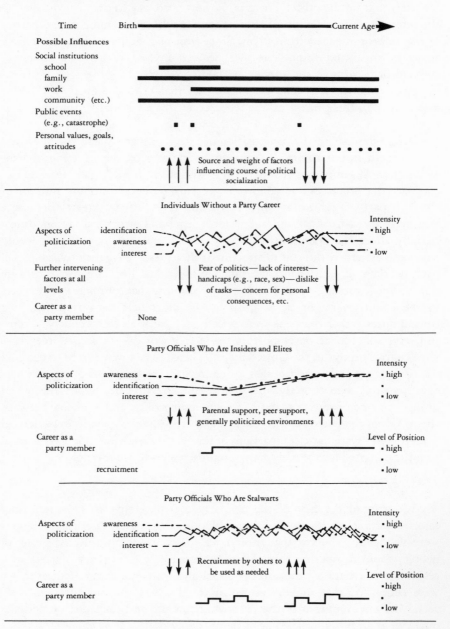

group of children into adulthood should be employed to study how a very small and exclusive subpopulation of adults eventually acquires or contends for party and public office. There is, however, no way to predict who among the tens of thousands of people born annually will either join political parties or rise to prominence within them. Since time and money constraints make a study of this kind impossible, we decided instead to adopt a relatively conventional form of the survey method to collect the same type of developmental information. The demonstration that critical aspects of relevant experiences in this process can be reconstructed is a distinctive feature of this book.

Before describing the composition of each study group and the questions put to them in our survey, a comment is in order on the selection of Vancouver and Winnipeg as research sites. The study initially was intended to compare the processes and conditions bearing on entry into and movement through party organizations in Canada and the United States.[21] Because a variety of cross-national and subnational legal and structural factors differentially affect the operation of parties in each country, however, it would have been extremely difficult to structure truly representative national samples of party workers of each country. Studies of individual local organizations were much more feasible. To guard against the possibility that community differences in the countries might be as great as the differences between them, two communities rather than one were selected for study in each country. Unfortunately, subsequent developments made it impossible to secure interviews with control groups in the United States. Therefore, we were forced to consider the advantages and disadvantages for addressing the questions of interest here of either a one country study with information on both party leader and control groups, or a comparative analysis of party leaders only, and to choose between them. Given the potential theoretical and methodological payoffs to be derived from precise, systematic comparisons of the party officials and nonparty control groups, we opted for the one country approach reported in this volume.

The Study Groups

We wanted the first of the nonparty control groups to be a randomly selected sample of the total adult population of each city. If our expectations were valid, we expected that interviews with a randomly selected group of people would reveal that they differed substantially from party officials with respect to conventional measures of social and economic status. However, we were concerned that differences which could reflect the more favored early social life environments of the party functionaries and such unique personal qualities as ambition or level of physical energy could not *by themselves* account for the status of party officials as officials. For example, although social back-ground advantages and personal values and skills might explain why a dispro-portionate number of party officials were highly successful lawyers, they could not explain why lawyers were party officials, since so many other equally successful lawyers are not involved in party work in any way.[22] In our case, we reasoned that more sensitive evaluations of the special factors that lead to and help maintain careers in parties could be obtained by matching and comparing party officials with *neighbors* alike in sex, age, and current life status, but differing with respect to the pursuit of party careers.[23] Residence, after all, is an important indicator of the station that a person has attained in life regardless of early life or other advantages. It reflects such factors as what one can afford, and the relation of location of workplace and type of job to residential alterna-tives. We term ths second control group "nigh-dwellers" throughout this book.[24]

The selection of an appropriate sample of party functionaries proved to be somewhat more difficult than we had anticipated. We initially had intended to draw a random stratified sample of members in each level of every party organization in the two cities. An examination of the lists of party officials supplied by provincial party secretaries and our own experience in these areas led us to abandon this plan. Among the practical problems encountered the most important was that the extent and form of the party organizations in each city varied substantially, the differences being a function of electoral success, and occasionally the idiosyncratic preferences of current party leaders. Coupled with this problem was a very substantial turnover in personnel at the lowest organizational level (i.e., the poll). There was a high rate of movement of people in and out of positions at that level. In addition to these considerations there was the conceptual problem of whether, in focusing only upon individuals holding positions in the formal party organizations, we were studying the "real" parties in the two cities. Off the record talks with party leaders and knowledgeable local academic observers gave us some perspective on the extent of congruence between the formal and real organizations.

To help insure that we were studying the real leadership of the parties and to circumvent the many practical problems in drawing representative random samples of each party in the two .cities, we decided to include *all* party officials who held positions in formal organizations *above* the level of poll captain and none below that level. We supplemented this group with individuals who in the opinion of a small coterie of local political "knowl-edgeables" played equally or more important roles in party affairs than did the holders of formal positions. In a few instances this resulted in the inclu-sion of individuals below our cutoff level, in others it led us to try to interview people who did not actually hold positions in their respective parties. To delineate further any possible informal influence structure in each city-party unit, we also decided to try to interview anyone not already on our lists who was considered one of the "most important people" in a particular party organization by six or more of the interviewees in the above two categories. (There were approximately twenty such people.) We listed approximately 750 people and were able to interview 625 of these formal position holders and informal party influentials in the two Canadian cities.

Although the selection and interviewing of the random sample of population in the two cities posed no unusual problems, we did experience considerable difficulty matching each party official with a neighbor. Since the great majority of the party officials were males it was particularly difficult to interview working males in appropriate age categories during the day. In some instances, after they were identified, interviews had to be secured at their places of employment. In most instances interviews had to be taken at home in the evening. Because evening interviews intruded upon their leisure time, a number of individuals who would have been appropriate matches either refused to be interviewed or would not complete an interview. Eventually, however, we did manage to complete 467 of 625 nigh-dweller interviews and 1,187 interviews with members of the randomly selected samples of population. The reader should note that when direct comparisons are made between party functionaries and nigh-dwellers, the latter sample has been augmented by including 158 cases from the random sample. We selected those members of the random sample who could have been matched with the 158 unmatched party officials. That is, we selected people from the random sample who matched the additional 158 party officials in terms of sex, age, and education or income. This procedure enables us to complete case-by-case matching of party officials with nigh-dwellers which is, of course, the most precise method for comparing them. However, because the 158 cases also continue to be included in the random sample, the procedure somewhat deflates differences between nigh-dweller and random samples, although it does not affect the representativeness of the latter.

The Interview

The field work was carried out in two stages. The first involved interviews averaging two hours in length with the party officials. We tried to frame questions that were based upon and in a sense encapsulated the major relevant theoretical concerns and empirical findings from previous research on political socialization, recruitment, and party careers. At the same time, by isolating and delineating fully the circumstances surrounding the critical events involved, we also tried to simplify and resolve some of the ambiguities and contradictions these findings present. Since the act of entering a party was conceptualized as a kind of threshold experience that would distinguish party functionaries from the two control groups, it served as the fulcrum around which the interview was organized. After the interviewee's sense of personal identity had been ascertained by means of a "Who Am I?" type of question and the respondent's educational, residential, and occupational histories had been recorded, the interviewee was asked the age at which he or she first became affiliated with a political party. Considerable effort was made to establish this age precisely since, once it was established, the questioning proceeded in terms of time segments prior and subsequent to affiliation.

After the respondents had indicated the age at which they initially joined a party, prior factors that might have led them to affiliate were explored. Despite the fact that the act of affiliation was treated as an attribute (i.e., respondents either were or were not in a party at a particular age), because of our theoretical interests we conceptualized entry as the culmination of a temporally drawn out and somewhat nebulous process that had begun much earlier in their lives. Accordingly, a major segment of the interview was devoted to delineating and illuminating that process.

Some thirty questions keyed to the period between birth and earliest childhood to time of joining were asked. To enhance each respondent's ability to reconstruct early life experiences accurately, we again used a strategy of trying to establish precise ages at which critical events took place. Thus, for example, we asked specific ages for such events as first awareness of politics and public affairs, first psychological identification with a political party, and any subsequent changes in identification. We also tried to key these events to especially salient periods of life (e.g., grammar school, university, going to work). In this manner, respondents were led through prejoining segments of their lives, a period we tried to recap with an open-ended "all-in-all" question in which they were asked to judge which experience, influence, or event was particularly important in moving them toward party work.

Our attempt to treat politicization, the joining of political parties, and the set of experiences within parties as developmental processes was motivated by our theoretical concerns and pragmatic considerations. Insofar as politicization was concerned, we tried to separate the process into three major components. Two of these, psychological identification with a party and political interest, have been extensively investigated. The third aspect of politicization, first political awareness, has not received much systematic attention. We tried to delineate the environments in which all three events occurred and to tie them to specific agents that triggered them.

Because of the rather amorphous quality that affiliating with a party has in Canada, a symbolic behaviorist[25] rather than a structural conception of joining was utilized. We tried to make clear that the act was to be viewed as a social and psychological rather than as a formal or legalistic event. The concept of joining a party was a construction imposed upon reality. For some people it described without distortion a relatively simple act; for others it involved fitting a complex process into an overly simple and somewhat unrealistic classification. To relate the experience to a coherent framework, we began with a pair of questions that were intended to reveal whether a respondent had volunteered or had been recruited into the ranks of the party and whether first activities on its behalf were task-specific or diffuse and general. These were followed by questions aimed at determining whether the party member who made the first contact or was contacted by the future official was known or related to the respondent. Among other matters about which respondents were questioned were the positions held by first party contacts, the levels of their own first party positions, the kind of work they initially were asked to undertake, their reactions to this initial experience, and whether they would have joined regardless of these initial contacts.

Joining presupposes organization. Accordingly, we tried to record the set of experiences and behaviors of individuals, which we term party careers, by leading interviewees through the positions they held in their parties from the time they entered them to the point at which the interviews were taken. We tried to key the holding of positions to specific ages and also to ascertain when, if ever, the interviewees had dropped out of their parties. For those who had interrupted their work we tried to determine the length of time they were out, the age at which they again began work, and the positions they held upon reentering. We also questioned respondents on such matters as the intensity of their commitments to the party vis-à-vis other matters; the levels of their participation in electoral campaigns and in party activities between elections; the levels of politics in which they were most interested; their perceptions of the effectiveness of party colleagues and their party organizations; their reasons for continuing to be active; their aspirations for higher party and public offices; and their expectations as to the continuation of their activities in the foreseeable future. We also obtained detailed familial histories for each interviewee, as well as information pertaining to their present social and economic statuses and activities.

As indicated, we tried to minimize the hazards involved in the use of data based upon recollection of events by forcing the interviewees to settle on specific ages at which critical events occurred and by orienting these events toward more universally shared experiences such as schooling and work. Another tactic we employed to minimize recall error was to include a number of interlocking questions designed to check the accuracy with which respondents were able to recall events and time periods. Whenever inconsistencies were detected during the processing of the data they were noted and resolved. In some instances this required reestablishing contact with the individuals concerned. Apart from these tactics, during the analyses the data obtained were checked against several models of systematic error and bias in recall. No such models were found to fit.

The focus of the interview with the random sample and the nigh-dwellers was the noninvolvement of these two groups in party affairs. The intent was to identify factors inhibiting participation in political parties. Consequently, questions were designed to elicit the following information:

1. What proportion of the two groups at some time in their lives had been asked to work for a party but had refused?
2. How many people in each group had never been asked to work for a party but would have refused if asked?
3. Why do or would people refuse to become involved in party-related activities?
4. What proportion of the two populations had never been asked to work for a party in the past but would have, and what proportion actually had worked for a party?
5. What reasons do people give for working or wanting to work in parties?

As with the party officials, a substantial proportion of the interview with nonparty groups was concerned with delineating the social and political milieux in which the respondents were reared and their political socialization experiences. The expectation was that both of these would differ substantially from those of the party officials and thereby provide support for our expectations regarding the link between these early life experiences and subsequent political activity.

Summary

This study focuses on two questions: 1) the conditions under which only some four percent of the population of a democracy such as Canada become officials of political parties; and 2) the conditions under which a small minority of officials rise to positions of political prominence whereas the majority are confined to carrying out routine but necessary electoral and organizational maintenance tasks. Our approach to these matters is informed by differing but complementary perspectives. For convenience, the label social structural may be applied to the theoretical orientation which assumes that people's current statuses have been strongly affected by the statuses, skills, and resources they have acquired since birth. Implicit in this orientation is the assumption that all other factors being equal, status begets status; for example, well-educated individuals engaged in prestigious occupations are more likely than other citizens to be recruited for positions in political parties and prestigious members of an already exclusive group are more likely to attain highest level positions in these voluntary organizations. Given that the *ceteris paribus* condition rarely obtains, entry into party organizations and the enjoyment of successful careers within them also are affected by impersonal societal forces and the structure and organization of parties. We have noted a number of structural factors characteristic of local parties that may affect participation within them.

Since activity within party organizations is a relatively exotic form of political participation we also rely on a political socialization perspective to guide this investigation. Political socialization is a shorthand label for any √indirect impact that early political experiences may have on later life behavior. As an analytic perspective, it implies that people who currently manifest patterns of political behavior which differ markedly from those of others do so because they were reared in environments and acquired values, attitudes, and information that also differed. Thus, in the next chapter we not only shall compare the social statuses of party officials, their nigh-dweller matches and members of the general public, but we also shall systematically examine their political socialization experiences and the political settings in which they were reared. We rely on these two perspectives throughout the book, particularly in Chapters 4, 5, 7, and 8, in which we examine the recruitment experiences of party officials, the conditions that affect their placement in Elite, Insider, or Stalwart categories, and the role of women as officials within their respective parties.

NOTES

1. The literature on the socioeconomic characteristics of party activists is extensive. See for example, Dwaine Marvick and Charles R. Nixon, "Recruitment Contrasts in Rival Campaign Groups," in D. Marvick, ed., *Political Decision-Makers* (Glencoe, Ill.: The Free Press, 1961), pp. 193-217; Samuel J. Edersveld, *Political Parties: A Behavioral Analysis* (Chicago: Rand McNally, 1964), chap. 3; Mark Abrams and Philip Little, "The Young Activist in British Politics," *British Journal of Sociology*, 16 (1965): 315-332; G. Robert Boynton and Lewis Bowman, "Recruitment Patterns Among Local Party Officials: A Model and Some Preliminary Findings in Selected Locales," *American Political Science Review*, 60 (1966): 667-676; Henry Jacek, John McDonough, Ronald Shimizu, and Patrick Smith, "Social Articulation and Aggregation in Political Party Organizations in a Large Canadian City," *Canadian Journal of*

Political Science, 8 (1975): 274-298; John McMenemy and Conrad Winn, "Party Personnel—Elites and Activists," in Winn and McMenemy, *Political Parties in Canada*, chap. 9.

   2. Otis Dudley Duncan, David L. Featherman, and Beverly Duncan, *Socioeconomic Background and Achievement* (New York: Academic Press, 1972); Lorne Tepperman, *Social Mobility in Canada* (Toronto: McGraw-Hill Ryerson, 1975); Carl J. Cuneo, "Social Ascription in the Education and Occupational Status Attainment of Urban Canadians," *Canadian Review of Sociology and Anthropology*, 12 (1975): 6-24; John C. Goyder and James E. Curtis, "Occupational Mobility in Canada Over Four Generations," *Canadian Review of Sociology and Anthropology*, 14 (1977): 303-319.

   3. On the relationship, more generally, between social class and political participation in Canada and the United States see Lester Milbrath, *Political Participation* (Chicago: Rand McNally, 1965), chap. 5; Robert E. Lane, *Political Life: Why People Get Involved in Politics* (Glencoe, Ill.: The Free Press, 1959), pp. 326-334; Sidney Verba and Norman H. Nie, *Participation in America: Political Democracy and Social Equality* (New York: Harper & Row, 1972), chap. 8; Seymour M. Lipset, *Political Man* (Garden City, N.Y.: Doubleday, 1960), chap. 3; Van Loon, "Political Participation in Canada: The 1965 Election," 384-386.

   4. See, for example, Norman H. Nie, G. Bingham Powell, Jr., and Kenneth Prewitt, "Social Structure and Political Participation: Developmental Relationships, I,"*American Political Science Review*, 63 (1969): 361-378; and "Social Structure and Political Participation: Developmental Relationships, II," *American Political Science Review*, 63 (1969): 808-832; Stein Rokkan, *Citizens, Elections and Voters* (New York: David McKay, 1970), chaps. 1 and 12; Maurice Pinard, *The Rise of a Third Party* (Englewood Cliffs, N.J.: Prentice-Hall, 1971), chap. 7; Michael B. Stein, *The Dynamics of Right-Wing Protest: A Political Analysis of Social Credit in Quebec* (Toronto: University of Toronto Press, 1973), chap. 4.

   5. See Marvick and Nixon, "Recruitment Contrasts in Rival Campaign Groups"; Peter Pulzer, "Is There a Political Class?" in Pulzer, ed., *Political Representation and Elections: Parties and Voting in Great Britain* (New York: Praeger, 1967), pp. 67-72; Abrams and Little, "The Young Activist in British Politics"; Kenneth Prewitt, "Political Socialization and Leadership Selection," *Annals of the American Academy of Political and Social Science*, 361 (1965): 96-lll; Marvin E. Olsen, "Three Routes to Political Party Participation," *Western Political Quarterly*, 29 (1976): 550-562; and Robert H. Salisbury, "The Urban Party Organization Member," *Public Opinion Quarterly*, 29 (1965-66): 550-564.

   6. Eldersveld, *op. cit.*, p. 167.

   7. See, for example, Joseph Schlesinger, "Party Units," *International Encylopedia of the Social Sciences*, Vol. 11: 428-435.

   8. It is true that the national and provincial party organizations sometimes "parachute" candidates for the House of Commons or for a provincial legislature into constituencies. This practice, however, is not widespread in Canada. It is also true that national and provincial party organizations provide financial assistance, speakers, campaign materials, and other forms of assistance to local organizations and their candidates. These forms of support are welcomed since they usually cannot hurt and under certain conditions may even provide the margin between electoral success and failure.

   9. A visit to Ottawa and the ten provincial capitals and an inspection of the national and provincial organizations of the parties will confirm this assertion. The

national and provincial offices of the Liberal, Progressive Conservative, and New Democratic parties have minimum staffs that can be and are expanded immediately before elections. The Social Credit party lacks even this level of organization at either the federal or provincial levels. See Engelmann and Schwartz, *Canadian Political Parties: Origin, Character, Impact*, pp. 173-182.

10. The use of this metaphor reflects our experience with the reality of local party structures. Party positions are hierarchically organized in both cities; hence, the use of the term "pyramid." Although their paper tables of organization suggest that they can be fuller and more vertically developed than the metaphor implies, in fact, the majority of officials occupy positions at lower levels of these organizations (i.e., the base and middle of the pyramid). Hence, the use of the descriptive adjective, "squat." Finally, there are relatively few levels of office between the base and the apex of the pyramid, prompting us to describe them as "truncated." Although logically "squatness" can be independent of "truncation," empirically it is not. Consequently, "truncated" will be used as a shorthand description of both organizational features of local parties.

11. See Harold L. Wilensky, "Orderly Careers and Social Participation," *American Sociologial Review*, 26 (1961): 521-539.

12. Eldersveld, *op. cit.*, chap. 4; Jacek *et al.*, *op. cit.*, John Wilson and David Hoffman, "Ontario: A Three Party System in Transition," in Martin Robin, ed., *Canadian Provincial Politics* (Scarborough, Ont.: Prentice-Hall, 1972), pp. 198-239.

13. Eldersveld, *op. cit.*, chap. 4.

14. Eldersveld, pp. 1-13.

15. Joseph A. Schlesinger, "The Nucleus of Party Organization," in William E. Wright, ed., *A Comparative Study of Party Organization* (Columbus, Ohio: Charles E. Merrill, 1971), pp. 55-72.

16. Samuel H. Barnes, *Party Democracy: Politics in an Italian Socialist Federation Organization* (New Haven, Ct.: Yale University Press, 1967), pp. 241-253.

17. William E. Wright, "Comparative Party Models: Rational-Efficient and Party Democracy," in Wright, ed., *A Comparative Study of Party Organization*, pp. 17-54.

18. Engelmann and Schwartz, *Canadian Political Parties: Origin, Character, Impact*, p. 4.

19. Joseph A. Schlesinger, "Political Party Organization," in James G. March, ed., *Handbook of Organizations* (Chicago: Rand McNally, 1965), pp. 764-801.

20. Kenneth Prewitt, *The Recruitment of Political Leaders: A Study of Citizen-Politicians* (Indianapolis: Bobbs-Merrill, 1970), p. 8.

21. We opted for a "most similar systems" design (i.e., the comparison of societies generally alike that differ in certain respects) both because it was consistent with two of the three criteria of the comparative method distinguished by Emile Durkheim (cf. *The Rules of Sociological Method*, 8th edition, translated by Sara Soloway and John E. Mueller, edited by George E. G. Catlin [Glencoe, Ill.: The Free Press, 1950], pp. 125-140) and because it was more practicable than a "most different systems" approach. The two approaches are evaluated in Adam Przeworski and Henry Teune, *The Logic of Comparative Social Inquiry* (New York: Wiley-Interscience, 1969), chap. 2. Societal differences pertinent to the similar systems design that also led us to opt for community comparisons rather than a national sampling of party workers are discussed briefly in Joel Smith and Allan Kornberg,

"Some Considerations Bearing Upon Comparative Research in Canada and the United States," *Sociology*, 3 (1969): 341-357.

Having decided against national sampling, it was important to choose communities with organizational and contextual settings that matched across country lines well enough to justify the assumption that they are alike on some underlying relevant dimensions. Vancouver, Winnipeg, Seattle, and Minneapolis were selected because they appeared to meet these requirements. Their historic and demographic characteristics were sufficiently similar to offer reasonable assurances that any cross-national differences observed would be real. Moreover, both American cities contained flourishing Republican as well as Democratic party organizations. The selection of Vancouver and Winnipeg as the Canadian research sites was motivated by a similar consideration. In addition to having two well organized old-line parties, the two cities seemingly contained vigorous New Democratic and Social Credit parties. Other Canadian communities that were considered as potential research sites, particularly those east of the Great Lakes, usually lacked either a New Democratic or, more frequently, a significant Social Credit party. In addition, on the spot investigation indicated that in all four cities we would be able to secure the cooperation and support of local party leaders without which the study would have been virtually impossible to execute. However, subsequent funding pressures in the United States made it impossible to secure data for control samples in the two American cities and thus to complete the design.

22. Much has been written on the confluence of law and politics as careers. See, for example, Joseph A. Schlesinger, "Lawyers and American Politics: A Clarified View," *Midwest Journal of Political Science*, 1 (1957): 26-39; and Heinz Eulau and John D. Sprague, *Lawyers in Politics* (Indianapolis: Bobbs-Merrill, 1964). For a convenient summary of major findings in comparative perspective see Moshe Czudnowski, "Political Recruitment," in Fred I. Greenstein and Nelson W. Polsby, eds., *Handbook of Political Science*, V. 2 (Reading, Mass.: Addison-Wesley, 1975), pp. 204-209. In Canada, Kornberg and Mishler report that 33% of Canadian MPs have law degrees and Clarke *et al.* find that 11% of provincial MLAs are law school graduates. Only one quarter of one percent of Canadian adults are lawyers according to the 1971 census. See Allan Kornberg and William Mishler, *Influence in Parliament: Canada* (Durham, N.C.: Duke University Press, 1976), p. 65; and Harold D. Clarke, *et al.*, "Backbenchers," in David J. Bellamy, *et al.*, *The Provincial Political Systems: Comparative Essays* (Toronto: Methuen, 1976), p. 216.

23. Our reasoning is in accord with that of Herbert Hyman who in his pioneering discussion of political socialization contended that, "Ideally, one should compare individuals of the same age at different calendar points and match them in social composition. Then one can isolate the influence of the larger environment, controlling the chronological component of generations. This approach is rarely found in the literature of quantitative empirical studies of political development." Herbert H. Hyman, *Political Socialization: A Study in the Psychology of Political Behavior* (New York: The Free Press, 1959), p. 103.

24. We considered obtaining from a current group of party officials the names of childhood friends and then locating and interviewing these people. Since a control group of this kind would have been exposed during the presumably critical childhood years to the same general social, economic, and political environments as were party functionaries, to reconstruct critical events in their lives would have enabled us to identify the factors that make otherwise common origins significantly different. This procedure was impractical for two reasons. First, the costs involved in obtaining a list

of childhood friends, locating, and then interviewing them would have been staggering. We would have had to trace a substantial number of friends and associates of the party officials who either had not been born in Vancouver or Winnipeg or had moved from these areas. Second, the party officials might have been selective in their recall of childhood friends and acquaintances in ways that could have introduced unknown biases in our subsequent analytic comparisons.

    25. Cf., Jerome G. Manis and Bernard N. Meltzer, eds., *Symbolic Interaction: A Reader in Social Psychology*, 3rd edition (Boston: Allyn and Bacon, 1978).

Chapter Two

Social Structure and Political Socialization

Elites may be defined as that minority in any society who possess . . . disproportionate shares of scarce and highly valued resources.

Robert Presthus, *Elite Accommodation in Canadian Politics*, p. 60.

Early impressions, absorbed through willing pores, set lifetime priorities.
Peter C. Newman, *The Canadian Establishment*, p. 60.

W E have hypothesized that party officials in Canada and elsewhere can be distinguished from politically inactive citizens by distinctive socioeconomic and demographic characteristics and political socialization experiences which provide them with a complex and diverse set of resources that facilitate active involvement in party organizations. Similar to other propositions about real world phenomena, the social structure-political socialization-party activity hypothesis requires empirical testing. To this end, the present chapter presents an overview of the extent to which the Winnipeg and Vancouver party officials actually do have socioeconomic and related characteristics and political socialization experiences which differ from those of their fellow citizens who are not active in party affairs.

Structure and Socialization: An Overview

In Canada, the classic analysis of the relationship between social stratification and political power remains John Porter's *The Vertical Mosaic*.[1] Arguing that Canadian society is structured so that social, economic and political hierarchies tend to "fuse" or "agglutinate" at higher levels into a single overarching system of status and power, Porter provides ample documentation that those who occupy top level economic and political positions are highly unrepresentative of the Canadian public in several respects. Disproportionately, these elites tend to be native-born, of British heritage, and affiliated with high status Protestant churches. Educated in exclusive preparatory schools and in distinguished universities at home and abroad, they subsequently enjoy careers as corporate executives, proprietors of their own businesses, or partners in major law firms. Demographically, they are middle-aged or older with an overwhelmingly large proportion being men. Although based on evidence gathered largely before 1960, the essential accuracy of this portrait of Canada's national socioeconomic and political elite has been reaffirmed in more recent studies by Clement, Newman, and Presthus.[2]

It is difficult to specify the extent to which *local* party officials will mirror the socioeconomic, ethnic, religious and demographic characteristics of national elites. With regard to demographic characteristics, research on public office-holders and candidates and party activists repeatedly has documented that active participants in Canadian political life tend overwhelmingly to be middle-aged or older men.[3] The consistency of these findings and their consonance with those of Porter and others leads us to anticipate similar types of sex and age distributions among the officials of all four parties.

As for ethnicity and religion, the results of previous studies are less consistent. Most noteworthy in this regard is the disjuncture between the findings of Porter regarding the largely Anglo-Celtic and Protestant composition of top elite groups and those of Kornberg and others in analyses of the backgrounds and statuses of federal and provincial legislators and candidates for these offices. The studies of political officials and candidates have found that federal MPs and Cabinet ministers and provincial MLAs have ethnic and religious characteristics quite similar to those of the Canadian public as a whole.[4] Moreover, these tendencies are not simply a function of the inclusion of a substantial number of French-Canadian Catholics from Quebec in these samples. The consistency of the findings of the research on federal and provincial legislators (plus the fact that the works of Porter and others were focused primarily on socioeconomic rather than on political elites) suggests that, as a group, party officials likely will approximate the ethnic and religious distributions of the residents of Vancouver and Winnipeg.

There is another reason for expecting the parties to be relatively similar—at least in these regards—to both the population in general and to one another: the electoral imperative. Electoral victory in reasonably competitive, heterogeneous ethnic and religious social milieux requires, as Eldersveld has argued, that local parties become "alliances of sub-coalitions" that allocate at least some of their organizational positions to representatives of all major ethnic and religious groups within their communities, even those which do not normally give them strong support at the polls.[5] Nonetheless, the fact that the four parties usually have received varying levels of electoral support from different ethnic and religious groups[6] suggests that there will be some inter-party variations in these regards. More specifically, one might anticipate finding proportionately more Catholics in the Liberal party, with Protestants, particularly those from high status churches (United, Presbyterian, Anglican) gravitating to the Conservatives. The New Democratic and Social Credit parties also should contain larger proportions of Protestants than the Liberals and, given their democratic socialist ideological origins, one would expect the New Democrats to contain a larger percentage of persons professing no religious affiliation. Finally, the anti-Semitic pronouncements of the founders of the Social Credit party suggest that few, if any, Jewish Canadians will be found in its organizational ranks.[7]

Similar kinds of expectations can be advanced with respect to ethnicity. The Liberal party should contain more officials of French-Canadian descent. The other parties should have larger cohorts of members of Anglo-Celtic origin, but, given the relatively large numbers of persons of other than Anglo-Celtic or French ethnic backgrounds in both British Columbia and Manitoba, it can be expected that each of the parties will contain more of these types of officials than were found in the aforementioned nationwide studies of MPs and MLAs.

Regarding socioeconomic status, in a comprehensive review of the literature on political elites Robert Putnam has concluded that ". . . no matter how we measure political and social status, the higher the level of political authority, the greater the representation of high-status social groups."[8] Given this "law of increasing disproportion" and the arguments advanced in Chapter 1, one would anticipate that relative to the general public all four local parties will contain disproportionately large numbers of members of socioeconomic elite groups. Precisely how "elite" they will be in comparison with other groups of political actors (e.g., federal MPs), however, is an empirical question, although Putnam's "law" would suggest that the status of local party officials should be lower than that of national or provincial level political actors. In addition, studies of public officeholders and candidates in Canada have repeatedly shown that Liberals, and to a lesser extent Conservatives, are individuals of higher statuses, on average, than are New Democrats or Social Crediters.[9] These interparty differences reflect the tendency of the two older parties to recruit as candidates well-educated, high income-producing lawyers and business executives, and of the two minor parties to recruit lower status professionals, small businessmen, and, to a much lesser extent, white-collar and skilled blue-collar workers.

Given these considerations and the design of the research, it can be anticipated that the party officials will: 1) be drawn from virtually every stratum and major ethnic and religious group in the population; 2) be more representative of the distribution of ethnic and religious characteristics than of other status characteristics in the Canadian population; 3) overrepresent males and those of middle age in the population; 4) overrepresent those groups which usually have accorded their respective parties disproportionately heavy electoral support; 5) not be as elite a group as party colleagues who are public officials; and 6) be quite similar in the aggregate to their nigh-dweller matches.

In the first chapter we argued that the organizational activities of political parties disproportionately are carried out by the more politicized segments of the middle and upper-middle classes rather than by a random representation of these classes. This argument rested on two observations. First, higher socio-economic status is not a sufficient nor even a necessary condition of high levels of political participation. If it were, we would never find politically active working class people or upper status people who were not politically active. In no democracy is this the case. Second, studies of political participation in democratic societies in which citizens are not continually "mobilized" to become involved in prescribed and officially sanctioned activities by organs of the state indicate that public officeholders and party activists frequently report that their parents, relatives, or friends either were politically active or very interested in politics. For example, Eldersveld found that in the United States 22% of the Wayne County, Michigan, party workers reported that their fathers either were "quite" or "very" interested in politics.[10] Marvick and Nixon reported that nearly 40% of the Democratic and Republican campaign workers in Los Angeles came from families where at least one parent was politically active,[11] and in their comparative study of party officials in Massachusetts and North Carolina, Bowman and Boynton reported that as many as 49% of the officials had one or more parents who had been active in politics.[12] Comparable rates also have been reported in several studies of city councils and state legislatures.[13] In Canada there have been fewer systematic investigations but the tenor of relevant findings is similar. Kornberg, studying Members of the 25th Parliament, found that 42% of the MPs came from highly politicized familial milieux.[14] Clarke, Price, and Krause, in a survey of provincial legislators in all ten provinces, reported that 35% had parents or other relatives who had held public elective office.[15] Kornberg and Mishler's study of the 28th Parliament indicated that nearly two-thirds of the MPs had fathers with a strong interest in politics, and 38% had mothers with similar levels of political interest.[16] Finally, Clarke and Price found that fully 52% of the freshmen MPs in the 30th Parliament reported that their parents had been active in party work.[17]

What makes such rates intriguing is not their variation but the fact that the levels of political interest and involvement of parents and others during the childhoods of future political activists seemingly are so much greater than they are among members of the general public.[18] Atypical exposure to political stimuli is likely to have three effects. First, it may lead to the development and retention of an interest in things political and a predisposition toward political activity as a normal and desirable form of social interaction. In some cases, such exposure may result in a strong orientation towards politics as a full-time career rather than simply as an avocational pursuit. Second, people reared in familial environments in which extensive or intensive political activity is the norm may be located in the kinds of social networks in and from which some type of political recruitment is likely to occur. For the most part people of this kind are likely to seek opportunities for political involvement by virtue of predispositions developed in frequent contacts with politically involved people who may serve as socializing agents or positive role models. They also enjoy a social location that increases the probability of being approached to engage in political activities. The principal consequence of having been reared in a highly politicized environment, however, is to develop well-defined feelings about political participation. These feelings are positive for most such people, although they can be negative for some. Therefore, if approached to work, the latter may refuse strongly and consistently for what they feel to be well-founded reasons. However, on balance, most are likely to respond more positively than the average person.

The extent to which party officials report having spent their early lives in politicized settings is a major focus of the present analyses. In undertaking an appropriate examination, explicit comparisons between the party workers on the one hand and the nigh-dwellers and general public on the other are necessary, for as Prewitt has noted, ". . . studies which indicate that public officials received an abnormal dosage of political cues prior to their incumbency do not also tell us how many persons in the population received similar dosages but were never drawn into politics."[19] By comparing the party officials with nigh-dwellers matched in terms of social characteristics, as well as with a random sample of the adult population, we may understand better the potential significance of the politicization and other aspects of childhood environments for political socialization and the eventual recruitment of people into party organizations.

In itself, finding that party functionaries were reared in the most politicized environments would not illuminate concrete aspects of key socializing experiences. To comprehend these experiences requires a more direct investigation of the content, timing, and agents of political learning. Therefore, three phenomena will be considered. (1) The age of initial political awareness and its substance will be ascertained. Awareness of the political world, of course, usually is a precondition for political participation. It is reasonable to assume that this event will condition subsequent political development and thereby indirectly influence predispositions toward political activity. (2) Another concern is the development of political interest and how it varies over time. One reason such a small segment of the population becomes active in parties is that very few people are intensely and more or less continuously interested in politics. (3) The acquisition of party identifications will be considered. In Canada and elsewhere the direction and strength of psychological attachments to political parties repeatedly have been shown to be significant factors in explaining voting turnout and electoral choice by the public.[20] Moreover, partisan motives frequently have been cited by party activists as reasons for initiating party work, and the strength of partisanship is related to differential participation rates and career patterns within party organizations.[21]

To recapitulate, analysis will proceed as follows. Several social structural characteristics (sex, age, religion, ethnicity, education level, socioeconomic origin, current occupation, income) of party officials, nigh-dwellers, and the general public will be compared. The party officials will be considered both *en masse* and within their parties. We shall determine whether our effort to match party leaders with very similar persons was successful and whether the four groups of officials differ in ways that are consistent with their parties' public images and patterns of electoral support. This will be followed by an examination of the political socialization experiences of party officials and the two nonparty groups, to ascertain whether the officials have socialization experiences that are atypical. Let us turn, then, to the data.

Social Structure

Sex. Although party women are the subject of a detailed analysis in Chapter 8, it has been suggested that the relatively low levels of political participation by women in most Western societies may be explained by the fact that politics traditionally have been viewed as "man's work." Accordingly, male incumbency in political positions reinforces the expectation that political leaders should be men and prompts men to recruit other men, and women to conclude that the pursuit of political positions is not an appropriate activity for them. Other role constraints leading to lack of educational and occupational career opportunities further inhibit many women from acquiring the skills, resources and interpersonal contacts which facilitate the initiation and development of political careers.[22] The data support the expectations as to rates of participation. Although more than half of the population of the two metropolitan areas are women, their party organizations are distinctly masculine (see Table 2.1). Slightly less than 19% of the four parties' officials are women. The percentages in each party vary minimally; NDP-19.5%, Liberal-13.8%, Conservative-23.8%, and Social Credit-20.2%.[23]

Table 2.1
Selected Social and Demographic Characteristics of Party Officials,
Nigh-Dwellers and General Public

	Party Officials	Nigh-Dwellers	General Public
Sex			
Men	81.3%	81.3%	41.8%
Women	18.7	18.7	58.2
Total	100.0	100.0	100.0
	(N=625)	(N=625)	(N=1187)
Age			
Under 30	8.8%	11.0%	27.0%
30 to 59	56.5	51.2	42.3
60 or over	34.7	37.8	30.7
Total	100.0	100.0	100.0
	(N=625)	(N=625)	(N=1186)
Religious Affiliation			
United Church, Anglican, Presbyterian	48.1%	49.8%	45.3%
Other Protestant	12.6	10.5	12.1
Roman Catholic	14.4	15.9	17.4
Jewish	4.5	3.7	2.4
Other	8.5	6.8	9.2
No affiliation	11.9	13.3	13.6
Total	100.0	100.0	100.0
	(N=620)	(N=622)	(N=1165)
Ethnicity			
Anglo-Celtic	64.6%	61.7%	54.8%
French	5.0	3.8	5.9
Other Northern and Western Europe	9.6	10.8	12.8
Central and Eastern Europe	13.4	16.6	17.4
Other	7.5	7.0	9.0
Total	100.1	99.9	99.9
	(N=604)	(N=600)	(N=1129)

Age. It would be unrealistic to assume party organizations will mirror the age distributions of the adult public if for no other reason than that younger people generally are more geographically and occupationally mobile and may be unable or unwilling to give substantial portions of their leisure time to a party. Middle-aged people, in contrast, are more likely to have developed a firm sense of partisanship, established themselves sufficiently in their occupations to be able to participate in party work without jeopardizing their careers, and reared children who no longer require their more or less constant attention. Empirically, people under thirty years of age are significantly underrepresented in the local parties whereas those between the ages of thirty and fifty-nine are overrepresented. There are also substantial interparty differences among the officials. For example, although 30.2% of the NDP workers and 26.7% of the Liberals are fifty or over, 44.5% of the Conservatives and 43.4% of the Social Credit officials can be found in these ages. These differences are reflected in the mean current ages of the four groups: 42.9 for Liberals, 43.9 for New Democrats, 48.5 for Conservatives, and 48.7 for Social Crediters.

Religious Affiliations. The religious affiliations of federal and provincial legislators have been found to be quite representative of those of the Canadian population. Similarly, those of the party officials parallel the affiliations of the nigh-dwellers and general publics (Table 2.1). However, considerable differences exist among the officials of the four parties. A majority of New Democrats (50.2%) are Protestant, with much smaller and equal proportions being Catholic (5.4%) and Jewish (5.4%). A substantially greater percentage of New Democrats (28.1%) than of other parties' officials profess no religion. A majority of Liberals are also Protestant (54.1%), mostly United or Anglican church members. Consistent with the support Catholics historically have given the party, there is a larger proportion of Catholics (25.8%) in the Liberal than in the other parties (NDP-5.4%; Conservative-8.8%; Social Credit-13.4%). Again, consonant with historic patterns of political support, over three-quarters of the Conservatives (76.8%) are Protestants, 92.9% of whom belong to the Anglican, Presbyterian or United churches. Although two-thirds (68.0%) of the Social Credit officials are Protestants, the percentage affiliating with low status Protestant churches (23.7%) is greater than for other parties. Not a single Social Credit official is Jewish.

Ethnicity. Porter's use of a mosaic metaphor to describe the ethnic composition of the Canadian population is both familiar and felicitous. Significantly, he found the mosaic has a critical vertical dimension with political and economic power concentrated among Canadians of Anglo-Celtic origins whose families have lived in Canada for generations. As argued above, however, one need not necessarily expect local parties in Winnipeg and Vancouver to be composed exclusively of persons of Anglo-Celtic backgrounds. Indeed, approximately one-third of the officials (35.4%) are of non-Anglo-Celtic descent. However, the proportion of persons of Anglo-Celtic origin is higher in every party than in either the nigh-dweller or general public groups (see Table 2.1), being highest for the Conservatives (77%) and lowest for the Social Credit (58%). The New Democratic and Liberal parties contain somewhat higher proportions of officials of non-Western European origins (25% and 22% respectively) and the latter party, as anticipated, contains the largest proportion of people of French-Canadian descent (8%).

Education. It virtually has become a truism in contemporary sociopolitical analyses that in Western democracies high levels of formal education are associated with political participation generally and with party work and electoral campaign activity in particular.[24] Higher levels of education influence political involvement in several ways. Perhaps most important is that in advanced industrial societies education provides people with resources such as prestigious occupations, high incomes, flexible work schedules, and substantial leisure time, all of which are conducive to political activity. In terms of their psychological and intellectual impact, higher levels of formal education are assumed to enhance communication skills and feelings of self-confidence. Relatedly, some social scientists view education, particularly at the post-secondary level, as a process of social and cultural enlightenment whereby citizens develop a *Weltanschauung* conducive to political activity. As a consequence of a process intended to enhance reasoning skills and the ability to be comfortable with abstractions, as well as to increase concern for the humanistic aspects of society, individuals supposedly come to recognize the critical importance of political processes for maintaining or advancing their own and others' well-being. Another perspective, grounded in traditional notions of *noblesse oblige*, assumes that better-educated persons, because of their superior knowledge, develop a greater sense of responsibility for the conduct of political and social affairs in their community and nation.

Whatever the reasons, the average party official has enjoyed significantly more formal education than has the average citizen. As might be expected, however, the educational levels of party officials are closer to those of the nigh-dwellers than to those of the general public. Thus 20.3% of the general public, 13.8% of the nigh-dwellers, but only 10.7% of the party officials have eight or fewer years of formal schooling (See Table 2.2). At the other end of the educational continuum, 20.2% of the party officials have 17 or more years of education, as compared to 9.9% of the nigh-dwellers and only 2.9% of the citizenry at large. Equally impressive are interparty differences. The Social Credit party is largely composed (77.8%) of people with high school educations or less (i.e., a maximum of 12 years of formal education). Members of the New Democratic and Conservative parties are better educated, although approximately two-thirds of the former and one-half of the latter also ended their education at the high school level. The Liberals are the only party in which a majority of the officials (57.7%) has better than a high school education. Indeed, 29.0% of the Liberals as compared to 25.2% of the Conservatives, 11.8% of the New Democrats, and 8.1% of the Social Crediters have completed 17 years or more of formal schooling.

Among party officials with university degrees, salient interparty differences are again noticeable. For example, whereas 42.5% of all university graduate officials are lawyers (15.4% of all party officials), the proportion with law degrees varies from 61.8% of the Conservative degreee holders to 45.7% of the Liberals to 20.4% and 16.7% of the NDP and Social Credit respectively. The minor parties are also distinctive in that much larger proportions of their officials do not have advanced degrees. Of those with degrees, 42.9% of the New Democrats and 41.7% of the Social Crediters as compared to 26.7% of the Liberals and 16.4% of the Conservatives terminated their formal education with bachelor's degrees in the arts or sciences.

Socioeconomic Origins and Current Statuses. Putnam's "law of increasing disproportion" holds that the higher and more important a political position, the greater the status discrepancy that is likely to exist between an incumbent and the average citizen. As noted, it is difficult to advance precise hypotheses respecting the "eliteness" of local party functionaries. However, the four measures of socioeconomic status that are employed—father's principal occupation, respondent's principal occupation, annual family income, and Duncan's two-digit summary index[25] of occupational status—should certainly shed light on the matter.

Inspection of the data on father's occupation reveals substantial differences between the party leaders and the general public and more modest differences between officials and nigh-dwellers: 43.1% of the party leaders, 36.0% of the nigh-dwellers, and 27.4% of the general public had fathers who were professionals, executives, or proprietors of businesses. In contrast, 46.6% of the general public, 45.9% of the nigh-dwellers and 41.0% of the party officials had fathers who were blue-collar workers or lower status white-collar employees. These background differences among the three samples are reflected in the average socioeconomic status (SES) score assigned to father's occupation: 43.8 in the case of the party officials, 39.9 for the nigh-dwellers, and 34.0 for the members of the public. Interparty differences are also evident: 50.5% of the Liberals and 51.4% of the Conservatives had fathers who were professionals or businessmen as compared to 37.4% of the Social Crediters and 30.1% of the New Democrats.

Reflecting a basic proposition in stratification theory that one's opportunities in part are determined by one's socioeconomic origins, we find a

Table 2.2
Socioeconomic Status Characteristics of Party Officials,
Nigh-Dwellers and General Public

Education (Grade Completed)	Party Officials	Nigh-Dwellers	General Public
0–8	10.7%	13.8%	20.3%
9–12	46.6	57.6	64.2
13–16	22.6	18.7	12.6
17 or more	20.2	9.9	2.9
Total	100.1	100.0	100.0
$\overline{X}$ number of grades completed	13.4	11.9	10.8
	(N=625)	(N=625)	(N=1176)
Occupation			
Professionals	33.4%	24.5%	14.2%
Business proprietors and executives	25.8	22.5	11.2
Clerical, sales	13.3	14.8	22.4
Skilled and unskilled laborers	8.3	21.3	18.7
Service	2.1	6.3	8.6
Farmers and farm laborers	0.8	0.6	0.8
Not in labor force	16.3	10.0	24.1
Total	100.0	100.0	100.0
$\overline{X}$ SES score	63.6	54.5	46.4
	(N=625)	(N=621)	(N=1161)
Annual Family Income*			
Under 9,800	9.4%	10.9%	23.6%
9,801–19,500	38.8	39.1	46.2
19,501–29,300	25.6	28.2	20.4
29,301–39,000	11.6	10.5	4.6
39,001–48,800	6.4	5.1	2.7
48,801 and over	8.3	6.1	2.5
Total	100.1	99.9	100.0
	(N=614)	(N=588)	(N=1079)

* Income figures adjusted to 1978 dollars

monotonic increase in the proportions of people with a higher status occupation as we move from general public to nigh-dwellers to officials. 25.4% of the general public, 47.0% of the nigh-dwellers and almost 60% of the party officials are professionals, executives or business proprietors. Consonant with their occupational distributions are significant differences in mean SES scores of the three groups (63.6, 54.5 and 46.4 for party officials, nigh-dwellers and the general public respectively).

The magnitudes of these differences in comparison with those for father's occupation suggest that the average party official may have started life under somewhat more favorable circumstances than either the average nigh-dweller match or average citizen, and that he or she also has experienced more upward mobility. To obtain an estimate of intergenerational socioeconomic mobility, we subtracted the SES scores assigned to father's principal occupation from those assigned to respondents' occupations. The results show that the great majority of all three samples have achieved some upward mobility: 70.5% of the party officials, 65.8% of the nigh-dwellers, and 64.1% of the general public have scores higher than their fathers'. Given party differences in the distributions of current occupation, interparty differences in mobility are fairly substantial. The Conservatives and Liberals show the greatest upward mobility (21.9 and 21.4 points respectively). The New Democrats are the least mobile (15.3 points on average), and the Social Crediters fall between (17.9 points).

Insofar as principal occupation is concerned, the Liberals and Conservatives are generally similar. As Figure 2.1 illustrates, slightly more Liberals than Conservatives are either professionals (41.9% vs. 35.4%) or business proprietors or executives (27.6% vs. 23.1%). Both parties contain approximately the same proportion of blue-collar workers (Liberals-5.2%; Conservatives-4.1%). In contrast, not only do the New Democratic and Social Credit parties differ from the former parties, they also differ from one another. About one and one-half times as many Social Crediters as New Democrats are businessmen (34.3% vs. 20.7%), whereas the NDP contains a much larger group of professionals (30.8% vs. 16.2%). Nearly twice as many New Democrats as Social Crediters are employed as blue-collar workers (21.4% vs. 12.1%). White-collar workers in the latter party outnumber their occupational counterparts in the former by a margin of approximatly 3 to 2. Party variations in the occupations of members are reflected in differences in SES scores: 87.4% of the Conservative, 82.9% of the Liberal, 61.5% of the Social Credit, and 59.3% of the NDP officials have scores of 50 or greater. The differences in the average scores of the major as opposed to the minor party officials are particularly impressive: 72.6 for Conservatives and 70.4 for Liberals as opposed to 54.3 for Social Crediters and 53.2 for New Democrats.

A comparison of these scores with comparable data on MPs in the 28th Parliament (1968–72) indicates that with one exception socioeconomic status

Figure 2.1
Principal Occupations of Party Officials

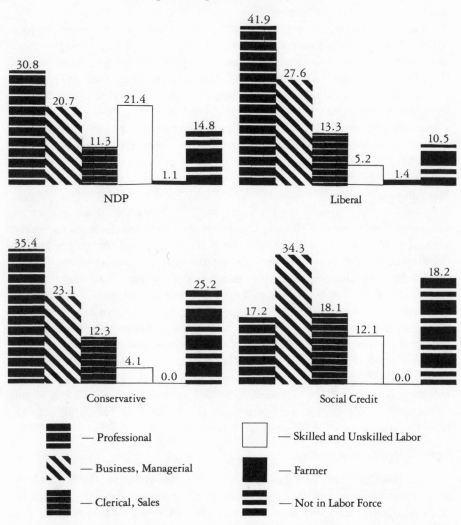

differences between the local party officials and federal MPs are quite modest. Overall, mean SES scores for MPs and local party officials are 69.4 and 63.6 respectively.[26] Similarly, for three of the parties, the Liberals, NDP, and Social Credit, these differences are in the direction predicted by Putnam's "law of increasing disproportion" (i.e., the MPs have higher mean scores). Specifically, Liberal legislators' scores exceed those of Liberal party officials by 5.7 points, with comparable differences for New Democrats and Social

Crediters being 8.1 and 5.9 points. For Conservatives, in contrast, the picture is quite different. The mean Duncan score of Conservative MPs is 61.7, fully 10.9 points *less* than that of Conservative party officials.[27]

The Conservative exception, as well as the other SES differences between MPs and party officials described above, might possibly be ascribed to factors idiosyncratic to the Winnipeg and Vancouver parties or to the composition of the 28th Parliament for that matter.[28] Although possible, these are improbable explanations. Rather it would appear that despite their local nature, local parties, particularly the Liberal and the Conservative but also (albeit to a lesser extent) the NDP and Social Credit, overrepresent upper SES groups. Indeed, even the mean SES scores of officials in the latter two parties exceed those of the general public by 6.8 and 7.9 points respectively, whereas comparable differences for Liberals are 24.0 points and for Conservatives 26.2 points.

Considering annual family income as a final measure of current socioeconomic status, we find that expected differences are manifested between the general public on the one hand and the party officials and their nigh-dweller matches on the other (see Table 2.2). At the lowest end of the income scale (under $9,800) the general public outnumbers the party and nigh-dweller samples by a margin of more than 2 to 1 whereas the converse obtains at the other end of the continuum ($48,801 and over). Also as anticipated, differences between party officials and nigh-dwellers are modest, and interparty differences, especially those between New Democrats and other party officials, are fairly large. Fully 69.0% of the NDP officials as opposed to 52.1% of the Socreds, 43.4% of the Conservatives, and 32.8% of the Liberals have annual income under $19,501. Conversely, 38.6% of the Liberals, 31.5% of the Conservatives, 21.8% of the Socreds, but only 9.0% of the NDP officials report annual incomes of $29,301 and over.

Political Socialization

Childhood Social Milieux. Let us examine first the extent to which the childhood social environment of the members of the three groups were politicized. Approximately four times as many party officials as nigh-dwellers or general public sample members have fathers or mothers who had been active in party work (Table 2.3). This holds for the officials of all four parties with interparty differences being no more than 6.6%. The politicization of milieux, of course, depends upon more than parental political activity. As children or adolescents, individuals may come into contact with a variety of other people who either are interested or actively involved in political life. In this regard, party leaders more frequently report having been acquainted with officeholders. Specifically,

Table 2.3
Extent of Politicization of Immediate Childhood Environment

	Party Officials	Nigh-Dwellers	General Public
Father Active in Party Work	43.8%*	12.0%	11.2%
Mother Active in Party Work	21.7*	5.0	5.1
Knew Public Officeholder(s)	42.4	35.4	31.1
Knew Party Activist(s)	51.0	39.5	35.3
Knew "Very Interested but Inactive" Individual(s)	53.6	35.8	35.0
Position on Politicized Environment Index			
0 (lowest)	21.6%	37.3%	42.3%
1	27.0	38.9	36.2
2	31.8	20.5	17.5
3 (highest)	19.5	3.4	4.0
$\overline{X}$	1.49	.90	.83
	(N=625)	(N=625)	(N=1187)

* (N=585) Questions not asked of party officials reporting first political awareness after age 18.

42.4% of the party officials, as opposed to 35.4% and 31.1% of the nigh-dwellers and general public respectively, indicate they had an acquaintance with a public officeholder (Table 2.3). Interparty differences are generally small, perhaps most noteworthy being the relatively high percentage of Social Credit party leaders (67.7%) who report having known no public officeholders.

Similar differences are evident in reports of acquaintances with party activists and other politically interested people during childhood. 51.0% of the party workers, 39.5% of the nigh-dwellers and 35.3% of the general public report having known at least one party worker, with 22.2% of the party officials, 11.5% of the nigh-dwellers, and 9.5% of the public having known at least two. The Social Credit party officials report the fewest acquaintances and their distribution differs only slightly from those for the nigh-dwellers and general public. Considering persons who were "very interested but not active" in politics, slightly over 50% of the party workers, as compared to approximately 35% of the nigh-dwellers and general public mentioned having known such people. Once more, the Social Credit party officials report having known fewer politically interested individuals than the other party workers. The detailed recollections reveal that there were a wide variety of types of such persons (e.g., neighbors, family friends, distant relatives), suggesting that the politicized environments in which officials were reared were more encompassing than those of the other two groups.

To gain a fuller appreciation of the extent of the differences among party workers, nigh-dwellers, and the general public with regard to their locations in politicized environments, a summary measure of parental party activity and acquaintanceships with public officeholders, party officials, and politically interested but inactive people was constructed.[29] The mean index score for all party workers is 1.49 (Table 2.3). Tests show more variance in scores within than between parties. For the nigh-dwellers and general public, the means are significantly lower (.90 and .83 respectively). The more politicized nature of the childhood and adolescent environments of the party officials is also suggested by the fact that as compared to 20% of the officials, only 3% of the nigh-dwellers and 4% of the general public have the highest possible score. Over half of the leaders (52%), but less than a quarter of the nigh-dwellers (23%) and general public (22%), are in the two top categories.

Initial Awareness of Politics. Unfortunately, previous studies of political socialization processes often have neglected the factors that go into the development of awareness of politics as a distinctive human experience.[30] Factors relevant to understanding why only some people eventually become politically active may be rooted in early cognitive experiences with political phenomena and affective orientations to them. In order to gather such information, the following questions were posed:

> Now, would you go back as far as you can remember to tell us two things. What is the first aspect of politics or public affairs (for example, an election outcome, a political issue, a party nominee, a party leader, the structure of governments) that you were aware of? And how old were you at that time?

Initial political awareness occurred significantly earlier for party officials (11.2 years of age on average) than for nigh-dwellers (12.8 years) or the general public (13.4 years). All three groups experienced a diverse set of events and conditions. Nearly one-third of the party officials, as compared to aproximately one-fifth of the nigh-dwellers and general public, mention events in terms of their own personal involvement (Table 2.4). Additionally, substantial numbers of respondents in all three groups mention specific federal, provincial, or local elections. Far fewer respondents mention general social events such as wars and depressions. The tendency not to mention general political or social phenomena is especially pronounced among party officials, 12.2% of whom make such references as opposed to 22.9% of the nigh-dwellers and 19.2% of the general public.

Table 2.4
Phenomena Associated with First
Political Awareness

Phenomena Reported	Party Officials	Nigh-Dwellers	General Public
Elections	20.8%	14.9%	18.8%
Other Specific Political			
Events or Specific Issues	12.0	14.9	12.0
Political Leaders	16.2	18.9	18.0
Personal Political Events	29.8	21.3	21.7
General Political Events	9.5	21.0	17.4
General Social Conditions	2.7	1.9	1.8
School Curriculum	6.4	3.2	5.9
Other	2.6	3.9	4.4
Total	100.0	100.0	100.0
	(N=624)	(N=619)	(N=1136)

Perhaps most important for understanding the processes leading to eventual political activism is that party officials more often recall their initial political awareness as being in some sense a personal experience. Thus, 27.4% of the officials as compared to 18.4% of the nigh-dwellers and 20.1% of the general public report direct active personal involvement in the event leading to initial awareness. More impressive intergroup differences can be found in terms of family influences where almost 36% of the party workers as opposed to slightly over 12% of the nigh-dwellers and general public indicate that a member of their family was involved. For over two-thirds of the party leaders, as compared to 36.1% of the nigh-dwellers and 38.2% of the general public, initial political awareness was marked by personal involvement; additionally, experiencing some emotional feeling in the situation is mentioned by 31.3% of the party leaders as compared to 21.3% of the nigh-dwellers and 20.9% of the general public.

Party Identification. Probably no single aspect of political socialization has received as much attention as the development of a psychological identification with a political party. Its significance for understanding electoral choice and a wide range of individual political attitudes, as well as its indirect relevance for explaining such systemic political phenomena as changes in party fortunes over time, has prompted scholars to focus attention on the processes by which partisan attachments are acquired and changed.[31] Relatively little is known, however, about the development of identifications among party officials or other elite political actors. The absence of pertinent data is especially troubling to those interested in understanding participation in party organizations. Given the overtly partisan character of their political participation, one might hypothesize that future officials acquire their preferences in a somewhat different fashion than the population as a whole and that the content of what they learn leads them to develop stronger partisan identifications. As a result, future officials may be more positively disposed than other people toward active participation in party organizations.

The data generally support these expectations. By way of introduction, whereas all 625 officials were identified with one of the four parties, 7.8% of the nigh-dwellers and 11.8% of the general public stated they had no identifications when they were interviewed and an additional 8.8% of the nigh-dwellers and 7.2% of the public thought of themselves as political Independents.[32] Moreover, 5.2% of the nigh-dwellers and 9.4% of the general public never at any time in their lives have identified psychologically with a political party. Among the respondents who did, fully 79.1% of the officials as compared to 60.4% of the nigh-dwellers and 52.8% of the general public had formed their initial identifications by the age of 20. Their greater precocity is reflected in the fact that the average party official initially had identified by the age of 15 (14.9 years) whereas the average nigh-dweller was almost three years older (17.8 years) and the average member of the general public almost four years older (18.8 years) when the event occurred.

Neither the strength nor the direction of partisan attachments are immutable. In Canada, a 1974 national election study revealed that over a third of the electorate (35.5%) had switched their federal party identifications at least once.[33] Similarly, neither the party officials nor the two samples of the public with whom they are compared were inextricably linked to the party with which they first identified. Nonetheless, the party workers were more constant in their loyalties as evidenced by the fact that 58.0% of them had had one and only one identification whereas only 45.9% of the nigh-dwellers and 46.9% of the general public had remained loyal to the party with which they first identified. Illustrative of both the duration and the greater intensity of the psychological commitment of the officials to their parties is that on the average they had identified with their *current* parties at age 20 and had maintained their identifications for 25 years. In contrast the members of the general public identified with their current parties at age 26 and had maintained these identifications for only 16.5 years. Since the party officials are older than the members of the general public, one might assume this striking difference largely is a statistical artifact of age. That it is not is indicated by the existence of similar differences in the duration of partisan commitments of party officials and nigh-dwellers. The latter group, of course, was deliberately matched with the officials on age. On average, however, nigh-dwellers identified with their current parties six years later and have continued these identifications for six years less.

Another indication of such differences in identification is found in data on agents associated with first and current partisan identifications. Party officials tend to cite more agents, on average, ($\overline{X}=1.9$) than do nigh-dwellers ($\overline{X}=1.7$), or members of the general public ($\overline{X}=1.6$), suggesting that the former were either more exposed or somewhat more sensitive to socializing agents in their environments than were the latter two groups. Perhaps more important are the kinds of agents cited; 81.3% of the officials compared to 66.8% of the general public and 63.0% of nigh-dwellers cite "family and close relatives" and "friends and neighbors" as agents associated with their first partisan identifications (See Table 2.5). For current identifications, the proportions citing these agents are 65.1%, 46.2%, and 41.4% respectively. Since the friends, close relatives, and friends and neighbors of the party officials far more often were public officials or in other ways politically active and interested, it is reasonable to assume that the content of what was imparted was more manifestly political.

Political Interest Patterns. Although many courses of political interest development are conceivable, undoubtedly, joining a party is facilitated by a continuing high level of interest in political affairs. Therefore, one would expect that the interest of future officials developed earlier and was sustained at higher levels than is the case for the other two groups. Looking first at *overall* levels of political interest from childhood to early adulthood, one finds sharp differences between party and nonparty groups; 36.8% of the party officials, but only 14.4% of the nigh-dwellers and 10.6% of the general sample report having followed politics "very closely" until the age of 26. And, whereas 85.6% of the party leaders mention having followed politics at least "somewhat closely" before joining a party organization, approximately 40% of the nigh-dwellers and 50% of the public paid very little or no attention.

To delineate specific patterns of development and change in political interest, respondents were asked to recall information for four age periods: a) 14-18 (or high school); b) 18-22 (or college); c) 22-26 (or profesional or graduate school); and d) 26 to present age, and individuals who reported either an increase or a decrease in interest during a particular interval were asked about agents or events associated with this change. Substantial, and in some instances, dramatically large differences obtain among the three groups' levels of political interest in all age periods (See Table 2.6). Particularly impressive is the fact that 40.5% of the party officials but only 19.1% and 14.7% of the nigh-dwellers and public at large respectively report increases

Table 2.5
Agents Stimulating a Partisan Identification

Agents of First Partisan Identification	Party Officials	Nigh-Dwellers	General Public
School	22.2%*	16.5%	13.4%
Family, other close relatives	54.6	43.6	51.4
Friends, neighbors	26.7	19.4	15.4
Public Figures	33.5	33.1	30.4
Important Events	25.0	27.1	17.5
Other	27.7	26.4	21.9
(N=)	(603)	(553)	(976)
Agents of Current Partisan Identification			
School	19.9%*	12.0	10.2
Family, other close relatives	37.9	23.5	31.6
Friends, neighbors	27.2	17.9	14.6
Public Figures	39.6	46.6	39.8
Important Events	32.9	32.4	25.3
Other	39.2	36.7	32.8
(N=)	(589)	(558)	(978)

* %'s sum to greater than 100 because more than one agent or event could be cited.

in political interest from ages 14-18. Moreover, atypical levels of and increases in political interest also characterize party workers in later age periods; nearly three-quarters of the officials as opposed to somewhat over one-half of the two public samples indicate increases in political interest after the age of 25. In short, a sustained strong interest in politics sharply distinguishes future party officials from others.

Regarding agents that spark changes in interest levels, with but one exception the several categories of agents (family, friends, and neighbors; school-related experiences; work-related experiences; experiences in voluntary associations; public figures; and public events) are more frequently cited by the party officials than by the two samples of public. (The exception is the more frequent mention by the public of work-related experiences.) The tendency of the officials to cite school-related experiences is not merely an artifact of the longer period of formal education that party officials have enjoyed. If one considers only those officials and nigh-dwellers who attended school during a majority of the periods under consideration (i.e., high school, college, post-baccalaureate),

Table 2.6
Respondents Reporting Increasing Political Interest During Various
Age Periods

	Party Officials	Nigh-Dwellers	General Public
High School or 14–18*	40.5%	19.1%	14.7%
University or 18–22	47.5	34.2	29.6
Graduate School or 22–26	47.2	42.0	36.7
26 till present age	72.4**	57.5	55.2

* Question asked for these age periods for those not in school.
** Only for party officials who had not joined a party by age 26.

discernible intergroup differences remain. In high school, 24.9% of the party workers, but only 8.4% of the nigh-dwellers referenced schoolmates, class materials or teachers as important factors leading to increased political interest. Comparable figures for those attending university and graduate or professional schools are 43.3% versus 32.5% and 30.7% versus 21.5%.

Socializing Consequences of Milieux. The inference we draw from these materials is that something like a "spread of positive affect" characterized the socialization experiences of most party officials. They appear to have been more sensitive and more receptive to a variety of political stimuli outside their homes because of the politicized character of the families in which they were reared. If this inference is valid we should find that among this homogeneous group of party officials, as well as among the nonparty groups, those reared in more politicized environments should have experienced certain socializing events, such as becoming politically aware, and developing an initial identification with a political party, at earlier ages. In effect, some of the socialization differences that distinguish the people in parties from people not in parties also should distinguish everyone reared in more as opposed to less politicized milieux—regardless of whether they are party officials.

Both of these expectations are confirmed. In all groups there are consistent decreases in mean age of first awareness and identification with a party and increases in the proportion interested in politics by high school age as scores on the politicized milieu index rise (See Table 2.7). Moreover, with minor exceptions the ages at which the event was experienced by people at each level of politicization are lowest for the party leaders, intermediate for nigh-dwellers, and highest for members of the general public. Politicization level also has the greatest relative impact on the party officials. For age of initial political aware-

Table 2.7
Timing of Political Socialization by Placement on
Politicized Milieux Index

| | Politicized Milieux Index | | | | |
	0	1	2	3	Total
$\overline{X}$ Age of 1st Awareness:					
Party Officials	13.1	11.8	10.5	9.5	11.2
Nigh-Dwellers	14.4	12.0	11.5	11.0	12.7
General Public	14.7	13.1	11.7	11.5	13.4
Age of 1st Party Identification:					
Party Officials	18.2	16.0	14.0	11.7	15.0
Nigh-Dwellers	19.6	17.7	15.4	15.6	17.8
General Public	20.7	18.6	15.8	15.2	18.7
% Interested in Politics by High School:					
Party Officials	50.4	67.5	80.9	83.6	71.2
Nigh-Dwellers	40.8	55.1	60.9	76.2	51.7
General Public	25.9	51.2	63.0	61.7	43.0

ness, the mean decreases by 3.6 years for the officials and by 3.4 and 3.2 years for the nigh-dwellers and general public respectively. For age of first identification the comparable decreases are 6.5, 4.0 and 5.5 years. Finally, the same sorts of relationships are present for development of an interest in politics by the time of high school. As Table 2.7 illustrates, the percentage of individuals reporting increased political interest during the high school (14-18) age period rises sharply as milieu politicization increases.

Summary

The purpose of this chapter has been to examine several basic social characteristics and political socialization experiences of Canadian party officials by comparing them with samples of nigh-dwellers and the general public. Party officials as a group tend to resemble nigh-dwellers and the general public in terms of ethnicity and religious affiliations. Unlike the nonparty groups, however, but similar to other groups of political actors, most officials in every party are middle-aged or older men. Further, in all parties, majorities of varying size are drawn from the upper socioeconomic strata of their communities. The strength of the tendency toward socioeconomic elitism is revealed in several ways. Particularly telling are comparisons of the occupational SES scores of party officials and federal MPs. For three of the parties the officials' scores are only marginally lower than those of colleagues who are MPs, and for the Conservatives the officials' scores actually exceed those of MPs by nearly 11 points. Overall, the fact that party officials' characteristics approximate those of national level political elites rather than those of a cross section from their communities indicates the pervasive importance of social structure in political recruitment.

It is clear, however, that social structural factors alone cannot explain why a small minority of persons become party officials, for socioeconomic status is neither a *necessary* nor *sufficient* condition for recruitment. There are officials with lower status, and most upper status people never become party officials. Following this logic, we also compared the political socialization experiences of party officials with those of nigh-dwellers and the general public. Perhaps the most important fact in this regard is that, as children, party officials had much more contact with politically involved individuals. Party leaders also report developing an initial awareness of politics earlier than do the two control groups, and that more often it was triggered either by direct personal involvement or by that of a family member or relative. They also report first identifying with a party and with their present parties earlier in life. Differences in political interest development patterns are equally impressive. In every age period the officials are much more likely to report increasing levels of interest.

In sum, recruitment to active roles within political parties is a complex process in which both social structural and political socialization factors play significant roles. In the next section we shall specify factors that influence recruitment into political work generally and party organizations in particular.

NOTES

1. Porter, *The Vertical Mosaic* (Toronto: University of Toronto Press, 1965).

2. Presthus, *Elite Accommodation in Canadian Politics* (1973) and *Elites in the Policy Process* (1974); Wallace Clement, *The Canadian Corporate Elite* (Toronto: McClelland and Stewart, 1975); Peter C. Newman, *The Canadian Establishment* (Toronto: McClelland and Stewart—Bantam, 1975).

3. See, for example, Florence Bird, *et al.*, *Report of the Royal Commission on the Status of Women in Canada* (Ottawa: Information Canada, 1970), pp. 340-343; Harold D. Clarke, Richard G. Price and Robert Krause, "Backbenchers," pp. 216-218.

4. See, for example, Allan Kornberg and Norman C. Thomas, "Representative Democracy and Political Elites in Canada and the United States," *Parliamentary Affairs*, 19 (1965-1966): 91-102; Clarke, *et al.* "Backbenchers," pp. 216-218.

5. Eldersveld, *Political Parties: A Behavioral Analysis*, chap. 4.

6. For data on the social bases of support for Canadian parties see Clarke, *et al.*, *Political Choice in Canada* (1979), chap. 4. See also John Meisel, *Working Papers on Canadian Politics*, 2nd ed. (Montreal: McGill-Queen's University Press, 1975), chap. 2

7. Stein, *The Dynamics of Right-Wing Protest: A Political Analysis of Social Credit in Quebec*, (1973), p. 34, n. 50.

8. Robert Putnam, *The Comparative Study of Political Elites* (Englewood Cliffs: Prentice-Hall, 1976), p. 33

9. Allan Kornberg, *Canadian Legislative Behavior* (New York: Holt, Rinehart and Winston, 1967), p. 46; Allan Kornberg and Hal H. Winsborough, "The Recruitment of Candidates for the Canadian House of Commons," *American Political Science Review*, 62 (1968): 1242-1257; Kornberg and Mishler, *Influence in Parliament*, pp. 63-68.

10. *Eldersveld Leadership Study Codebook*, mimeographed (Ann Arbor, Mich.: Inter-University Consortium for Political Research, 1970), deck 21, question 17, p. 17.

11. Marvick and Nixon, "Recruitment Contrasts in Rival Campaign Groups," p. 209.

12. Bowman and Boynton, "Recruitment Patterns Among Local Party Officials: A Model and Some Preliminary Findings in Selected Locales," 667-676. Computed from Table 4.

13. Prewitt, "Political Socialization and Leadership Selection," p. 107; John Wahlke, *et al.*, *The Legislative System* (New York: Wiley, 1962), p. 83; James David Barber, *The Lawmakers* (New Haven: Yale University Press, 1965), pp. 27, 71, 121, 168.

14. Kornberg, *Canadian Legislative Behavior*, data computed from Table 3.5, p. 52.

15. Harold D. Clarke, Richard G. Price and Robert Krause, "The Role Socialization of Canadian Political Elites: A Note on Provincial Legislators," unpublished paper, Department of Political Science, University of Windsor, 1976, p. 6.

16. Kornberg and Mishler, *Influence in Parliament*, p. 67.

17. Harold D. Clarke and Richard G. Price, "A Note on the Pre-Nomination Role Socialization of Canadian Freshmen Members of Parliament," *Canadian Journal of Political Science*, 10 (1977), 398.

18. Milbrath, for example, summarizing the findings of political participation research in the United States, states that only 4% or 5% of the general adult population participates in party activities during election campaigns. See Milbrath, *Political Participation*, p. 19. More recent research by Verba and Nie, although documenting the existence of several distinct modes of political participation and somewhat higher levels of political activism in the American population, again clearly indicates that only a relatively small proportion of citizens (8%) are members of political clubs or organizations, *Participation in America*, p. 42. Canadian data are similar. For example, in a 1974 national survey of the Canadian electorate, although 16.6% of the respondents reported having done something on behalf of a candidate or party at some point in their lives, only 3.7% said they engaged in these activities "often." (See chap. 3, Table 3.2).

19. Prewitt, "Political Socialization and Leadership Selection," p. 106.

20. Clarke, *et al.*, *Political Choice in Canada*, chap. 5.

21. Clarke, Price, Stewart and Krause, "Motivational Patterns and Differential

Participation in a Canadian Party: The Ontario Liberals," *American Journal of Political Science*, 22 (1978): 139-151.

22. For a discussion of constraints on female political participation see Jeane J. Kirkpatrick, *Political Woman* (New York: Basic Books, 1974), chap. 1.

23. Some of the data reported in this and subsequent chapters, particularly those involving interparty analyses, are not shown in tabular form. Details concerning these analyses are available upon request.

24. Milbrath, *Political Participation* (1965), chap. 5.

25. The rationale and method for computing these scores are described in Albert J. Reiss, *et al.*, *Occupation and Social Change* (New York: The Free Press, 1961).

26. Data on MPs are taken from Kornberg and Mishler, *Influence in Parliament*, p. 65.

27. In evaluating SES differences between MPs and local party officials, it should be noted that a substantial minority (30.1%) of the latter are or have been candidates for either legislative or appointive offices. Intraparty status differences are explored in detail in chap. 7.

28. One might expect, however, to find relatively more people of lower SES in samples of entire local party organizations. In this respect, the design of the present study which involved attempting to interview all party officials at the "middle" and "upper" echelons of local organizations may have included a disproportionately large number of upper SES party workers. This does not obviate the basic finding that local parties do contain a substantial proportion of such people.

29. The index sums dichotomies based on information regarding: 1) the presence of parental political activity; 2) knowing persons active in politics during childhood or adolescence; and 3) knowing individuals who were not active but "very interested" in politics during childhood or adolescence. Adding a respondent's scores on all items yields a summary index ranging from 0 - 3. This index will be used in ensuing analyses, so it should be noted that despite its sensitivity in reflecting differentials in the timing of socialization experiences, the differences in the intensity of the same measures are considerable. For example, the index gives equal credit for having known *anyone* active or interested in politics, but, in fact, the party leaders knew *more* of both types of people. The same is true of parental activity; more of the leaders had two active parents. Thus, if each level of each measure could be thought of as a range, the party leaders would be at its peak, the nigh-dwellers in the middle, and the general public at its bottom. This is pertinent for interpreting analyses in the following chapter. We shall observe that even after controlling for such matters as previous experience participating in politics, being approached to work for a party, and status differences, socialization differences still help account for participation levels among persons who otherwise would appear to be likely candidates for party membership.

30. For example, only one of the articles in Dennis' reader on political socialization deals explicitly with the development of political awareness and that article is a preliminary report of the data used in this study. See Allan Kornberg, Joel Smith, and David Bromley, "Some Differences in the Political Socialization Patterns of Canadian and American Party Officials: A Preliminary Report," in Jack Dennis, ed., *Socialization to Politics* (New York: Wiley, 1973), chap. 18.

31. The classic study is Angus Campbell, *et al.*, *The American Voter* (New York: Wiley, 1960), chaps. 6 and 7. On party identification in different Western democracies see Ian Budge, Ivor Crewe and Dennis Farlie, eds., *Party Identification and Beyond* (New York: Wiley, 1976). For data on party identification in Canada

and references to relevant Canadian research see Clarke, *et al.*, *Political Choice in Canada*, chap. 5.

32. In the nigh-dweller sample 24.4% describe themselves as strong identifiers. 22.0% describe themselves as weak identifiers and 35.9% are self-styled "Independent" partisans. Comparable figures for the general public are 23.8%, 28.6%, and 27.7% respectively.

33. Clarke, *et al.*, *Political Choice in Canada*, chap. 5.

Chapter Three

Participants and Nonparticipants

Canadian political culture may be characterized as being 'quasi-participative.'

Robert Presthus, *Elites in the Policy Process,* p. 6.

C ANADA, as other Western democracies, has an "open" political system and anyone who wishes to participate in politics ostensibly is free to do so. Some people work for a political party or a candidate for an elective public office even though they are not party officials. Local party organizations, relatively skeletal and somnolent between elections, generally welcome the temporary assistance of sympathetic members of the public. Indeed it is doubtful if local parties could wage effective campaigns without such assistance. In addition, some of the more efficient and vigorous part-timers become targets of subsequent recruitment efforts by party organizations.

What induces these unaffiliated part-timers to participate? Are participants distinguished from nonparticipants by distinctive social and political attributes? Also, why do most citizens refrain from doing anything more than voting? Can their lack of participation be explained by their antipathy toward political parties and public officials? Do some people fail to participate because their assistance is not solicited by representatives of parties? Would they participate if they were asked, and do some persons take part in campaign activities even though they are not asked to do so?

In this chapter we shall address these questions. Their answers obviously bear on the more general issue of who joins and remains in political parties. We first shall delineate the extent of participation in electorally-related types of political activity using data derived from national surveys and from our study of nigh-dwellers and members of the general public in Winnipeg and Vancouver. We then shall report the reasons the latter two groups offer to explain either their willingness or unwillingness to engage in one or more political actions beyond voting. Next, the social, political, and attitudinal profiles of those in each sample who have or have not been approached by representatives of the parties, as well as profiles of those who do and do not participate in such activities will be presented. These profiles will show that the parties are quite selective in their requests for public help and, further, that somewhat different attributes characterize the individuals whose assistance each of the parties solicit. They also will demonstrate that those who participate in one or more political actions are quite different from those who confine themselves to voting. Finally, we shall consider the effects of a variety of pertinent factors—childhood politicization, prior campaign participation, previous approaches to work for a party, and adult socioeconomic status—on the willingness of nonmembers of parties to work for them.

Participation: An Overview

The proportions of nigh-dwellers and general public who report *ever* engaging in several electorally-related political activities are displayed in Table 3.1. Large majorities of both groups report voting in federal and provincial elections with rates of voting in local elections being somewhat lower. Far fewer respondents report engaging in other types of political activity. For example, apart from voting, the most frequently reported action (by 48.1% of nigh-dwellers and 31.7% of the general public) is attending a political gathering of some kind, and the second most frequent (cited by 26.1% of nigh-dwellers and 18.6% of the general public) is displaying a political symbol such as a badge, a political poster, or a bumper sticker. Over one-fifth (21.3%) of the nigh-dwellers at some time have made a financial contribution to a political party or candidate. Approximately one-sixth (16.7%) report poll watching and a similar proportion (16.3%) report helping a party or candidate to "get out the vote." Members of the general public have not engaged in these most common activities as often, equivalent rates for them being respectively 9.8%, 10.2%, and 6.5%. Soliciting as opposed to giving funds is the least reported activity for either group (nigh-dwellers-6.4%; general public-2.0%). In both samples giving outweighs soliciting by a ratio of over three-and-a-half to one. More generally, not only does a larger proportion of nigh-dwellers report having participated in activities other than voting, but also the *number* of activities in which they have engaged is greater, an average of 3.4 as opposed to 2.6 for the general public.

Data derived from a 1974 national study[1] indicate that the relative frequency with which the general public of Winnipeg and Vancouver has participated in the several electorally-related political actions described above is not atypical of

Table 3.1
A Comparison of the Political Activities Engaged in by
Nigh-Dwellers and General Public

	Nigh-Dwellers	General Public	Differences between Nigh-Dweller and General Public Participation Rates
Nonvoting Activities†			
Attended a political meeting or rally	48.1%	31.7%	16.4%
Displayed political sign, poster, bumper sticker, wore political badge, etc.	26.0	18.6	7.4
Contributed money to a party or candidate for public office	21.3	9.8	11.5
Was a poll watcher or scrutineer	16.7	10.2	6.5
Drove people to polls on election day	16.3	6.5	9.8
Canvassed door-to-door	13.2	5.9	7.3
Telephoned people on behalf of party or candidate	12.7	6.9	5.8
Mailed out party and campaign literature	12.0	7.0	5.0
Performed general tasks for party or candidate	11.6	6.9	4.7
Lent home for party meetings, cocktail and coffee parties for party, candidates, etc.	8.5	3.8	4.7
Did clerical work for party or candidate	7.5	4.0	3.5
Solicited money for party or candidate from others	6.4	2.0	4.4
Was involved in other activities	3.6	2.1	1.5
Voting			
Always votes in national elections	81.7	71.0	10.7
Always votes in provincial elections	79.4	66.5	12.9
Always votes in local elections	62.0	46.5	15.5
	(N=619*)	(N=1146*)	

† Percentages of samples who ever have participated in a particular activity

* Missing data removed (respondents previously ineligible to vote also removed from vote frequency computations: general public [N=22], nigh-dwellers [N=2]).

the Canadian electorate in general. As Table 3.2 shows, the only activities other than voting in which majorities of the electorate ever have taken part are reading about politics in newspapers (87.1%) and discussing politics with other people (82.9%). In contrast, at all levels of politics (national, provincial,

Table 3.2

Political Activities of 1974 National Sample of the Canadian Electorate

How Often Does Respondent:*	Participate in Federal Politics				Participate in Provincial Politics				Participate in Local Politics			
	Often	Sometimes	Seldom	Never	Often	Sometimes	Seldom	Never	Often	Sometimes	Seldom	Never
Read about politics in the newspapers	40.8	28.7	17.7	12.9	41.7	29.0	16.4	12.9	39.3	27.0	17.7	16.1
Discuss politics with other people	23.7	37.2	22.0	17.1	26.0	36.4	20.1	17.5	23.5	32.7	21.9	21.9
Try to convince friends to vote the same way	8.4	12.7	10.0	68.9	9.1	13.5	9.4	68.1	6.5	12.3	9.4	71.7
Work with other people in community to try to solve some local problem	5.1	15.4	12.4	67.2	5.7	15.3	11.1	68.0	7.4	17.7	11.3	63.7
Attend a political meeting or rally	4.9	14.9	11.7	68.5	5.2	14.6	11.4	68.7	5.4	11.8	11.6	71.3
Put a sticker on car or put up a sign, etc.	4.5	9.1	4.4	82.0	4.9	9.4	4.0	81.8	3.4	6.1	3.7	86.9
Spend time working for a political party or a candidate	3.7	6.9	6.1	83.4	3.6	7.0	5.4	84.0	2.7	5.0	6.1	86.2
Contact public officials or politicans	3.0	11.2	13.9	72.0	3.1	11.7	11.4	73.8	4.3	14.3	10.5	71.0

Distributions on Federal and Provincial Participation Scales

	Totally Inactive	Vote Only +	Discuss Politics +	Convince Friends or Attend Meetings +	Campaign Activity	(N)	Coefficients of Reproducability	Coefficients of Scalability
Federal	11.0%	29.0	29.8	20.9	9.4	(1203)	.95	.77
Provincial	16.8%	25.2	26.7	21.9	9.5	(1203)	.93	.70

*Horizontal percentages are based on weighted half-sample (N=1203) with missing data removed.

Table 3.3
Distribution on Politicization Index
of Party Officials, Nigh-Dwellers
and General Public

Politicization Index	Party Officials	Nigh-Dwellers	General Public
0 (Low)	5.8%	13.3%	21.2%
1	11.2	20.8	22.8
2	13.1	24.2	20.7
3	20.3	21.9	15.8
4	19.0	12.8	12.7
5	21.1	5.6	5.8
6 (High)	9.4	1.4	0.8
N =	(625)	(625)	(1187)
$\overline{X}$ =	3.37	2.23	1.97

local) less than 10% report doing anything else and approximately two-thirds to nine-tenths state that they *never* have engaged in such activities. Particularly pertinent to the present inquiry is the fact that approximately 85% state that they never have worked for a political party or candidate *in any type of election at any time* and less than 4% mention that they do such work "often." These data confirm a finding from a 1965 national election survey which indicated that only 5.1% of the electorate was involved in that campaign with only 4.4% being a member of a political club or organization.

More detailed analyses of the 1974 election study data not only indicate that a minority of Canadian citizens involve themselves in politics but also that electorally-related forms of political participation tend to be hierarchically ordered. Thus people who engage in campaign activities such as "getting out the vote" also tend to be the ones who attend political meetings and discuss politics with their friends. Because of this, it is possible to form Guttman scales of political participation which meet or exceed conventional statistical standards.[2] (The distribution of the 1974 electorate on two such scales is shown in Table 3.2.) Further, in every province there is a strong correlation between the extent of participation in federal and provincial politics; active campaigners in federal elections also tend to be active in provincial elections and vice versa. In brief, data from two national studies confirm the present findings and support the argument advanced in the first chapter that party work and related campaign activities are relatively exotic forms of political behavior in which only a minute proportion of the Canadian population engages.

Table 3.4
Proportions of Highly Politicized and Less Politicized Nigh-Dwellers and the General Public Who Were Asked and Who Participated in One or More Political Activities Other Than Voting

	Nigh-Dwellers			General Public		
	Highly Politicized	Not Highly Politicized	Total	Highly Politicized	Not Highly Politicized	Total
Asked to participate and did	46.0%	33.2%	38.6%	34.2%	19.4%	24.6%
Asked to participate but would not	7.3	7.1	7.2	7.4	5.7	6.3
Were not asked to participate but did voluntarily	24.5	18.4	21.0	25.1	14.6	18.3
Were not asked to participate and would not have participated if they had been asked	22.2	39.6	32.3	32.8	55.3	47.3
NA	0.0	1.6	1.0	.5	5.1	3.5
(N =)	(261)	(364)	(625)	(418)	(769)	(1187)

Participation: Nigh-Dwellers and the General Public

Just as the extent of childhood politicization helps to account for who joins a party, it also has a role in explaining the political participation of some members of the nonparty groups. At the end of the last chapter we showed that politicization of the childhood milieu was related to the occurrence of such socializing experiences as becoming aware of politics, becoming identified in a partisan sense, and becoming politically interested. Joining both sets of information by dichotomizing the ages of first awareness and identification at approximately the medians for the party officials (i.e., 11 and under vs. older for first awareness; 15 and under vs. older for first partisan identification) and taking into account the existence of an interest in politics by the high school age period (14-18), permitted us to create a seven-level politicization index. Table 3.3 indicates that party officials, nigh-dwellers, and members of the general public vary in their distribution from high to low on this index as one would expect in light of what we already know of their relative eliteness and commitment to politics.

By dividing the distribution so that nigh-dwellers and general public members with scores of three or more are designated as having been highly politicized in their youths, it is apparent that politicization does have an impact both on being asked to participate and actually having done so. 53.3% of the highly politicized nigh-dwellers and 41.6% of the highly politicized members of the public as opposed to 40.3% and 25.1% of their less politicized counterparts were asked to do something for a party. Of these, 46% of the politicized nigh-dwellers and 34.2% of the politicized general public as opposed to 33.2% and 19.4% of the less politicized agreed to do so. Further, approximately a quarter of the politicized members of each group did something more than vote even though they had not been asked whereas only 18.4% and 14.6% of the less politicized did so.

Status also makes a difference. Chapter 2 indicated that as a group the nigh-dwellers are more of an "elite" than are members of the general public. We find that 45.8% of the nigh-dwellers but only 30.9% of the general public had been asked to perform one or more of the activities listed in Table 3.1 and that 84.3% of the former and 79.6% of the latter agreed to do so. Indeed, consideration of the less politicized groups in the two samples suggests that in the absence of a politicized background there is no substitute for status. (See Table 3.4.)

It should be noted that the level of childhood politicization also is associated with differences in political participation rates. The average number of different activities among the highly and less politicized nigh-dwellers is 2.5 and 1.7 with comparable figures for highly and less politicized members of the general public being 1.6 and .87. If only participants in one or more activities are considered, in the nigh-dweller sample the mean number of activities is 3.6 for the more politicized and 3.2 for the less politicized. Among general public participants, the equivalent means are 2.7 and 2.5 respectively.

Three inferences can be drawn from the data presented in Table 3.4. (1) Party officials appear to have fairly detailed information about the people to whom they turn for assistance. Status characteristics are visible but political socialization experiences are not. Nonetheless, the more politicized members of both the nigh-dwellers and public groups are more often asked for their help, suggesting that party leaders know something about their backgrounds. (2) There is support for our assumption that political participation going beyond voting is facilitated by being reared in a politicized milieu. A politicized background does seem to place people in a social network from which they are more likely to be recruited (even if it is for part-time campaign help) and it does increase the likelihood of their responding positively to a solicitation for assistance. (3) There also is support for the assumption that being reared in a politicized background does not *invariably* result in individuals becoming politically involved. Approximately one in ten among the highly politicized of both groups refused their help when asked.

Although the data are not presented in tabular form, it may be noted that the Liberal party and its candidates for elective office in the two cities have been the principal beneficiaries of the work done by members of both the general public (26.9%) and the nigh-dwellers (32.1%). The proportions of the public who have worked for the NDP and the Conservatives are almost equal (15.9% and 14.7% respectively), but among the nigh-dwellers a larger percentage (21.9%) have worked for the Conservatives than for the NDP (16.8%). Only 2.4% of both nigh-dwellers and the general public have carried on some form of activity on behalf of Social Credit. Another 6% of each sample have worked for other parties and the remainder refused to say for whom they have worked.

When asked why they stopped doing party work, approximately two-thirds of the general public (66.3%) and the nigh-dwellers (64.7%) said they simply had "dropped out" or they "had not been approached again and didn't volunteer." An additional 30% of each group said they lacked time, they had moved, the activities interfered with their jobs, or they had been asked to work at times that were not convenient for them. Additionally, 3.6% of the general public and 5.8% of the nigh-dwellers report not liking the "whole business of politics"—the people, the organizations, the candidates, and so forth. Although 60% to 70% of those in each group account for the termination of their political activities by reference to drift or inertia, slightly larger proportions of the more rather than of the less politicized members of the nigh-dweller and general public groups (differences of 9.1% and 2.8% respectively) offer reasons of substance. These considerations reflect the possibility that politicization can make one more discerning of dislikes, as well as likes, and of conflicts that lead to the realization that other demands on one's time can be more important than politics.

The mixed feelings of Canadians about political participation is further emphasized by the contrasts in their views as to why others participate and why they themselves might or might not do so. All respondents were asked what they thought were the "most important reasons people have for working in political parties?" A majority of both the nigh-dwellers (58.1%) and the general public (51.1%) ascribe to party leaders the commendable and public-spirited motive of wanting to improve government, but about 40% of each sample also attribute a somewhat crasser motive to people who have become party workers (i.e., the desire for personal material gain). The third factor most frequently cited by both groups (28% of the nigh-dwellers and 21% of the general public) is a desire for fun, excitement, and social gratification. Relatively similar proportions of nigh-dwellers and members of the general public also ascribe party or candidate support reasons (17%), a desire to launch a political career (12%), and a response to pressure (10%) as motives inducing people to become party activists.

Those respondents who indicated a willingness to engage in some form of political activity if they should be asked to do so at some future time were queried concerning their reasons for involvement. Their responses differ from the motives they ascribe to party workers in a number of ways. Only a small proportion of the respondents (3%) say they would participate in party work because they hope to derive some material benefit from their actions, and an even smaller proportion (1.5%) say they would become a party worker in response to pressure applied by others. In contrast, the majority cite good government-citizen duty reasons (70%) and loyalty to a party, its candidates, and to party officials soliciting their help (68% of the nigh-dwellers and 56.5% of the general public) to explain why they would participate. Finally, approximately a third of the two samples state they would engage in party activities simply because they are interested in politics.

We asked the members of both samples who indicated that they would not work for a party if approached to do so: "Which of the reasons on this list would be important to you in not participating?" Their responses reveal that the largest group in each sample simply may not have adequate time to devote to such work. Thus 39.1% of the nigh-dwellers and 38.3% of the general public feel they are too busy, lack the time, and so forth. An additional 20% of the nigh-dwellers and 16.8% of the general public report they would not work because they dislike politics and politicians, whereas 20% of each group give a closely related reason, such as politics are something they would not get involved in, or something they would not do.[3]

Table 3.4 indicates that the more extensive participation of nigh-dwellers may be facilitated by the fact that their assistance is more frequently solicited by party representatives. The personal recognition implied by being asked is a rather significant inducement to comply in a system that is not highly politicized, in which participation is voluntary, and in which campaign activities ostensibly go financially unrewarded. This is a point to which we shall return at the end of this chapter. For the present it may be observed that despite the rather substantial differences in their participation rates, as groups, approximately the same proportions give similar reasons for their decisions to work, not to work, or to stop working for a political party. These similarities and the stereotypic character of the responses of both groups, we suggest, reflect and may well be consequences of both the distinctive organizational features of political parties and the commonly shared unflattering public image of parties, their roles, and who is in them. Thus, in explaining why they stopped party work, people give the kinds of answers one could expect from anyone who had done something on behalf of a relatively inefficient organization that did not compensate them financially for their efforts, that only asked for and accepted their help at infrequent and widely spaced intervals, and that may have contained officials whom they did not find especially congenial associates.

It also is not surprising, given the supposedly conservative, pragmatic, and non-participatory character of Canadian political culture,[4] that so many non-active members of both samples give as reasons for not wanting to participate such answers as too busy, not interested, and dislike of politics and politicians. At best the features of the Canadian political culture cited above may leave people with mixed feelings about politics and politicians.[5] Consistent with this climate of ambivalence are the reasons former workers give to explain their own—as opposed to party officials'—reasons for working in political campaigns. They explain their own willingness to participate with socially acceptable reasons (e.g., citizen duty, desire to improve government, sense of obligation to another person). They attribute to other workers such mixed motives as the desire to improve government *and* to secure material rewards. Before examining some of the characteristics of these participants let us explore further the attributes of people whose help is solicited and those whose services seemingly are not required.

Who Is Approached?

Another aspect of the impact of both relative social status and degree of politicization on political participation is afforded by information on who is approached to do what by representatives of political parties. Regarding who is approached, nigh-dwellers on the average are asked to perform twice as many tasks for the parties as are members of the general public ($\overline{X}$s are 2.0 and .94). Within each sample the more politicized are asked to do substantially more things than the less politicized (2.2 vs. 1.4 for the nigh-dwellers and 1.4 vs. .68 for the general public). If those who are not approached to do anything are excluded from consideration, the comparable averages become 4.2, 3.4, 3.4, and 2.7. These figures provide additional support for our assumption that party officials may possess intelligence that transcends generations as to who are the people who have the sorts of backgrounds that may make them susceptible to party blandishments.[6]

Table 3.5 contains data on the backgrounds of the 286 nigh-dwellers and 367 members of the general public who were approached to engage in work for a party during an election campaign. The first section of the table compares them with the remaining 333 nigh-dwellers and 779 members of the general public in terms of backgrounds and current status characteristics. The middle section presents political background characteristics, and the final section summarizes their current political attributes and attitudes. As may be seen from the top panel of the table, the parents of those approached are more often native Canadians of Anglo-Celtic ethnic origins. Those approached come from higher socioeconomic backgrounds (insofar as these are measured by fathers' SES scores); they are better educated; they more frequently are high-income-producing members of a profession or are executives and proprietors of businesses; and they more often are "joiners" of social organizations and "consumers" of printed media.

Not surprisingly, in view of the material already reviewed, the data in the second section of the table indicate that those approached were reared in far more politicized settings. Also, large differences in the current political attributes and attitudes of the approached and non-approached may be observed. (See the last section of the table.) Among both the nigh-dwellers and the general public the group that had been asked to work contains larger proportions of individuals strongly identified with one of the political parties, larger proportions of Independents, and smaller proportions with weak or no party identifications. Particularly striking is the fact that the largest percentage of the nigh-dwellers and general public who were approached are self-described "Independent Liberals," "Independent Conservatives," and so forth. Those who do have partisan identifications have maintained them for longer periods, and their provincial and national partisan identifications more often are congruent. In addition, more of the approached group personally are acquainted with elected public officials and party functionaries. They follow politics more closely than those not approached and their feelings toward political parties

Table 3.5

Differences in Selected Social and Political Characteristics of Those Who Were Asked and Who Were Not Asked to Work for a Political Party

Selected Social Background and Current Status Characteristics	Nigh-Dwellers		General Public	
	Approached	Not Approached	Approached	Not Approached
% Anglo-Celtic ethnic background	38.1	35.7	39.0	33.9
X̄ SES scores of fathers	42.6	35.8	35.9	32.8
% Male	83.9	79.3	41.7	41.7
X̄ Age	45.0	45.1	41.7	41.9
% Who are affiliated with high status Protestant denominations	23.8	22.5	20.4	19.4
% Who belong to three or more organizations other than church	52.8	37.8	27.5	21.9
X̄ Years of formal education	12.6	11.7	11.3	10.7
% Who are university graduates	25.5	19.5	11.4	7.6
% Who are professionals and executives or proprietors of businesses	56.6	42.6	35.7	29.4
X̄ SES scores of occupations	57.5	51.0	48.4	43.9
% With incomes over $34,200	17.5	11.4	8.9	5.9
% Who read three or more magazines, journals, etc.	38.5	28.5	36.0	22.5
Political Background Characteristics				
X̄ Age of first awareness of politics and public affairs	12.4	13.1	12.6	13.8
X̄ Age of first psychological identification with a political party	16.7	19.7	17.6	19.8
% Whose parents both identified with a political party	67.5	58.6	65.7	57.3
% With at least one parent who worked for a political party	16.4	13.2	18.0	10.9
% Who as children knew three or more political figures	32.5	21.3	31.6	21.1
% Who had some interest in politics during high school (or ages 14–18)	61.5	48.0	56.1	42.7

	(N=286)	(N=333)	(N=367)	(N=779)
% Who had some interest in politics during university (or ages 18–22)	79.4	71.8	80.7	67.9
% Who had some interest in politics from age 26 to present	95.1	82.9	80.9	67.3
% Who had followed politics very closely from the time they became politically aware to age 26	17.5	11.1	15.5	7.8
% Who feel their information about politics had been above average level from the time they became politically aware to age 26	29.7	17.7	21.8	12.5
Current Politically Relevant Attributes and Attitudes				
% Who are strong Liberal, Conservative, NDP, and Social Credit identifiers	26.9	20.1	27.2	20.2
% Who are Independent Liberals, Conservatives, etc.	40.2	28.8	32.2	23.5
% Whose national and provincial party I.D.s are the same	61.2	56.5	62.9	57.1
$\bar{X}$ Years duration of current party identification	20.2	15.3	17.3	14.6
% Who know political figures personally	67.8	46.2	47.1	28.8
% Who currently follow politics very closely	39.9	25.8	29.7	17.7
% Who feel people like them really don't have a say about what government does	14.3	18.9	17.7	23.7
% Who feel public officials don't care about what people like them think	14.0	20.1	16.1	25.3
% Who feel government is too complicated to really understand	35.7	46.5	47.1	57.5
% Who feel they usually can get sympathetic hearing and help from a public official	59.4	52.9	52.3	45.4
% Who feel they are more likely than others to be asked for their political opinions	33.9	18.0	22.1	11.6
% Who feel their political opinions were recently asked by others	49.0	35.1	40.9	23.2
% Who feel their information about politics is above average level	45.1	31.5	28.3	17.5

more often are positive. Further, they tend more often to feel politically competent; to consider themselves opinion leaders; and to vote in elections, regardless of the level of the contest.

Since aggregate differences between individuals who have and have not been approached by any political party might mask substantial differences among the groups approached by specific parties, people who have been approached by the Liberal, the Conservative, and the New Democratic parties were compared in terms of the same qualities. (The comparisons could not be extended to those approached by the Social Credit party since there were so few in the sample.) In fact, only three observations pertinent to our concerns are suggested:

(1) Liberals and Conservatives tend to approach community notables whereas the New Democrats tend to approach lower-middle class people.

(2) From one-third to one-half again as many NDP as Liberal or Conservative approachees are persons who support the same party at both the federal and provincial levels.

(3) All three parties find it either desirable or necessary to turn to those who may be described as political "leaners," i.e., Independent Liberals, Independent Conservatives, and Independent New Democrats. This was particularly true of Liberals and New Democrats when approaching nigh-dwellers and less the case for these two parties in approaching members of the general public. Conservatives approach "leaners" about forty-five percent of the time in both control groups.

Other than these patterns, differences among those approached are minimal and random.

Who Participates?

There was less than perfect overlap in the membership of the group whose assistance was solicited by representatives of the political parties and those who actually did something for them, whom we will term "participants." For one thing, 45 of the nigh-dwellers and 75 members of the general public had refused to do anything for a party, when asked. For another, fully 131 nigh-dwellers and 217 members of the general public whose assistance had *not been solicited*, nonetheless, voluntarily undertook one or more political actions beyond voting.[7]

It was judged that the differences between the proportions of those approached for and those who actually performed party work were sufficiently large to make a systematic comparison of the social and political characteristics of participants and nonparticipants worthwhile. Analysis indicates that the participants in both the nigh-dweller and the general publics differ from nonparticipants in the same ways the approachees differ from those not solicited. Particularly striking are the differences in the average ages, occupations, incomes, memberships in social organizations, and the rates at which nigh-dweller participants and nonparticipants monitor printed media.[8]

As might be anticipated, given the materials already presented, a wide range of even more striking differences characterize the political backgrounds of participants and nonparticipants among both the nigh-dwellers and general public. Participants more often followed politics closely, judged that their information about political affairs was above average, and more often stated that in the past following politics had been important to them. Substantial differences continue to characterize their *current* political attitudes and attributes. Particularly impressive are the different proportions who now follow politics closely (44.6% vs. 13.8% of the nigh-dwellers and 33.8% vs. 11.8% of the general public), who personally are acquainted with politicians (68.5% vs. 37.7% and 49.1% vs. 23.1%), who feel their political opinions are likely to be asked for (37.1% vs. 7.7% and 23.8% vs. 7.8%), and who feel their information about politics is above average (51.3% vs. 17.4% and 32.0% vs. 12.1%).

The differences observed between people who do or do not participate in the political life of their communities, provinces, and country beyond the act of voting in periodic elections offer strong support for the assumptions underlying the Chinese box designation of political participation (depicted schematically in Chapter 1). These differences support our expectations that: a) there is a relationship between socioeconomic status and the extent to which people are exposed to political stimuli; and b) the more politicized the milieux in which individuals are reared, the more likely it is that as adults they will be implicated in and positively oriented to politics as a process. Their significance is heightened by the fact that fully 30.4% of the nigh-dwellers and 37.3% of the general public whom we have labeled participants confined participation beyond voting to relatively undemanding activities, such as attending a political gathering or displaying a political symbol (e.g., a badge, bumper sticker, or lawn sign). The limited attraction of politics for most people is further dramatized by the finding that even a political action as trivial as attending a political meeting apparently generates enough of a reaction so that some people have no desire to repeat it. Obviously, these are not the kinds of individuals who are likely to become party officials.[9]

Responses to the question on whether they would work, however, indicate that 48.4% of the nigh-dwellers and 44.5% of the members of the general public might be induced to participate. Indeed, as Table 3.6 reveals, more than

Table 3.6

Willingness to do Political Work when Asked, According to Prior Experience, Sample, and Early Politicization

% Who Would Work if Asked to Do So

Prior Political Experience	General Public	Nigh-Dwellers	Highly Politicized		Not Highly Politicized	
			General Public	Nigh-Dwellers	General Public	Nigh-Dwellers
Asked to participate and did	62.5% (248)	61.7% (201)	68.3% (123)	61.4% (101)	56.8% (125)	62.0% (100)
Asked to participate and did not	50.8 (193)	54.1 (111)	63.2 (95)	60.0 (55)	38.8 (98)	48.2 (56)
Not asked, but participated	32.5 (40)	18.7 (27)	23.5 (17)	25.0 (12)	39.1 (23)	13.3 (15)
Neither asked nor participated	34.7 (531)	35.6 (194)	47.3 (131)	38.2 (55)	30.5 (400)	34.5 (139)
Total % would work if asked	44.5	48.4	57.4	53.6	37.2	44.8
N =	(1012)	(533)	(366)	(223)	(646)	(310)

half to almost two-thirds of those who have participated would acquiesce if asked to do so again. Further, the data, in their aggregate form, suggest that on this issue nigh-dweller status is not a critical factor. Since the parties simply do not approach members of the general public to the same extent that they approach nigh-dwellers (although the results might be as satisfactory), either the task is too difficult or less elite members of the general public are not as wanted. Given that previous participants among the general public are likely to be as accessible to the parties as nigh-dwellers, the scales would seem to tip in favor of the latter alternative.

The last four columns of Table 3.6 indicate that prior politicization not only has a marked role in increasing the likelihood of working (if asked), but that it also interacts to obscure the overall patterns related to status. On the first point, the data are obvious. At all combinations of prior experience (with two minor exceptions) the highly politicized are the more likely to indicate that they would work, if asked, without regard to sample. At comparable levels of politicization, however, there are two systematic but different patterns of sample variation. With the minor exception of the small group who earlier had participated without having been asked, among the highly politicized, members of the general public are more likely than nigh-dwellers to indicate they would work if asked. Among the less politicized (with the same small exception) it is the nigh-dwellers who are more likely to give a positive response. Parenthetically, it should be noted that the same inversion takes place with regard to the proportions willing to donate funds to a party or candidate of their choice. Among the highly politicized, the members of the general public are more likely to indicate a willingness to contribute, whereas among the less politicized, it is the nigh-dwellers who are the more willing.

The analyses that began in Chapter 2 and have continued through this chapter also provide some clues to understanding *why people do not join political parties*. Nigh-dwellers and members of the general public tend to grow up in less politicized milieux than do party officials and to report that various aspects of political socialization occur somewhat later and with lesser personal impact and affective involvement. Nonetheless these two groups do include individuals who would appear to be good candidates to join a party because they possess facilitating attributes. The problem is that they tend to possess them to a lesser degree. This, then, is one dimension of an explanation for the nonaffiliation of those who otherwise might be party officials.

There are alternative explanations. One involves the possibility that "party official-like" nonjoiners consistently differ from "real" officials in ways not yet examined. A second is that some persons who are potential grist for party organizational mills have status attributes that either make them unwanted by parties, or make them *feel* they would be unwelcome. A third possible explanation is that persons otherwise likely to join do not do so because they have negative sentiments about some aspects of politics and party work. It is not that they are simply uninterested, ill-equipped, or victims of political inertia, but that they consciously dislike political parties or politics as a process. If this were the case, it would seem likely that such negative sentiments would be concentrated more among people likely to work but who chose not to do so, than among individuals who would not be likely to work under any conditions.

We examined the data for evidence of these possibilities. Regarding the possibility that individuals who are potential joiners, in fact, do not affiliate because they differ from current officials in ways that are relevant, we created a "protoparty" group in both the nigh-dweller and general samples of the public. The two groups consisted of 124 nigh-dwellers and 153 members of the general public who had been asked to work for a party, had responded positively, and indicated that they would respond in a similar fashion if asked to work again. Since they obviously were wanted by the parties and since they had responded positively to their solicitations, why, one may ask, were these people not party functionaries? One explanation appears to be that the 124 protoparty nigh-dwellers lack the kind of partisan commitment that appears to be a requisite for joining and staying in a party. More specifically, 43% describe themselves as Independent Liberals, -Conservatives, -New Democrats, and -Social Crediters and an additional 18% label themselves "weak" partisan identifiers. Moreover, two of every five of those who do have a party identification identify with party "A" at the federal level and with party "B" in provincial politics.[10]

The protoparty group in the general public are more committed partisans. More often than their nigh-dweller counterparts they have a party identification, especially a strong identification. In addition, they more frequently identify with the same party at the national and provincial levels. They less often engage in cross-party voting and disapprove more of people who term themselves political Independents. Further, they are more interested in politics at all levels than their nigh-dweller counterparts. At the same time, however, they lack the upper-middle class status that distinguishes party officials, especially those of the two major parties. For example, only one in ten is a university graduate and only about one-third are members of the professional or business communities. Only 7% have annual incomes of $34,200 or more. Nonetheless, since they also were wanted by the parties, one may speculate that a kind of self selection process is operative; that many members of this group, despite a keen interest in and knowledge and concern about politics and the fortunes of a particular party, are reluctant to commit themselves to joining a party "full time" because of possible psychic discomfort they might feel in organizations predominantly composed of people with higher statuses than their own.

Table 3.7

Percentages of Various Subgroups Expressing Negative Sentiments as Reasons for Not Engaging in Political or Party Work if Asked

| | Previous Participants | | Not Previous Participants | |
	Highly Politicized	Not Highly Politicized	Highly Politicized	Not Highly Politicized
Nigh-Dwellers				
Approached previously	25.6	13.5	31.3	16.7
Not approached previously	40.9	35.7	24.2	15.6
General Public				
Approached previously	28.9	13.2	25.9	34.4
Not approached previously	28.6	25.4	26.9	11.1

To assess the possibility that people who otherwise might join do not do so because of negative attitudes toward political parties, we examined the reasons for their choices given by those who indicated they would not engage in political work if their participation were to be solicited. The proportions who selected at least one of the alternatives from among "fear of politics," "dislike of politics and/or politicians," "dislike of the kind of work that is required," "dislike of the kind of people who work in parties," and "concern for the personal consequences" were calculated for the several subgroups in order to detect any systematic differential distributions of negative sentiments. The difference between the nigh-dweller and general public samples in the rates selecting such negative reasons are minimal, 22% for the nigh-dwellers and 19% for the general sample. Within each group, however, the differences increase when the several controls are applied. The data show that those more likely to be experienced and discerning on the basis of their training and party experiences also are the more likely to express antipolitics or antiparty reasons for not working if approached.

Evidence for this interpretation and for the particular role of early politicization is provided by the data in Table 3.7. Of the eight comparisons that are possible when status, previous participation, and having been approached to participate are controlled, in seven the people with the more politicized backgrounds give reasons that express negative feelings for politics and parties at a higher rate than those who come from less politicized backgrounds. None of the other possible sets of controlled comparisons produce such a consistent pattern. In the other comparisons many of the paired differences are very small, within one or two percent of each other. The large ones, however, also suggest some tendency for those with previous experience in political work—particularly those who had worked when they had *not* been asked to do so—to explain their disinterest in future participation with the expression of antipolitical sentiments. These patterns are consistent with the suggestion that persons seemingly most inclined to work for a party may be more discerning and, hence, more likely to make negative as well as positive judgments. The patterns also suggest that the past experiences of former workers who had not been invited to do so were rather unhappy. Perhaps the volunteers were made to feel unwelcome and this provided them with an experiential basis for developing and retaining antiparty work sentiments.

One other point about involvement in party affairs is worth making. Early in this chapter we observed that the personal recognition implied in being asked to work for a party can be an important inducement to comply in a society such as Canada. Analyses of political socialization experiences suggest that party officials may possess rather extensive information about the lives of people to whom they turn for assistance. A majority of the nigh-dwellers (51.8%) when asked if they knew the specific party officials with whom they had been matched replied that the latter were known to them. 17% say they were "close friends," 17.5% state they were "friends," and 17.3% report they were "acquaintances." An additional 27% indicate that although they were not personally acquainted, they had heard of the persons with whom they had been matched. Also, the closer the relationship between party official and nigh-dweller, the more frequently they discussed politics. 39.5% of the acquaintances, 63.3% of the friends, and 88.3% of the close friends have engaged in such discussions. More relevant to the matter of recruitment to party work, both solicitations of assistance and frequency of participation in party work vary directly with the closeness of the party official–nigh-dweller relationship. Fully 62% of the nigh-dwellers who are close friends of the officials had been approached to work whereas only 38% of those who do not know their party matches had been solicited. Equivalent figures for those who actually had participated in a campaign are 78% and 42%. These data[11] provide additional confirmation for our assumption that there is an important social dimension to political recruitment; to a substantial degree it takes place within a network of personal relationships of varying closeness. If we can extrapolate from these findings, and from our analysis which indicates that some people would not work for a party, if asked, because they have an active dislike for political work that is enhanced by the sensitivity that extensive politicization can engender, it would appear that party officials use their knowledge about friends and acquaintances to divide those among them who would be appropriate recruits into two groups. The first contains individuals who are likely to be receptive to their appeal for help. The second is made up of friends and acquaintances who are likely to resist any enticement or blandishment. Obviously, this is information well worth having.

Summary

In this chapter we have examined several aspects of the political participation of nigh-dwellers and cross sections of the general public of Winnipeg and Vancouver. Similar to the findings of national surveys of the Canadian electorate, only relatively small minorities of the general public in the two cities ever had participated in party work and related campaign activities. Not surprisingly, given their generally higher socioeconomic statuses, participation rates among nigh-dwellers are somewhat greater. Motives cited to explain either willingness or unwillingness to engage in one or more political activities that extend beyond voting were delineated, and data on the social and political backgrounds and current statuses of the individuals in the two samples of the public whose assistance was solicited by representatives of the parties in the two communities were presented. Similar data were presented for those who accepted an invitation and those who worked even though their help was not formally solicited.

The data reveal, particularly among the nigh-dwellers, that participants and nonparticipants differ in ways that generally support the assumptions that political activities that go beyond voting are disproportionately engaged in by people who derive from middle class backgrounds, who are themselves members of the middle and upper-middle class, who are reared in relatively politicized milieux, and who currently are psychologically implicated in various ways in the political process. These findings are particularly impressive because approximately one-third of the individuals whom we classified as "participants," in fact restrict their actions (other than voting) to routine and undemanding tasks or to minor symbolic gestures.

Finally, additional analyses indicate that some people who have the requisite attributes of party officials are not formally affiliated because they do not have strong psychological attachments to political parties. Others have very negative images of political parties, their officials, and politics as a process. Still others, whom the party organizations apparently want to recruit, may *feel* they lack the social statuses to be comfortable in organizations predominantly composed of upper-middle class and middle class people. And still others, who might work, apparently are never asked. Being asked in itself is an important element in the recruitment process; observations on the role of being asked in the nigh-dwellers—officials relationship foreshadow our findings in Chapters 4 and 5 that co-option is an element in the recruitment of party officials themselves.

NOTES

1. For more detailed analyses of the 1965 and 1974 national survey data on political participation see Burke, Clarke and LeDuc, "Federal and Provincial Participation in Canada: Some Methodological and Substantive Considerations," *passim*; and Rick Van Loon, "Political Participation in Canada: The 1965 Election," 376-399. Participation in electorally-related activities constitutes only one "mode" or "type " of political activity. On this point see William Mishler, *Political Participation in Canada: Prospects for Democratic Citizenship* (Toronto: Macmillan, 1979), *passim*.

2. Clarke, *et al.*, *op. cit.*, pp. 64-66.

3. An additional 17% of the nigh-dwellers and 20% of the general public say they would not work because politics and politicians hold no interest for them, while 8% of the nigh-dwellers and 12% of the general public say that, if asked, they might do something for a party but feel handicapped by their sex, advanced age, or some physical disability. Another 6% of the nigh-dwellers and 5% of the general public say they would not engage in political work because their personal lives might be adversely affected, and the remaining members of the two samples whose political activities had been limited to voting cite a number of other reasons that are so diverse they defy categorization.

4. See *inter alia*, John Porter, *The Vertical Mosaic*, chaps. 1, 7, 12, and 13; Gad Horowitz, "Conservatism, Liberalism, and Socialism in Canada: An Interpretation," *Canadian Journal of Economics and Political Science*, 32 (1966): 144-171; Van Loon, "Political Participation in Canada"; Presthus, *Elites in the Policy Process*, chap. 1; William Christian and Colin Campbell, *Political Parties and Ideologies in Canada* (Toronto: McGraw-Hill, 1974); Paul Sniderman, H. D. Forbes and Ian Melzer, "Party Loyalty and Electoral Volatility: A Study of the Canadian Party System," *Canadian Journal of Political Science*, 7 (1974): 268-288; Richard Simeon and David J. Elkins, "Regional Political Cultures in Canada," *Canadian Journal of Political Science* 7 (1974): 397-437.

5. On this point see Canadian Institute of Public Opinion data noted in Allan Kornberg, "Parliament in Canadian Society," in Allan Kornberg and Lloyd D. Musolf, eds., *Legislatures in Developmental Perspective* (Durham: Duke University Press, 1970), pp. 55-58. See also Clarke *et al.*, *Political Choice in Canada*, chap. 1.

6. That politicized backgrounds also may make people more sophisticated, discerning, and independent in their own decision making, more able to pick and choose among available alternatives and to say "no" when they feel it appropriate, is suggested by the fact that systematically people reared in more highly politicized environments actually agree to perform a smaller proportion of the tasks they are approached to do than do those who derive from less politicized backgrounds.

7. The principal difference between the volunteers and those whose help has been solicited was that the former had done fewer things—an average of 2.8 as opposed to 3.6 activities by the nigh-dwellers—and, among the members of the general public, 2.2 as opposed to 2.8 activities.

8. For example, nigh-dweller participants on average were three-and-one-half years older, and had SES scores that were 11 points higher than non-participants. 18.5% of the participants but only 7.7% of the non-participants had annual incomes over $34,200. Amost 40% of the participants but only one-quarter of the non-participants read three or more magazines or journals and more than twice as many of the former as the latter (56% vs. 27%) belonged to three or more organizations other

than a church. Equivalent differences between the participants and non-participants in the general population were of similar magnitudes.

9. However, other than age (they tend to be three to four years older) people who would not engage in political activities again do not differ in any significant fashion from Canadians who have carried out some campaign activity and who said that they would do so again if asked.

10. On the holding of different party identifications at the federal and provincial levels of government, see Clarke, *et al.*, *Political Choice in Canada*, chap. 5. They find that 34.6% and 21.4% of the British Columbia and Manitoba electorates respectively have different identifications in federal and provincial politics.

11. The data are explicated in greater detail in Joel Smith and John Zipp, "Social Relationships and Politics: Some Consequences of Friendship for Political Involvement," a paper presented at the Annual Meeting of the Canadian Sociology and Anthropology Association, London, Ontario, June 1978.

Chapter Four

Affiliation:
An Overview

> At levels below national or provincial offices the party structures
> virtually cease to exist between elections. The local strategists retire
> to their Kiwanis Club, neighbourhood committees or union halls,
> the local workers retreat to their households. . . . Except for the
> local M.P., a small office, and a few hyper-active local strategists,
> the party disappears.
>
> Van Loon and Whittington, *The Canadian Political System,* pp.
> 237-238.

THE recruitment of people to fill positions in party organizations in liberal democracies can be a complex process. To understand it one must bear in mind that political parties are more amorphous than most informed laymen or journalists assume. Canadian parties frequently do not maintain constituency offices between the election campaign periods that are their major *raison d'être* and they may be totally inactive in particular constituencies between contests.[1] It is not surprising, therefore, that usually there is no single, well-defined method for joining these organizations. Accordingly, ascertaining the initial recruitment experiences of party officials is not as simple a matter as one might assume. Since, however, how the process of joining is experienced may reveal not only a great deal about who is in parties and why, but may also help clarify the subsequent development of careers in politics, a major portion of the interview schedule was allocated to what had been conceived of as "the act of joining." In this and the following chapter several aspects of the data relevant to understanding this act will be examined. Here we shall consider some of its more accessible features.

On Matching

The previous chapters have dealt with a number of factors and personal qualities that may explain who does and does not participate in party organizations. These discussions reflect certain difficulties involved in trying to pinpoint key qualities that are particular causes of joining a party. Causes should be phenomena that both a) precede or coincide with joining and b) are relevant to joining and not just to having a high social status. To satisfy the first standard an age of first joining was established and used as a reference point on which to focus various prior and coincidental explanatory matters. To deal with the second criterion, data from interviews with the control sample of matched nigh-dwellers were employed. Matching on the basis of current age and status permits more focused comparisons of critical points in the earlier lives of matched pairs that can help explain why one but not the other holds a party position.[2] Case-by-case matching largely solves the problem created by the fact that the antecedent conditions of varying levels of political interest also may create other major current differences between party and nigh-dweller groups. Finally, matching offers a statistical advantage because the average differences between the officials and nigh-dwellers can be somewhat smaller than that between unmatched groups and still attain the same level of significance.[3]

To avail ourselves of these advantages, party leaders and their matching nigh-dwellers have been contrasted on a case-by-case basis. The various respects in which they are compared derive from the social structural and socialization approaches articulated previously. The socialization perspective suggests searching for evidence that party officials have undergone political learning experiences that differ from those of nigh-dwellers. Greater exposure to positively charged political stimuli as well as variations in the process by which political awareness, interest, and a sense of partisanship are acquired, constitute indicators of important socialization differences between officials and other citizens. The social structural approach suggests that party leaders will have possessed more prestigious statuses prior to joining. From an individual perspective, status advantages indicate both the possession of skills and resources needed to perform the tasks required by parties and the likelihood of being located in social milieux from which recruitment is facilitated. From an organizational perspective, it can be expected that officials will have status advantages because the parties need substantial economic resources and social capital to operate effectively and to present attractive images to voters. Some forty-three socialization and status characteristics from birth to the point of joining a party are employed to determine whether such differences between leaders and their nigh-dweller matches can help to explain affiliation.[4] Since some of these variables reflect aspects of both social structure and socialization experiences, the classification of specific measures is approximate and involves judgment. However, since the questions from which the measures are derived are keyed to specific periods of life, they can be placed in an approximate temporal sequence.

Table 4.1

Status Attributes of Party Officials and Nigh-Dwellers
from Birth to Age of Joining a Party

	Party Officials	Nigh-Dwellers	t*
Early Life Status Attributes			
% with both parents born in Canada	25.4	32.5	−2.71b
% with fathers born in province	13.3	9.8	1.95c
% with mothers born in province	10.9	9.3	.95
% born in Canada	81.4	77.1	1.93c
Mean family socioeconomic situation in childhood relative to local standards	3.2	3.0	2.78b
Father's mean Duncan SES score during R's childhood	43.6	39.8	2.74b
Status Attributes at Age of Joining			
Mean number of children	2.2	1.9	2.56b
% married	61.1	58.0	1.76b
% married with children	51.0	43.4	3.84a
% married with children under 5	27.7	26.2	.66
Index of closeness to present community of residence when joined (higher score— further away)	1.9	2.0	3.02b
Head of Household's mean Duncan SES score	54.6	40.7	9.10a
% with Head of Households who were:			
Professional	22.2	16.5	2.94b
Business executives	16.3	13.8	1.35
Blue collar workers	18.6	28.6	4.68a
Students	14.6	8.0	4.17a
Mean years of formal education	13.4	12.0	7.78a

*one-tailed t tests
a p ≤ .001
b p ≤ .01
c p ≤ .05

Pre-Affiliation Differences

As a set the socioeconomic measures in Table 4.1 indicate that the officials started with only minimal advantages over the nigh-dwellers, but that at the time of joining status differences had widened discernibly. Party leaders tend to recall slightly better familial economic conditions during childhood,[5] and the mean Duncan scores for the occupations of the fathers of party officials and nigh-dwellers are 43.6 and 39.8, respectively. At the age of initial recruitment, however, the widening of status differences is evidenced by the gap of 13.9 points in mean Duncan scores of respondents' occupations. A direct comparison of years of education completed when the officials joined was not possible, but since 80 to 90% of the members of both groups were out of school by that time, information as to total education was employed as a substitute. In this regard, the difference of nearly one-and-a-half years in favor of the officials (13.4 vs. 12.0 for nigh-dwellers) is consonant with the general pattern of status differences.

Other selected non socioeconomic aspects of the respondents' statuses that may have affected both their ability to affiliate and their attractiveness to parties are included in Table 4.1. The comparisons indicate, by and large, that at the time of joining the statuses of the officials facilitated affiliating with a political organization more than did those of the nigh-dwellers. For example, as the time of first affiliating approaches, the impact of local residential stability becomes apparent, with nigh-dwellers being somewhat less likely to have been community residents than party officials.[6] More of the party officials were in school when they joined, a difference that probably has two sources. Canadian parties normally have affiliated groups in colleges and universities that need students to run and staff them. In addition, many of the party activists who still were in school (particularly the Liberals and Conservatives) were law students who may have joined campus party organizations as a first step toward establishing useful professional contacts. Party officials also are further along in the family life cycle than are nigh-dwellers, being more likely to have been married. If they are married, they are more likely to have been parents, and, if parents, to have had older children. Thus, even though nigh-dwellers currently are quite similar to party officials, these comparisons suggest that when the officials first joined, the nigh-dwellers simply had not attained both the familial and status attributes that permit the luxury of joining or attract those who recruit new party members.

The role that socialization plays in explaining joining parties was evaluated by comparing the party members and nigh-dwellers in terms of the twenty-six variables displayed in Table 4.2. With two exceptions, only one of which is puzzling, these tests emphasize the major importance of a) spending one's childhood and adolescent years in a politicized environment, and b) the sensitivity to political phenomena which being reared in such an environment may promote. In accord with findings in Chapter 2, party officials tend to have had parents with party preferences that were known to the respondents and which are congruent with officials' current party affiliations. The party workers also

Table 4.2
Political Socialization Experiences of Party Officials
and Nigh-Dwellers from Birth to Age of Joining a Party

	Party Officials	Nigh-Dwellers	t*
Initial Political Awareness			
Mean age of initial political awareness	11.2	12.8	5.15[a]
% Reporting awareness of an overtly political event	38.6	25.3	14.22[a]
% Reporting awareness of different types of events:			
Elections	20.8	14.7	2.99[a]
Socioeconomic events (e.g., depression)	19.2	34.4	−6.33[a]
Specific political figures	16.1	18.7	−1.23
Political materials at school	6.4	3.2	2.69[b]
Personal contact with politicians	13.1	11.0	1.13
Specific political issues or events	5.0	3.0	1.73[c]
% Recalling first political awareness of event for which respondent:			
had no personal connection	32.0	63.0	−11.72[a]
had relatives involved	40.5	17.8	9.09[a]
was personally involved	27.4	18.2	3.81[a]
Party Identification			
Mean age of first identification	14.9	17.8	−6.48[a]
Mean number of identifications	1.7	1.9	−1.05
Parental party identification patterns:			
neither parent had identification	15.2	38.2	−9.55[a]
one parent had identification	17.4	.6	10.86[a]
parents identified with same party	54.5	44.8	3.56[a]
% with identifications different from parents	29.0	66.7	−14.22[a]
Contacts with Politically Involved People			
While R was in elementary school:			
% with politically active relatives or family friends	36.6	19.0	7.21[a]
% knowing no one politically active	49.0	60.5	−4.11[a]
Mean number of political activists known	.9	.6	6.03[a]
% with politically interested but inactive relatives or family friends	38.7	20.2	7.18[a]
% knowing no one interested in politics	46.4	64.2	−6.33[a]
Mean number of politically interested but inactive people known	1.1	.6	6.58[a]
% with friends interested in politics during:			
high school (14−18) age period	17.8	26.2	−3.63[a]
college (18−22) age period	27.4	17.0	4.71[a]
graduate or professional school (22−26) age period	15.4	4.6	6.63[a]

*one-tailed t tests   [a]p ≤ .001   [b]p ≤ .01   [c]p ≤ .05

are more likely to have known more relatives or family friends actually active or greatly interested in political matters. With the exception of the high school period, as they proceed with their educations (or during equivalent age periods if they had left school), higher proportions of party leaders than nigh-dwellers report having known people who were interested in politics. All of these differences are statistically significant.

The only exception to this pattern of heightened political exposure for the future leaders is the proportion of high school age friends interested in politics. Slightly over 26% of the nigh-dwellers but only 17.8% of the party workers report that their high school friends were politically interested. In a context in which all other findings are consistently and substantially in the other direction, this datum is anomalous. However, it does counter the possibility that the differences in the data are so large and consistent only because party officials retrospectively align their pasts with their present interests and values. The essential realism of their responses is further supported by the fact that the officials indicate that at a minimum almost 25% of their fathers and 10% of their mothers were formally affiliated with and active in party organizations. This is substantially above the proportion of nigh-dwellers' parents who engaged in such activities. Overall, the large number of statistically significant differences strongly indicate that the officials were socialized in considerably more politicized environments than were the matched nigh-dwellers.

As befits people reared in more politically-charged social environments, the party officials also report having shared earlier and more clearly in a number of political events and experiences. These occasions not only reflect the very early impact of environments but also reinforce perceptions that their environments included a significant political component. Thus the first event with political content (i.e., age of first awareness of politics or public affairs) is reported as occurring almost a year-and-a-half earlier by officials than by nigh-dwellers (at 11.2 vs. 12.8 years of age). From their descriptions, the event experienced by future party workers was more likely to have been explicitly political and they were more likely than the nigh-dwellers to have been closely involved either personally or through members of their immediate families. They report having formed their first partisan identifications a full three years earlier than the nigh-dwellers (at 14.9 vs. 17.8 years of age), but there is no marked difference in the number of such identifications reported. In this one regard the data suggest that as compared to their neighbors the officials are neither more close-minded inflexible party loyalists nor more manipulative pragmatists looking for the best political "deal." With this one exception, all these differences between officials and nigh-dwellers, again, are statistically significant.

It is possible that because the comparisons have treated the leaders of all the parties as a single group, important variations among parties are masked. This possibility was explored by examining the same materials for each party separately. The results are somewhat cumbersome to interpret because nigh-dwellers were matched not for party but for status. Variations could occur because differences between a party's officials and their non-party social equals do indeed diverge from the overall pattern or because their matched nigh-dwellers include a mixture of non-identifiers, Independents, and supporters of opposition parties. Checks on these numerous possibilities required several regrouped comparisons, none of which systematically contradict the results presented.[7] Thus the evidence indicates that both socialization and social structural factors facilitate or impede the joining of political parties. The fact that these conclusions are derived from the use of a control sample of matched nigh-dwellers suggests that these factors operate in addition to any special resources party officials have as members of an advantaged socioeconomic stratum.

The Experience of Joining

In one sense, only party officials can explain why and how joining occurs. Comparisons with nonjoiners may help focus on what to look for, but, never having joined, nigh-dwellers can say little at firsthand about the experience of entering a party organization. It follows that the most obvious way to learn about joining parties is to ask those who have done so what happened and why. And in a number of ways this strategy was adopted in the interview. The direct approach, however, is not without difficulties. For example, people may not know some or all of the reasons for their actions and, in addition, may have great difficulty verbalizing even those of which they are aware. On such stuff psychiatry thrives. Even were this not a problem, the question "why" usually yields an unsatisfying assortment of responses because, as a probe for explanation, it is often ambiguous. Some responses are necessary preconditions that apply equally to many outcomes (e.g., "I lived next door to 'X' at the time."). Other responses recount events that make the outcome plausible (e.g., "I was asked."). Moreover, responses at times are incomplete because an honest self-accounting would be socially unacceptable (e.g., "I really didn't care a hoot about parties or all the things that my co-workers said that they wanted to achieve, but at the time it seemed like a good way to get my law practice off the ground."). Given these possibilities, investigators often try to explain outcomes indirectly by fitting data to models that employ factors that may not happen to be salient in the actor's consciousness but still may be eminently sensible and important from the perspective of theories and explanations generated in previous research.

Knowing in advance the various sorts of problems that can arise in asking "why" directly, the question was approached in a number of ways. First it was asked as an unstructured open-ended question and the response probed for more details. After probing, lists of generally accepted reasons were offered and respondents were asked which applied to them. Responses solicited by this technique provide the basis for the following analyses of the party officials' own perceptions of their reasons for initially affiliating.[8]

Perceived Reasons for Joining

A major focus of the political recruitment literature[9] is the motives that people have for initiating and sustaining political activity. Research on party activists has revealed that individuals start and continue party work in response to a variety of what Clark and Wilson have designated as purposive (i.e., ideological, policy), material (i.e., patronage, preferments, other economic rewards), and solidary (i.e., social) incentives.[10] More concretely, these studies document that people become party workers because of a strong sense of partisan allegiance, to help their party implement specific policies or more general ideological goals, to make useful business contacts, to obtain patronage, or to enjoy the social and psychological gratification deriving from interaction with like-minded persons.[11] Also, virtually all of the relevant research suggests the presence both in aggregate and individual terms of what Eldersveld has called "motivational pluralism." Stated simply, party workers tend to report that not one but several factors motivated their decisions to become active.[12] Analytically, the types of motives reported by party activists correlate with a number of social, demographic, and political variables, and there is some evidence that the types and strength of motives are related to behavior within party organizations and attitudes towards various aspects of party work.

In order to avoid response-set bias, in asking respondents to indicate from a preset list their reasons for joining a party,[13] the sequence of choices was randomized. The alternatives summarized in Table 4.3 have been regrouped for interpretative purposes into four categories: political considerations, personal considerations, governmental improvement, and responses to pressures.

Turning first to political considerations, nearly half (47.0%) of the respondents cite party loyalty, with the percentage ranging from a low of 32.3% for Social Credit to a high of 55.6% for New Democrats. Other political considerations, including loyalty to candidates, to other party activists, and the desire to launch a political career, are mentioned by fewer respondents (27.2%, 13.4%, and 11.7% respectively). That only about one party leader in ten admits to personal political ambitions might be attributed to reluctance on

Table 4.3
Officials' Reasons for Joining a Party

Types of Reasons	% selecting reason as applicable*					most important reason†
	NDP	Liberal	Conser-vative	Social Credit	Total	
To Improve Government:						
At all levels	66.9	42.4	46.3	66.7	53.8	21.1
At national level	45.0	48.1	51.7	50.5	48.5	15.8
At provincial level	49.7	34.3	38.8	64.6	44.3	9.1
At local level	36.1	22.4	25.9	41.4	29.9	1.6
sub-total						47.6
Response to Pressures from:						
Immediate family	9.5	8.6	7.5	9.1	8.6	2.9
Close friends	7.7	16.2	12.2	13.1	12.3	4.3
Distant relatives	1.2	.5	1.4	—	.8	.2
Neighbors, acquaintances	5.3	6.2	5.4	10.1	6.4	1.3
Civic, fraternal groups	1.8	4.3	1.4	4.0	2.9	—
Employers	2.4	4.8	.7	1.0	1.1	.2
Co-workers	7.1	10.0	8.2	7.7	8.3	1.3
Unions, profesional assns.	11.2	1.4	1.4	4.0	4.5	1.0
sub-total						11.2
Political Considerations						
Loyalty to party	55.6	48.1	45.6	32.3	47.0	13.6
Loyalty to candidate	21.9	27.1	34.7	25.3	27.2	6.1
Loyalty to party official	13.6	12.4	18.4	8.1	13.4	1.4
To launch a political career	8.9	15.7	10.2	10.1	11.7	3.4
sub-total						24.5
Personal Considerations						
Personal satisfaction, enjoyment	56.8	60.5	58.5	49.5	57.3	16.0
To expand social life	8.9	15.2	12.2	14.1	12.6	.8
sub-total						16.8
(N)	(169)	(210)	(147)	(99)	(625)	(625)

*%'s add to more than 100 because of multiple responses
†for entire sample

the part of aspiring politicians to admit them in a cultural context which supplies little normative support for the legitimacy of politics as a career. It also might reflect the avocational nature of party activity for officials, few of whom ever will become serious contenders for public office.

Considering "improve government" reasons, large numbers of individuals in each of the four parties indicate that they played a part in the decision to affiliate. It may be that improving government is not a focused motivating force for most respondents, but represents a socially acceptable reason. Supporting this interpretation is the fact that the "all levels" response is chosen somewhat more frequently than those which refer to specific levels of government. It also is possible that a substantial proportion of party officials *do* want to improve government. Party work may not be perceived as qualitatively different from nonpartisan community and service work.[14] And, since officials conduct much of their activities locally and voluntarily, it is quite possible many are, in fact, acting out a community service orientation.

Regarding "personal considerations," a majority (57.3%) of the respondents, ranging from 49.5% for Social Crediters to 60.5% for Liberals, expected party work to provide them with "personal satisfaction and enjoyment." The frequency with which this reason is offered suggests that some new affiliates see party activity as providing opportunities for the sort of rewarding social interaction available in any voluntary association. If so, they may give less consideration to ideologies, policies, and local competitiveness than is assumed in most discussions of political recruitment. Alternatively, choice of the response "personal satisfaction and enjoyment" may have been motivated by the anticipated satisfaction of achieving a party's traditional goals, the election of its candidates, and the implementation of its policy positions.

Only relatively few party workers cite "pressures" from various individuals or groups as a reason for affiliating with a party. Family, friends, co-workers, and, to a slightly lesser extent, neighbors and acquaintances are the most frequent sources of such pressure. With a few understandable exceptions, their degree of importance is similar for the members of the four parties. The relatively small percentage of respondents citing these reasons may reflect, in part at least, the negative connotations associated with the notion of responding to "pressures" even when they are real. In addition, subtle pressures in the form of "helpful suggestions" may not be recognized and, therefore, may go unreported.

These data can yield additional knowledge by considering them in the context of both whether the respondents described themselves as recruits or volunteers and whether the tasks initially performed were of a general or

Table 4.4
Mode of Entry into Party Work for Officials Selecting
Political, Personal or Other Considerations as
Most Important Reason for Joining Party

| | Type of Reason | | | |
	Political	Personal	Other	Total
Mode of Entry				
Recruited – Specific Task	32.7%	22.9%	24.8%	26.4%
Recruited – General Work	17.0	11.4	15.0	14.9
Volunteered – Specific Task	7.2	10.5	10.4	9.6
Volunteered – General Work	43.1	55.2	49.9	49.1
Total	100.0	100.0	100.1	100.0
(N)	(153)	(105)	(367)	(625)

specific nature. Since respondents tend to select a number of reasons for joining, only the data on "most important reason" for joining a party will be utilized. Presumably these are the reasons with the greatest motivating force.

Analyses relating mode of entry to the choice of "improve government" responses support the previous suggestion that these responses may express commitment to a genuine desire to achieve social and political betterment. First, the data reveal that as the focus of the government to be improved changes from a more to a less personally accessible and practicable target (i.e., from "local" to "provincial" to "national" to "all"), the mode of entry shifts from recruitment for specific tasks (40.0%, 29.8%, 15.2%, 22.0%) to volunteering for general work (30.0%, 42.1%, 56.8%, 53.8%). This suggests that people with more concrete and realistic goals are sought out by parties to work on distinct tasks rather than at general labor. Second, the distributions of the particular reasons selected by members of different parties indicate that a strain of realism underlies the selections. Thus, over 20% of the Social Credit officials select the provincial alternative, a realistic one since that is where the party has been most successful. In contrast, 16.7% and 21.8% of Liberal and Conservative officials respectively select the national government, the level at which they have had their greatest electoral success over the years. The "improve all governments" alternative, probably the most formula-like expression of a good government or political altruism ideology, is selected by Social Credit (29.3%) and New Democratic party (31.4%) officials at twice the rate it is chosen by Liberals (13.8%) and Conservatives (14.3%). This distribution is consonant with the tendency of the minor parties to be the more ideological.

With regard to respondents who mention pressures from others as most important, those who identify the source of the pressure as immediate family members are more likely to have volunteered for general work (61.2% as opposed to 35.3% for those reporting other sources of pressure) while those who responded to pressures from anyone else are more likely to have been recruited for special jobs (45.1% vs. 16.6% of those reporting pressure from family). From this we may infer that the closer the source of pressure the greater the likelihood that personal contact as a mechanism works as co-option—in the sense that prospective party workers may be "induced" to "volunteer" by an already active family member. The more distant the contact the more the relationship may be perceived as analogous to the proferring of an attractive, and perhaps negotiable employment offer. In any case, the label "volunteered" ought not to be taken as synonymous with the absence of personal pressure or contact. Conversely, the designation "recruited" should not be associated invariably with the application of unpleasant pressures. Indeed, for some people the distinction between recruitment and volunteering may say more about their own feelings about the experience than its actual character.

Relationships between the several categories of motives and modes of entry are clear, if not especially sharp. (See Table 4.4). Those giving political reasons are less likely to have volunteered than those giving personal reasons, and the converse is true of those who were recruited. Similarly, recruits in both job types are more likely to express political and volunteers personal reasons. When the distributions of persons choosing specific political reasons are examined, fairly sharp differences emerge. (See Table 4.5). Those who initially are assigned specific tasks as opposed to general work are relatively more likely to mention wanting to launch a political career. Loyalty to parties or persons is relatively more important to recruits than to volunteers. There also is an indication that those who on entry receive special jobs select party loyalty less, and, on balance, choose it relatively less in comparison to initiating personal political careers than do those who are assigned general work.

The lower panel of Table 4.5 reveals clear differences among the parties. The officials of the more overtly ideological parties, the NDP and Social Credit, tend to give fewer political reasons, particularly with regard to a personal career. Although the NDP officials almost reach the average number of political responses for all functionaries, they do so only because of their frequent choice of party loyalty as their reason. Overall, officials of the minor parties whose primary reasons for initiating party work involve political considerations, express loyalty to the party over persons at greater rates, relatively speaking, than do officials of the major parties.

Finally, respondents vary with regard to how impelling their reasons

Table 4.5
Proportion of All Respondents in Each Mode of Entry, and
Proportions by Party Selecting Political Considerations
as Most Important Reason for Joining

| | Specific Political Reasons Chosen | | | Total % Choosing a Political Reason | N |
	Party Loyalty	Loyalty to a Person	To Launch a Career		
Mode of Entry					
Recruited – Specific Task	15.2%*	10.3%	4.8%	30.3%	(165)
Recruited – General Work	17.2	9.7	1.1	28.0	(93)
Volunteered – Specific Task	6.7	5.0	6.7	18.4	(60)
Volunteered – General Work	13.2	5.8	2.6	21.6	(307)
Party					
New Democrat	16.6	5.3	1.8	23.7	(169)
Liberal	14.3	8.5	4.8	27.6	(210)
Conservative	13.6	10.9	4.8	29.3	(147)
Social Credit	7.1	4.0	1.0	12.1	(99)
All Party Officials	13.6	7.5	3.4	24.5	(625)
(N)	(85)	(47)	(21)		

*%'s are computed in terms of number of people in a mode of entry category or party mentioning a particular political reason.

were for first affiliating. Presumably, pressure from a spouse or parent calls for immediate action much more than does one's interest in developing a political career. Similarly, a desire to improve the provincial government seems a more immediate and realizable goal than the general improvement of all governments. Therefore, options were grouped according to how likely they were to have had forceful meaning for the respondent, and were related to mode of entry. In keeping with the possibility that recruitment and volunteering may be euphemisms for describing how respondents feel about the experience rather than descriptions of what actually transpires, those with high valence reasons are more likely to have been recruits for specific tasks whereas those responding to other concerns tend to have volunteered and to have undertaken general work. The notion that volunteers are people who present themselves in response to some compelling internal pressures simply is not sustained by these data. Pressure seems to operate on those whom the party officials want to become active; they may be attracted by knowing in advance what they will be doing.

In summary, this examination of most important initiating reasons suggests that Canadian party officials, as a group, diverge considerably from a model of committed politicians, consumed by politics, ideologies, and programs. Some obviously are. Nonetheless, there is a frequent absence of passion, on the one hand, and of distinctive political motivations and world views, on the other. For many of the respondents, joining appears to be a response to decisions by others that they were needed. For other officials it is a personal act whose time has come, but by drift as much as by compulsion. Consideration of the reasons respondents give for initiating party work is a useful first step for understanding the joining process. However, as explanations these reasons are not totally adequate. In part, they explain why people join *any*, not just a political organization, and in part they are interpretations, expressions of feelings and emotions. The introduction of additional facts about initial entry indicates that there may be a "how" that is at least as important for understanding what happens as is the "why."

Thinking About Joining

Apart from the facts that people do have different motives for the same action, or experience the same situation differently, another major source of the considerable variation in reasons given, and for the frequent tendency to select reasons that do not relate specifically to the act of joining a political party *per se*, is that the phrase "joining a party" is ambiguous and diffuse. Thus, individuals either may respond to and articulate different parts of a complex experience, or they may not know what part of the complex to select for explanation. Indeed, in countries such as Canada, the idea of "joining a political party" may be a construction imposed on reality by layman and scholar alike. For some people the phrase describes, without distortion, what it usually connotes: a simple act of affiliation involving a status change symbolized by the taking of an oath, the payment of dues, the signing of a membership card, or some other clear-cut action. For others, however, affiliation is a more amorphous process involving enhanced political interest and activity associated with increasing participation in more or less formally structured party organizations. And, for still others, party membership—without either being sought or acepted—can be conferred on the basis of having attended the most routine constituency annual meeting, or even, in some instances, as the result of a brief conversation with someone already active in a party.

Despite these ambiguities, in our study joining was construed and is treated as a clearly defined, abrupt event involving an explicit acquisition of membership; not as an extended process of becoming or ceasing to be a member, or as a matter of one's feeling more or less a member. Although a conception of membership acquisition as an abrupt change in status might hardly apply to a cross section of all members of Canada's parties, it does seem warranted for studying a group of officials, many of whom hold the highest ranking positions in their respective local organizations. Their very status as officials implies and derives from the existence of organizational structures that they must have entered.

A few respondents' reports do indicate that our view of joining may have imposed an analytic concept upon their actual personal experiences. For example, respondents who report first being politically active in organized groups outside the party proper sometimes stated that prior affiliations with such paraparty organizations as youth, student, and women's groups constituted "membership" and should be taken into account in arriving at their ages of first joining. In contrast, other manifestly political activities, such as participating in the election campaign of a family friend or neighbor, almost uniformly were considered prior experiences and, therefore, not factors in defining their age of joining.

The vagueness that characterizes the shading of political experience inside and outside the confines of a party reflects the amorphousness of the organizations themselves. A good rule of thumb is that the more local the unit or the more distant an election, the more ill-defined will be the organizational structure. In part this is because parties often lack the personnel to fill all the positions specified in their tables of organization; in part it reflects the relatively volatile and amorphous nature of the organizations; and in part it is a product of the heavy emphasis placed on the conduct of periodic electoral campaigns. The absence of detailed records at the local level is both a reflection of and a contribution to these conditions. The vague nature of local Canadian party organizations is not without significance in its own right. A high-ranking member of one local party confided to us that since the organization can be changed readily to accommodate the wishes and needs of a newly-installed leader or executive secretary, a mechanism exists that simultaneously can continue past workers in positions of prestige and provide new supporters with rewards for meritorious activities in the new leader's service. Although such structural flexibility is probably necessary in view of the special organizational problems of parties in rewarding and maintaining the psychic loyalties and resource commitments of their members, unfortunately, efforts to explain joining systematically are rendered less successful (in terms of statistical standards) than they would be if party organizations were more like conventional public and private bureaucracies.

Learning About Joining

As indicated, prior to reconstructing circumstances and developmental experiences that antedated the party career, an age of first joining any party was established. A symbolic behaviorist rather than structural conception of joining was used and the following question was asked:

> Finally, in the columns on the right are spaces for describing your various positions as an active political party worker. We'll start at the age at which you first became a regular active and committed party worker—in the sense that you *both* thought of yourself and were thought of by others as an active, available, and reliable worker for a particular party. The affiliation could have continued for more than a single campaign but it doesn't have to have been with your current party. It could have been with any. If you worked for a party for a few years, then stopped for a while and started again, it's that first beginning we're talking about.

The wording was chosen to emphasize the view that membership is more a social and psychological than a formal legal matter. The ability of respondents to fix upon an age of first joining and, hence, to accept an imposed framework for what could have been a considerably drawn out process is consistent with the related data. Most respondents acquired membership, as distinct from simply identifying with a party, during election campaigns or other specific periods of heightened political significance and activity. Such events obviously intensify party activity. It is not surprising, therefore, that respondents were able to locate the time and reconstruct the events.

Probing of the circumstances surrounding entry into a party started with a pair of questions asking whether respondents had volunteered or had been recruited by others. Respondents also were asked to judge whether their first activities were rather clearly delineated and task specific or diffuse and general.[15] (These two qualities of joining already have been used in interpreting officials' expressed primary motives.) Among the aspects of joining delineated by the subsequent questioning were: 1) whether the party member with whom the first contact was made was a person closely related to the respondent (e.g., family member, relative, good friend); 2) whether this person held a high level party position; 3) whether the respondent occupied a high level first party position;[16] 4) whether the respondent's first tasks as a party member included any of the more prestigious or glamorous political activities;[17] 5) whether there was strong independent personal motivation to start party work irrespective of the actual mode of recruitment;[18] 6) whether any special activities or events in public affairs were taking place at the time of joining; and 7) whether at the time any special activities or events were taking place within the party itself. These, plus the age of joining, the recruited-volunteered and general work-

Table 4.6
Selected Aspects of Joining a Party

	Party				
	NDP	Liberal	Conser-vative	Social Credit	Total
X̄ age of first joining (in years)	28.4	29.4	30.8	36.0	30.5
% reporting independent personal impetus to join a party	79.3	67.6	68.0	68.7	71.0
% reporting significant activities in public affairs at time of joining	54.4	42.9	48.3	50.5	48.5
% reporting significant activities in party affairs at time of joining	31.4	28.1	29.9	30.3	29.8
% who were volunteers	69.2	52.4	55.1	59.6	58.7
% whose first contact was in high party position	37.3	43.3	45.6	41.4	41.9
% whose first contact was a close personal associate	46.2	61.9	57.1	55.6	55.5
% whose first party position was at a high level	18.9	16.2	22.4	21.2	19.2
% whose first tasks were general and diffuse	71.6	62.4	61.2	58.6	64.0
% whose first activities included interesting functions	26.0	15.2	24.5	35.4	23.5
(N)	(169)	(210)	(147)	(99)	(625)

specific task items, provide information on ten aspects of the affiliation process that will be considered below.

Joining Canadian Political Parties

To test the assumption that Canadian parties are typical of those in other Western democracies, and to establish some point of reference in interpreting the data, comparable information was examined for United States party officials.[19] On balance, it was clear that the process of joining a party is quite similar in both countries. In fact, there are more pronounced interparty differences in Canada than there are differences between the joining experiences of Canadian and American officials. The average age of 30.5 years for first joining a Canadian party masks a range of seven-and-a-half years (See Table 4.6), the Social Crediters being distinctly older on average (36.0 years) than are the other

Table 4.7
Mode of Entry into Party Work

Mode of Entry	Party				
	NDP	Liberal	Conser-vative	Social Credit	Total
Recruited – Specific Task	17.2%	30.5%	27.9%	31.3%	26.4%
Recruited – General Work	13.6	17.1	17.0	9.1	14.9
Volunteered – Specific Task	11.2	7.1	10.9	10.1	9.6
Volunteered – General Work	58.0	45.2	44.2	49.5	49.1
Total	100.0	99.9	100.0	100.0	100.0
(N)	(169)	(210)	(147)	(99)	(625)

officials. The officials of the NDP report volunteering and embarking initially on general work at considerably higher rates than do those in other parties (See Table 4.6). There also are substantial interparty differences in rates of glamorous initial task performance, the Liberals having the lowest rate, the Social Credit officials the highest. The New Democrats were more sensitive and responsive than were major party members to public and party events at the time they affiliated and less likely to have dealt with friends or relatives. They also report higher personal motivation and less glamorous, more general task activities than do the members of the other minority party, Social Credit. Additionally, the data suggest that more than the other parties, the Liberal party recruits its future officers through a network of personal contacts, and that recruits must work their way up from low status routine jobs to the rewards of accomplishment and position.

These dynamics of joining can be considered utilizing recruitment-volunteering and generality-specificity of work as controls within the sample. They are used concurrently because of their high interrelationship, as demonstrated by the data in Table 4.7. In each party, officials volunteer for general work rather than specific tasks at rates ranging from approximately 4 to 1 (Conservatives) to 6 to 1 (Liberals). Recruits, in contrast, are selected primarily for specific tasks rather than general work, the overall rate being a little less than 2 to 1. For all party respondents the most frequent mode of entry types are the "general work-volunteers" and the "specific task-recruits" in that order, the first outnumbering the second by almost 2 to 1. Approxi-

Table 4.8
Selected Aspects of Joining a Party and Mode
of Entry into Party Work

Aspects of Joining a Party	Recruited		Volunteered	
	Specific Task	General Work	Specific Task	General Work
% whose first contact re: joining held high party position	48.5	44.1	43.3	37.5
% having first contact re: joining with close associate	75.8	79.6	46.7	39.1
% reporting independent self-motivation for joining	31.5	35.5	86.7	100.0
% reporting special public affairs reasons for joining	26.0	24.7	65.0	54.5
% reporting special party affairs reasons for joining	15.7	18.3	41.7	38.4
% whose first position in party was at high level	18.8	11.8	26.7	20.2
% whose first party tasks were interesting	43.6	14.0	45.0	11.4
(N)	(165)	(93)	(60)	(307)

mately one-quarter of the leaders fall in the two remaining categories of "general work-recruits" and "specific task-volunteers." The proportion in each mode of entry category does vary by party, but such variations tend to be minimal.

Data in Table 4.8 reveal that mode of entry helps clarify several aspects of joining. Since it is the recruits for special work who most frequently report a first contact with a person in a high party position, one may infer that in Canada high ranking party officials are centrally involved in the process of bringing people in to take care of particular tasks,[20] be it actually finding or only welcoming and training them. Seemingly, special tasks are attractive, for those who join to engage in them are more likely to report that their initial work involved "glamorous" jobs. As might be expected volunteers more than recruits report having been motivated to join, whereas recruits more than volunteers report that the person with whom they were first in contact was someone with whom they shared a close social relationship. Finally, and somewhat surprisingly, volunteers are more likely than recruits to have held a higher level first position in a party. Thus, in contrast to the apparently rational but perhaps naive expectation that recruitment primarily is a tactic used to insure that high level party positions are filled by handpicked people, the data suggest that such positions also may be used to stimulate volunteers to offer their services. If so, this may be a very subtle form of co-option.

First Position-First Task

The precise conditions of joining varied considerably for individual party officials. Some started in important positions, others did not. Some did exciting, appealing work such as writing speeches, making public appearances, soliciting money, or being a candidate for public office; others carried out activities that most charitably may be described as routine. Some appear to have presented themselves hat-in-hand, others on their own terms, and still others were sought after by the parties. Some knew their party contacts well in nonpolitical circumstances, others had no such personal relationships. Some dealt with "people in high places" in the party, others did not. Some would have joined even if they had not been sought out, others probably would not have done so. Some joined when significant political or social events were occurring, others entered party work when prevailing conditions might best be described as "politics as usual." The availability of such an array of information for each official makes it feasible to address a number of intriguing questions. One may ask, for example, what proportion of a party's new affiliates receive both a high level organizational position and an interesting task to perform upon joining? What proportion receives neither? Is it the recruits or the volunteers who generally start their party careers under auspicious circumstances? Are those who join to perform specific tasks as opposed to general work more often rewarded with high level positions as well as with prestigious jobs? Does a party's national stature affect is permeability? Is "cronyism" the order of the day in political parties? Do high level positions and interesting jobs go disproportionately to new affiliates who are socially connected to high ranking incumbent officials? Questions such as these can be addressed by a further examination of the relationships among the features of entry.

First, as previous analyses already have suggested, securing a high level first position or a prestigious task assignment is the exception rather than the rule. Only 19.2% state they began in high level positions, and only 23.5% report being given an interesting first job. A very small minority of officials (7.2%) receive both high level positions and interesting tasks, whereas, in contrast, fully 64.5% indicate first having performed routine work in low level positions. With respect to the advantages and disadvantages of recruitment and volunteering, recruits are almost twice as likely to receive an initial job that is interesting (32.9% vs. 16.9%). (However, volunteers, as was indicated above, are slightly more likely than recruits [21.3% vs. 16.3%] to occupy high level positions initially.) Overall, recruited officials begin their careers under more favorable circumstances than their party colleagues who are volunteers because they are somewhat less likely than the latter (59.3% vs. 68.1%) to start by doing routine work in a low level position, a combination that is the norm in each of the organizations. The probability of securing an immediate payoff in the form of a prestigious task, as Table 4.8 has shown, is strongly related to whether the entrant begins by doing specific or general work. 44.0% of those in the specific work category as compared to 12.0% in the general category report prestigious initial task assignments. Although persons undertaking specific tasks are only marginally more likely than those doing more general work (20.9% vs. 18.2%) to be placed initially in high positions, an indication of the fact that they fare better is that less than half of such officials (48.0%) as opposed to almost three-quarters of the generalists (73.8%) begin by doing routine work in low positions.

If type of initial task and level of first position are considered by party, it appears that a party's stature in national politics is related to its permeability. Thus, although the four parties place a preponderance of their new members in low level, routine work positions, the ratio of low to high placements varies from 4 to 1 in the Social Credit, to approximately 8 to 1 in the Conservative and New Democratic parties, to over 20 to 1 in the Liberal organization (compare the first and fourth columns in Table 4.9). Although the difference in ratios may reflect the fact that Canadian parties are not subject to federal or provincial legal controls and consequently have considerable organizational flexibility, it also may reflect the parties' relative success in national elections. In terms of patterns of interparty competition, it is not too great an exaggeration to describe the Liberals as Canada's dominant party nationally, the Conservatives as the perpetual loyal opposition, the NDP as a "third party" which poses little real threat to the Conservative's competitive position, and the Social Credit as a negligible force in national politics. The party order of the ratios of available high level-attractive to lower level-unattractive new positions reflects these facts of Canadian political life.

The processes by which parties acquire new members also are illuminated by the distribution of officials in the middle categories where there can be trade-offs between positional status and task attractiveness. The two major

Table 4.9
Relationship Between Type of Initial Task and Level
of First Position by Party
(Horizontal Percentages)

	Type of Initial Task				
	Routine Task Level of First Position		Prestigious Task Level First Position		Total
Party	Low	High	Low	High	
New Democratic	63.9	10.1	17.2	8.9	100.1
Liberal	71.9	12.9	11.9	3.3	100.0
Conservative	60.5	15.0	17.0	7.5	100.0
Social Credit	55.6	9.1	23.2	12.1	100.0
All Party Officials	64.5	12.0	16.3	7.2	100.0

national parties, the Liberals and Conservatives, are as likely to offer new entrants high level positions as interesting work (Liberals, 16.2% vs. 15.2%; Conservatives, 22.5% vs. 24.5%). (See Table 4.9.) In contrast, the NDP and Social Credit parties more often give new entrants interesting work than high level positions (NDP, 26.1% vs. 19.0%; Social Credit, 35.3% vs. 21.2%). They may do so because they have different organizational needs or because they utilize their personnel differently than do the two major parties. For example, the minor parties, particularly the New Democrats, have been troubled over the years by a lack of money. Both minor parties generally have depended for such assistance on large numbers of small contributions from friends and supporters, whereas the two major parties more often have looked to a small number of "big givers" to fill party coffers. Consequently, the former may need to involve more of their personnel in fund raising (classified here as an interesting task) than the latter. The greater number of Social Credit and New Democratic officials initially engaged in carrying out interesting tasks also may be a consequence of the expectations of prospective recruits to these parties. Individuals considering affiliating with them may expect to be integrally and immediately involved in the conduct of important party affairs because this kind of involvement is gratifying. Given their lack of access to federal patronage, an interesting first job may well be one of the few "payoffs" a prospective Socred or New Democrat realistically can anticipate. Alternatively, their expectation of immediately being involved in interesting work may be grounded in ideologically oriented views of what party work "is all about." Or, it simply may be that higher level positions in the minor parties are less often perceived as attractive inducements to new members. Whatever the reasons, the minor parties may be forced to offer interesting tasks as incentives to prospective affiliates more frequently than do the Liberals or Conservatives.

On Cronyism

Since the majority of officials receive neither high level positions nor interesting work as rewards for joining a party, the question arises as to how such rewards are dispensed. Both social scientists, sensitive to the importance of social networks in decision making, and average citizens, tending to view politics cynically as a closed system of cronies, might entertain the hypothsis that a close personal association with someone in a high party position determines who receives immediate payoffs for joining. To test this hypothesis the data were examined for evidence of a positive association between the existence of close personal relationships with the persons in the party with whom respondents were first in contact, on the one hand, and the level of their first party position and the attractiveness of the work associated with it, on the other.

In brief, there is a relationship between status of first position and a prejoining acquaintance with one's first party contact. The relationship, however, is exactly opposite to what the cronyism hypothesis posits. A larger proportion of those who start their party work in a low level position than of those who start higher up are personally acquainted with their party contact (57.8% vs. 45.8%). There is no relationship between engaging in prestigious first activities and knowing one's party contact. Another test of the cronyism hypothesis examined the relationship between the status in a party hierarchy of a respondent's contact and the nature of the position first assigned the respondent. As with closeness of personal relationships, if the cronyism hypothesis is valid one would expect a contact with a high status party member to result in preferential treatment for the entrant: either a prestigious initial assignment or a high level office. However, this, too, is not the case. With respect to a reward in terms of high first position, there are only minimal differences in the levels of the first party positions obtained by respondents whose contacts are in higher as opposed to lower party positions, and the directions of these differences are inconsistent when controls are applied.[21] This also is the case with respect to a payoff in the form of attractive initial work. Indeed, in not one of 25 possible controlled conditions is there a statistically significant relationship between attractiveness of first task and the status of the respondent's first party contact.

Instead of cronyism it appears that a close personal contact substitutes for a lack of strong self-motivation. Repeatedly, those who are personally involved with their first party contacts more often report that they had no independent motivation to join a party, and it is safe to assume that at least some of them joined because of their personal relationships with one or more people already in a party. In short, from an organizational perspective, it seems more appropriate to describe the overall function of prior contact and personal acquaintance with people in a party as exploitative rather than rewarding.

This assessment of the relation between personal acquaintance and level of motivation also raises the question of the influence of public and party events at the time of joining. A respondent's awareness of such events could have been part of a complex of compelling stimuli to join at that time. Slightly over 80% of the respondents report that public rather than party events were salient factors in their entry. Consistent with the role of govermental improvement motives for initiating party work, it can be speculated that the tendency to emphasize public rather than party phenomena suggests, in some instances at least, that joining may be as much an instrumental as an expressive act. Thus, although a sustained level of interest in politics generally plays a role in the decision of many individuals to join a party, some individuals may affiliate principally because they view a party as a means to an end, an organizational vehicle that facilitates involvement in a personally salient political situation.

When age of first affiliation is related to the several other aspects of joining, we find that an independent self-motivation to initiate party work is a strong correlate of early joining. Persons who join at a time when events in the world of parties or public affairs are salient for them, and who also have no prior close relationship with their party contact—in brief, those who are highly self-motivated—are from one-and-one-half to three-and-one-half years younger on the average than the others when they affiliate. Although the strongly self-motivated are the earliest joiners, factors in the political environment seem to interact with motivation in a comprehensible manner. Those who report both self-motivation and important public and party activities transpiring at the time join three years earlier on the average than do those without either of these characteristics. This pattern obtains for the officials in all four parties, being especially sharp for the Liberals and NDP.

Summary

The analyses in this chapter were initiated with a case-by-case comparison of the party workers and their nigh-dweller matches. Comparisons reveal that the officials are precocious in almost every regard. Their environments and experiences are more politicized, they become aware of politics and public affairs earlier, and they acquire higher social status at a more rapid rate than those who subsequently become their social and economic peers. Analyses of perceived reasons for initiating party work then were undertaken, and showed, as has other research, that Canadians join parties for a variety of reasons. Governmental improvement reasons loom particularly large, but a substantial minority emphasize party loyalty and other more specifically political considerations. Since a large number of officials cite anticipated personal social and psychological rewards as motives for joining it seems that for some persons party work is analogous to participation in other types of voluntary associations.

To investigate other aspects of joining, distributions of and relationships among ten aspects of joining a party were examined in some detail. These indicate that in Canada most officials appear to join during periods marked by heightened political significance and activity. Also, although the officials report initially being assigned interesting work somewhat more frequently than they report holding high level party positions, there are substantial differences among the parties with regard to these two aspects of joining. Additionally, it would appear that the incumbents of high level organizational positions are centrally involved in the induction into their parties of people who will undertake particular tasks. However, volunteers are more likely than recruits to be given high level positions, at least initially, suggesting that offering these positions at times may be used as a co-optive tactic to induce people to volunteer. Among volunteers, those who join for specific tasks are rarest in the Liberal party. In contrast, the NDP includes the largest group of people who volunteer to do any work necessary.

Tests of the hypothesis that cronyism is a significant mechanism in recruiting new officials indicate this is not the case. If anything, the relationship between recruiter and recruit is more often exploitative than rewarding. Another inference that can be drawn is that the national stature of a party affects its permeability. Although all the parties place a majority of their new members in low level, routine work positions, there is substantial interparty variation in this regard. Congruent with their stature in national politics, the Liberal party organization is the most difficult to enter anywhere but at the bottom, the Conservative and the NDP less difficult, and the Social Credit the least difficult.

In sum, parties appear to proceed with the business of acquiring new members much as do other voluntary organizations. People are sometimes co-opted, more often exploited. Personal contacts are traded on, and when these do not suffice, the prospect of holding a high party position or engaging in interesting and exciting work is held out as an inducement to join. The processes and interpersonal relations involved in the officials' initial induction into party work are frequently subtle and complex. To understand them more adequately, analyses of joining party organizations will be continued in the next chapter.

NOTES

1. On the structural weakness of Canadian parties see Engelmann and Schwartz, *Canadian Political Parties: Origin, Character, Impact,* pp. 176-185; and Winn and McMenemy, *Political Parties in Canada,* chap. 10.

2. The importance of using matched samples in political recruitment research has been noted by others. See, for example, Kenneth Prewitt, "Political Socialization and Leadership Selection," *The Annals of the American Academy of Political and Social Science,* 361 (1965), 106; Moshe Czudnowski, "Political Recruitment," in F.I. Greenstein and N.W. Polsby, eds., *Handbook of Political Science,* v. 2 (Reading, Mass.: Addison-Wesley, 1975), p. 189.

3. Tests on data from matched pairs involve averaging the difference within pairs on a given measure for all pairs, and testing the observed average difference against the alternative of no real difference (i.e., the difference between observed and no difference will be no greater than would be expected on the basis of sampling variability).

4. The instructions for locating matching persons minimized present occupation, educational, and income differences by specifying the selection of nigh-dwellers living in residences as near and as comparable in appearance as possible to the officials'. In a potential matched residence, an interview was conducted only if a person could be found who was of the same sex and within three years of age of the official being matched. The age and sex specifications were maintained rigorously because the questions pertaining to socialization were keyed to specific years, events, and ages. This assured that the historical, social, and cultural context of the age or event was approximately the same for each member of the pair, permitting a fair comparison of each official and matched nigh-dweller. Similar though somewhat looser constraints applied to socioeconomic and family status attributes.

5. The question used to measure subjective perceptions of socioeconomic status during childhood was:

"By and large, how would you describe your family's situation in your childhood by the standards of that time?"

Response categories included 1) very badly off, 2) somewhat below average, 3) average, 4) somewhat better than average, and 5) very well off. Responses are coded from 1-5 with higher scores indicating higher socioeconomic status.

6. Those living farthest away from their present community at the time of initial affiliation received higher scores. The index ranged from 1 (lived at same address in present community) to 3 (lived outside their present community).

7. Included were comparisons of each party group with its matched nigh-dwellers, only pairs in which the matched nigh-dweller supported the official's party, and three-way contrasts among party officials, same party supporting matched nigh-dwellers, and same party supporting nigh-dwellers who happened to have been selected to match officials of other parties. Some by-products of these analyses are worth noting. With the exception of the small Social Credit group, a plurality of nigh-dwellers are supporters of the matching official's party. In addition, varying patterns confirm that the officials are not typical members of the social groups that support their parties, but tend to be of higher status.

8. These reasons, given after the fact, are of the sort Alfred Schutz designated "because of" reasons. He observes that an individual's account of an act after its execution may differ considerably from that same person's view of the reasons for the act when it was being projected as a possible course of behavior. The latter Schutz designates "in order to" reasons. He argues that in the everyday world people try to appear reasonable.

However, what is projected as reasonable, in fact, may not turn out to be so. Consequently, hindsight can be used later to produce a new set of reasons that make the action appear reasonable, intelligible, and hence more acceptable to one's self, and perhaps to others. Cf. Alfred Schutz, "Common-Sense and Scientific Interpretation of Human Action," in Maurice Natanson (ed.), *Philosophy of the Social Sciences: A Reader* (New York: Random House, 1963), pp. 302-346.

Both these sorts of accounts of reasons are given from the perspective of the individual. They constitute different aspects of what Abraham Kaplan calls "act meaning." There is also a meaning and explanation of action that can be developed from the perspective of an uninvolved observing analyst. Kaplan refers to this perspective as "action meaning." It must be arrived at and evaluated by other means. Cf. Abraham Kaplan, *The Conduct of Inquiry* (San Francisco: Chandler, 1964), p. 32. In the next section the public explanations of these particular respondents of why they joined are considered. Thereafter and throughout Chapter 5 we specify and evaluate explanations that would fit these respondents or any others working for similar parties in similar circumstances.

9. Representative studies include Wilson, *The Amateur Democrat*; Eldersveld, *Political Parties: A Behavioral Analysis*; Bowman and Boynton, "Recruitment Patterns Among Local Party Officials: A Model and Some Preliminary Findings in Selected Locales," 667-676; Philip Althoff and Samuel Patterson, "Political Activism in a Rural County," *Midwest Journal of Political Science*, 10 (1966): 39-51; Conway and Feigert, "Motivation, Incentive Systems, and the Political Party Organization," 1159-1173; Glen Browder and Dennis S. Ippolito, "The Suburban Party Activist: The Case of Southern Amateurs," *Social Science Quarterly*, 53 (1972): 168-175; and M. Margaret Conway and Frank B. Feigert, "Incentives and Task Performance Among Party Precinct Workers," *Western Political Quarterly*, 27 (1974): 693-709. The only comparable published Canadian studies are Henry Jacek, *et al.*, "The Congruence of Federal-Provincial Campaign Activity in Party Organizations: The Influence of Recruitment Patterns in Three Hamilton Ridings," 190-205; and Clarke, *et al.*, "Motivational Patterns and Differential Participation in a Canadian Party: The Ontario Liberals," 132-139.

10. Peter B. Clark and James Q. Wilson, "Incentive Systems: A Theory of Organizations," *Administrative Science Quarterly*, 6 (1969): 135-137; Dennis S. Ippolito, "Political Perspectives of Suburban Party Leaders," *Social Science Quarterly*, 50 (1969): 808; Thomas H. Roback, "Recruitment and Incentive Patterns Among Grassroots Republican Officials: Continuity and Change in Two States," *Sage Professional Papers in American Politics* (Beverly Hills: Sage Publications, 1974), p. 6.

11. Eldersveld, *Political Parties*, p. 275; Althoff and Patterson, "Political Activism in a Rural County," p. 45. See also Raymond E. Wolfinger, "Why Political Machines Have Not Withered Away and Other Revisionist Thoughts," *Journal of Politics*, 34 (1972): 365-398. For Canadian data see Van Loon and Whittington, *The Canadian Political System*, p. 236; Clarke, *et al.*, "Motivational Patterns and Differential Participation," 133-139.

12. Nearly one-third (31.1%) selected five or more reasons for joining a party and only 4.5% gave just one reason. For all officials the mean number of reasons given was 3.9. These figures vary only slightly from one party to the next.

13. The question asked was:

"Here is a list of reasons which may lead a person to embark on a career in party work. Which of them applied in your case?" "Which *one* of these was the most important?"

14. Prewitt, for example, found that the demarcation between political and community service activities often was quite blurred in the minds of many Bay Area council members. See Prewitt, *The Recruitment of Political Leaders*, chaps. 4 and 5.

15. The questions asked were as follows:

"When you finally did go to work that *first time* for the ———— party, were you approached with a specific offer or request to go to work for the party by a party worker or official, or did you pretty much decide on your own to volunteer your services: If you had to say it was more one than the other, what would you say?

[If approached] "Was there a particular position or job to do that they wanted you for, or did they just want you to become affiliated and active regardless of what you did?"

[If volunteered] "Did you have some specific task or job in mind that you could do for the party when you volunteered your services or did you simply expect to do whatever was needed or you were asked to do?"

16. "High level" first positions are described in Chapter 6.

17. "Glamorous" initial tasks included fund raising, speech writing, giving talks, taking a party office, and becoming a candidate for public office.

18. A strong independent personal motivation was assumed if a respondent: a) volunteered for general service, b) indicated he or she would have started party work at that time even if not approached (for those recruited for particular services or general work), or c) would have volunteered for particular services not knowing whether the party required such tasks to be performed.

19. The same interview schedule was administered to the 627 party officials studied in Minneapolis and Seattle. See Chapter 1.

20. More generally, the significance of party officials as recruiters is suggested by the fact that 42.9% of the respondents reported being encouraged to start party work in the year prior to the time they joined a party. Fully 88.1% of those encouraged reported that their encouragement came from a party official. This pattern applies to all parties.

21. The analyses were performed with controls for party, recruitment-volunteering, and general work-specific tasks.

Chapter Five

Affiliation:
Components of Joining

A multistage and multivariate model [of political recruitment] is difficult to handle. . . .

Moshe Czudnowski, "Political Recruitment, *Handbook of Political Science*, V. 2, p. 229.

THIS chapter examines more specifically how social structural factors and political socialization experiences together bear upon how individuals are initially recruited into party organizations. Previous chapters have established that aspects of social structure and socialization systematically distinguish between those who do and those who do not join parties. Party officials were shown to be a socioeconomic elite. Further, officials had socialization experiences distinctively different from those of ordinary citizens, more frequently having been reared in highly politicized environments and having acquired an awareness and interest in politics and a sense of partisanship earlier and through different sorts of experiences. Analyses in Chapter 4 have revealed that joining a party in Canada is a multifaceted and oftentimes amorphous event which is subject to considerable variance both between and within particular parties. Since the social structural and socialization perspectives articulated earlier are broad in their scope of applicability, they may explain patterns of variance not only in who joins parties, but also in how joining occurs.

It is difficult, however, to assess the utility of social structural and socialization explanations of the "hows" of initial recruitment before satisfying two conditions. First, we need to condense the large array of available information on initial joining by identifying any major dimensions or components that may underlie the detailed data presented in Chapter 4. Second, we must construct a relatively parsimonious and cogent model of joining that includes both strategic social structural and political socialization variables. We then can test the explanatory power of this model for the party leaders *in toto* and in their individual organizations.

Identifying the Components of Joining

The philosopher, Abraham Kaplan, in discussing several qualities of concepts, proposes, among others, the terms "constructs" and "indirect observables."[1] They refer to easily comprehended terms and features of everyday life that pose knotty problems in research. He uses the former term to designate complex summary entities that do not exist in a concrete sense even though we are accustomed to dealing with them as if they did (e.g., the government). The latter term, indirect observables, refers to phenomena that are real but that can not be apprehended directly (e.g., dreams, which only can be observed through reports, brain measurement, or observation of sleepers). If joining a Canadian political party were akin to joining one of the Communist parties of Western Europe, problems of conceptualizing and measuring initial recruitment would be minimal insofar as joining such a party normally is a single, overt, uniform, and observable (at least in principle) act at a specific time and place.[2] In Canada, however, local parties generally lack clear organizational boundaries, members may "drift" in and out, and, as a result, recruitment experiences are diverse and complex. As part of the process of explanation, the analyst must build a construct of entry from a variety of less than striking details. Thus, particular attention must be given to the analytic procedures to be used in subsequent explanatory efforts.

A comparison of the constructs "joining" and "athletic ability" may help clarify why special attention has to be given to analytic procedures. In everyday life no difficulty is experienced in communicating about athletic ability. Professional football coaches frequently rationalize their drafting of a particular player in words such as, "He's an athlete." Similarly, sportscasters describe one back as a great passer or another as a powerful runner. Nor is there much difficulty in drawing up lists of the varieties of athletic abilities required for certain sports. It can be stated with relative confidence that quickness is a requisite of outstanding performance in basketball, and that excellent vision is a *conditio sine qua non* for hitting a baseball. However, an effort to identify and measure systematically such components of general athletic ability as strength, agility, speed, quickness, and stamina, would reveal that a number of these qualities may overlap in outstanding athletes (e.g., A's ability as a great passer may rest not only on his ability to throw a football accurately but also on his quickness in releasing the ball and his strength in throwing it a long distance). Therefore, when we use actual performance in a sport as the indicator, we would find it impossible to measure one of these qualities in an athlete without partially measuring another. It also is possible that only one aspect of general athletic ability is a sufficient condition for greatness in some sports (e.g., speed for a 100 meter sprinter). Additional possibilities are that a combination of attributes (e.g., in pole vaulting) or that exceptional development of one or two attributes but only normal development of others (e.g., in javelin throwing) may be sufficient for achieving outstanding sports performances. In short, systematic research on general athletic ability would require that data be collected for a variety of components which in different combinations affect the quality of performance in individual sports.

The problems involved in analyzing initial entry into a party organization are similar, since joining a party, like athletic ability, is a construct whose analytically distinct components are not entirely separable in reality. There is an additional difficulty. For simplicity, the discussion of athletic ability assumed its components were known and that there were valid and reliable procedures available for measuring them. This is not the case with joining a party. The ten aspects of joining considered in the last chapter were specific items in our interview schedule. They might not apply equally well to other parties in other places at other times. Nevertheless, patterns in the answers may reflect unobservable underlying elements that are present in some guise in a much broader range of political systems.

Fortunately, there are multivariate statistical procedures that not only permit one to represent the complexity of an unobservable synthetic construct, but also to delineate and measure its underlying dimensions. The procedure used here is canonical correlation.[3] The pertinent difference between the canonical approach and more conventional factor analytic techniques is that canonical variates are identified in terms of being maximally correlated with other clusters of variables in a particular set of explanatory data. In the present analysis, these explanatory variables measure the socialization experiences and social structural characteristics of the party leaders. The canonical procedure can provide insight into any underlying structure in the phenomenon of their joining a political party in a context that is relevant to our interest in explanation.[4]

Some Procedural Considerations

Any canonical variates that may be estimated and interpreted will be measures of joining and they will then be explained by multiple regression and path analysis. Multiple regression estimates how much of the variance in components of joining (the dependent variable) the independent variables in a model can explain (indicated by the coefficient of determination, the square of the coefficient of multiple correlation) or, alternatively, how well a set of empirical observations fit a hypothetical model.[5] Path analytic techniques estimate the magnitudes of all direct and indirect links among variables included in a model.[6] These linkages and their path coefficients, estimated using regression weights, constitute an explanation of joining.[7]

Since the features of joining combine to form a synthetic concept with overlapping components that are not completely separable in the real world, and because a developmental explanation of the concept, joining, involves chains of cumulating and sequential influences, certain cautions are necessary for understanding the meanings and restrictions on meanings of the results of these several multivariate analyses. More specifically, an unobservable but real underlying component of the synthetic concept may partially measure other components. This is the case with the canonical variates that are derived to represent the components of joining a party, because the estimated variates must be statistically independent[8] even though they really may be associated. Therefore, the first variate that is derived not only will measure all of that variate but also will contain elements of subsequent variates. It is the "first plus," so to speak. The second variate will measure all that remains of the second, but it too will have a plus—parts of any subsequent variates to which it is related. After the first variate, then, each succeeding variate will measure the residual of a variate, plus its overlap with subsequent variates.

A hypothetical version of the situation is depicted in Figure 5.1. The encompassing circle represents all possible information, measured or unmeasured, about joining. The four interior circles represent hypothetical variates that can be derived by a technique like canonical correlation and that are to be interpreted as elements of joining. Based on the patterns of loadings of individual variables on which we have information, the variates derived in this study will be designated age of joining, self-motivation, expertise, and co-option.[9] For labeling purposes, these four variates are given the acronyms AGE, SEMOT, EXPERT, and COOPT respectively. The sizes of the circles reflect the order of their extraction—age, self-motivation, expertise, and co-option. Each variate extracted after the first is represented by that sector of its circle not overlapping with previously extracted variates, the condition of independence restricting measurement to only the residual of the variate. In the case of self-motivation this excludes a proportion approximately equal to its overlap (i.e., unknown correlation) with age.[10] However, it includes parts of the two variates to be extracted subsequently, that is, expertise and co-option. The residual area of the larger surrounding circle reflects information in the original items not absorbed by the four variates plus other aspects of joining not measured at all. Finally the bars represent the original items and suggest how the information in each is distributed among the variates and the residual circle.

The possibility of overlap has two disadvantages: a) it cannot be deter-

Figure 5.1
Relationships Between Canonical Variates and Original Variables

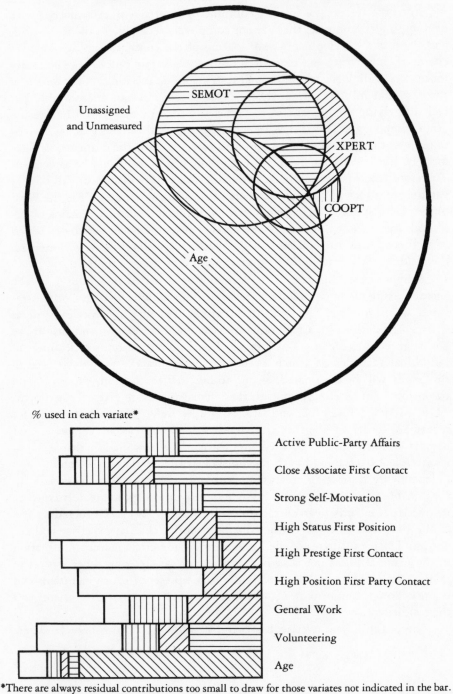

% used in each variate*

Active Public-Party Affairs

Close Associate First Contact

Strong Self-Motivation

High Status First Position

High Prestige First Contact

High Position First Party Contact

General Work

Volunteering

Age

*There are always residual contributions too small to draw for those variates not indicated in the bar.

mined if each variate needs to be or can be explained separately; and b) it prevents estimating the real relationships, if any, among them. Essentially, the explanation of each variate is confounded because it also may include partial explanations of the unknown amounts of overlap with those that follow. Similarly, if, as in our case, the same model is to be used to explain each, the explanatory power of the model also partly and increasingly will be used up as analysis proceeds from the first to the last variate. Thus, the meaning of separate explanations of each is ambiguous.

To help clarify the situation, assume that Figure 5.1, rather than representing information about joining a party, instead represented information about the athletic ability of 625 people. The large circle would indicate all the information we could have about their abilities; a variety of measures of how they are able to use their bodies, including, for example, weights they could lift and distances they could run in various times. Canonical correlation would relate these measures, as a set, to other information that might explain differences in the several aspects of ability. This information might include matters such as the heights and weights of parents, whether their parents had taken part in athletic competition, the heights and weights of respondents, their pulse rates, and the lengths and thicknesses of their limbs. The four interior circles would represent components of athletic ability that had been derived from this information (e.g., speed, agility, quickness, and strength, extracted in that order). Although one may not know the extent, it is known that in the real world such attributes are related to one another. But since the canonical technique dictates that variates extracted to represent aspects of athletic ability are not associated, the circle representing a component such as agility, although it would include unknown proportions of the still to be extracted variates, quickness and strength, would exclude the proportion of agility which overlapped with speed. Similarly, the circle representing quickness would include an unknown proportion of the still to be extracted strength, but would exclude the proportion of quickness that overlapped with speed and agility. Moreover, since information about height and weight, pulse rate, and so forth was being used to explain all four components of athletic ability, if the model really applied in varying ways to all four, speed probably would be better explained than would strength since available information would have been used up as the analyses proceeded.

The reader may well inquire why the canonical technique is used if it has these disadvantages; more specifically, if a factor analytic technique not requiring extracted factors to be independent of one another might not be preferable. The answer is that the canonical technique, despite the special problems it presents, enhances meaning for it extracts variates directly in the

Chart 5.1
Variables in Model to Explain Joining a Party

Variable Name	Meaning
RFSES	Respondent's family's economic situation during childhood by the standards of that time (higher score, situation better)
DSESF	Duncan socioeconomic status score of respondent's father (high score, high status)
RESTAB	Stability of residence at birth, age six, and when first became politically aware (lower score, less residential mobility)
NIGHPTY	Consistency between respondent's current party and the most prevalent party in his childhood neighborhood (high score, different)
PENCH	Factor score summarizing presence of politics in immediate environment during childhood (positive score, politicized environment)
CLUBS	Total number of political clubs belonged to prior to joining a party
STABPTY	Whether there was a change in party identification before first party affiliation (high score, change)
IMPORT	Importance of politics prior to joining a party (higher score, greater importance)
INTER	Respondent's interest in politics followed a "normal" course of development (e.g., once the respondent became interested in politics, interest continued and/or increased until the time of joining the party) (higher, normal)
POLCY	Did (a) the platform and policies and/or (b) the leadership, membership, or candidates, of a particular party influence respondent to work for party (higher score, more influence)
PRESR	Did (a) respondent's relatives' interest in politics or pressure from friends or family, and/or (b) co-workers, teachers, or associational memberships, influence respondent to work for a party (higher score, more influence)
ENCOR	Influence of encouragement by others and degree of personal passivity on entry into party work (0, joining just happened to 4, encouraged and respondent actively interested)
EDUC	Educational level measured in terms of highest grade or grade equivalent completed
CHILD5	Was respondent married with youngest child under five at time of first becoming a party worker (highest score, both; middle score, married; lowest score, unmarried)
BSEXC	Was head of household in business or an executive when respondent first began party work (higher score, yes)
BLUEC	Was head of household a blue collar worker when respondent first began party work (higher score, yes)
PROF	Was head of household a professional when respondent first began party work (higher, yes)

context of other factors expected to relate to it. For example, although it may not be known whether a component of athletic ability such as speed really can be isolated empirically from the other three, one can be more confident from the context that a derived component *labeled* speed, really is that. Further, since the uncorrelated variates that are extracted in a canonical analysis are nonredundant pieces of a larger entity, they can be added together to form an explanation of the whole. Thus, an explanation of athletic ability could be generated by adding together the separate though possibly partial explanations of speed, agility, quickness, and strength.

It should also be noted that factor analytic techniques which extract related variates have their own problems. Perhaps most pertinent is that extracted factors often are extremely difficult to interpret because the loadings of the first are grouped with those of subsequent factors to which they are related. Consequently, if such a technique had been employed to delineate the components of joining a party (or athletic ability) one might not have been able to recognize a component such as self-motivation (or speed in the case of athletic ability) for what it is.

A Model to Explain Joining

Canonical correlation identifies any underlying dimensions in a given set of variables that are related to a second set. Here the second set is a group of items that comprise a model to explain joining. They reflect the socialization and social structural perspectives adopted to explain why only some people join parties. However, the explanatory variables employed in Chapter 4 had to be refined and compressed. Not only would it be confusing to employ so many measures in a model, but also it would be a mistake to assume that *all* measures pertinent to whether people join parties also are pertinent to why those who join, join differently. The selection, reduction and refinement processes yielded seventeen variables for the model and these were employed in the canonical analysis. The measures are listed in Chart 5.1. Some were constructed from several other measures, some by factor analyses (e.g., degree of politicization of childhood environment [PENCH], importance of politics to respondent prior to joining a party [IMPORT]), and some by combining patterns of information into types on an *a priori* basis (e.g., pattern of development of political interest [INTER]). Others are based on direct answers to single questions or codes of those answers (e.g., family's economic situation during respondent's childhood [RFSES]).

The model is organized as a flow of influence through time and is depicted in Figure 5.2.[11] The temporal sequence (reading Figure 5.2 from left to right) and cumulation of influences represent the experiences of a hypothetical

Figure 5.2
General Model of Components of Joining a Party

Model Stages

One	Two	Three	Four	Five	Components of Joining
		Pattern of Political Interest Development (INTER)		Educational Level (EDUC)	AGE
Father's Duncan Score (DSESF)					
	Degree of Politicization of Childhood Environment (PENCH)	Political Club Memberships (CLUBS)	Policy-Leadership Reasons for Joining (POLCY)	Marital/Family Status (CHILD5)	SELF-MOTIVATION
		Importance of Politics (IMPORT)	Pressure to Join (PRESR)	Head of Household: Business, Executive (BSEXC)	EXPERTISE
Family's Relative Economic Situation (RFSES)	Consistency of Neighborhood-Respondent Party Identification (NIGHPTY)				
		Stability of Party Identification (STABPTY)	Encouragement-Personal Interest in Joining (ENCOR)	Head of Household: Blue Collar (BLUEC)	CO-OPTION
Residential Stability (RESTAB)				Head of Household: Professional (PROF)	Initial Entry

Flow of Influence Through Time →

average respondent. Some of the measures cluster at certain points in time, others do not. Some refer to an instant or a short time span, others to much broader periods. Nonetheless, the variables are arranged in a plausible overall temporal sequence, and all those measures in the same column of Figure 5.2 are treated as if they refer only to the same period or point in time. The temporal sequence permits one to interpret the model in causal terms, a necessary caveat being that the temporal order is an approximation which may not fit the sequence of experiences of each respondent equally well. Specific predictions regarding level and direction of net and gross effects of each independent variable with each dependent variable will not be offered because, as the model depicted in Figure 5.2 implies, such predictions depend on potentially complex causal linkages involving several intervening variables.

The two columns on the left side of the model include early life attributes of a future party official. Those in column one deal with general structural matters: family's general economic level relative to standards of the time (RFSES), father's occupation (DSESF), and stability of residence between birth, age six, and time of first joining a party (RESTAB).[12] Since they influence most people's experiences from birth to young adulthood, including opportunities for youthful socializing experiences, it is quite likely that there may be a considerable gap between their gross and net effects. Indeed it may be that they have no net (i.e., direct) effects whatsoever. The second column from the left contains two measures that refer to political qualities of this early life environment. The first measure (NIGHPTY) describes whether the dominant party in the respondent's childhood neighborhood was the same as his or her present party. The second (PENCH) is a factor score that summarizes the presence of several politically oriented stimuli and role models (e.g., family, friends, schools, neighbors) in the respondent's immediate childhood environment.

The third column from the left contains four measures that focus on adolescent and early adult political behavior and interest. The first two indicate the extent of participation in paraparty and nonparty political organizations from birth to joining (CLUBS) and changes in partisan psychological identification between first identification and actual joining (STABPTY). The other two variables indicate how important politics and political matters were to the respondent (IMPORT) and whether his or her interest in politics developed normally (i.e., was sustained or increased and never declined) during that time (INTER).

The fourth column measures pertain to awareness during the year immediately before affiliation of certain factors that might have moved one toward a party affiliation. The first (POLCY) refers to awareness of attractive party features (e.g., leadership, platform), and the second (PRESR) to awareness of pressure to affiliate by significant others (e.g., family members, friends, co-workers). The last (ENCOR) is a scale of the respondent's judgment of his or her progress toward affiliation during the period, ranging between unconscious drift, at one extreme, to active interest in joining and encouragement to do so, on the other. These measures describe the nature and strength of relatively short-run factors that may overcome inertia and generate the actions necessary for joining.

The measures immediately to the left of the joining variates describe several attributes that could have impeded or facilitated particular modes of entry into a party. These variables include educational level (EDUC), three measures of occupation of head of household (business or managerial [BSEXC], blue collar [BLUEC], and professional [PROF]), and an index of marital and family status (CHILD5). They also may be significant because party officials size up prospective recruits. From their perspective, such matters as attractiveness to the public, time available for party work, and possession of skills needed in the organization, all may influence a potential member's attractiveness.

These seventeen measures were selected from a considerably larger number of possible explanatory variables after sustained preliminary analyses. A number of measures that might have added substantially to the explanation in statistical terms purposely were eliminated. Some, like party, obviously are important but will be treated differently for technical reasons. Others, like sex and ethnicity, have a continuous or spasmodic impact and cannot be placed in a temporal model. Still others that antedate joining and can be located temporally might not have been independent of some aspect of joining.[13] Since these exclusions diminish the completeness of any explanation, this approach to specifying the model constitutes a conservative explanation of joining.

Variates Dervied from Canonical Analysis

In the canonical correlation analysis, the ten measures of aspects of joining were reduced to eight by two adjustments. First, age of joining was not included but was treated as a unique dimension because several preliminary tests indicated it was unrelated to any of the other items, and because its removal simplified interpretation of the other underlying dimensions. Second, the items concerning party and public events at the time of joining were merged because of their strong relationship. The analysis of the remaining eight measures produced three canonical variates (components of joining) that were statistically significant and distill much of the information in the original items. Table 5.1 summarizes these results.[14] Age and these three variates will be treated as the "real" components of joining because they reflect elements of the process suggested by analyses reported in Chapter 4.

Table 5.1
Statistically Significant* Weights of the Canonical Variates that
Summarize Aspects of Joining

| Items | Canonical Variates | | | % of item Variance Explained by the Three Variates |
	Self-Motivation	Expertise	Cooption	
Volunteered	.47	−.34	.39	49.2
General Work	(+)**	−.62	.57	78.0
High Position First Contact		.50		27.5
High Prestige First Task		.38	−.31	24.7
High Status First Position	.46	.41		38.6
Strong Self-Motivation	.64	(−)**	.65	83.9
Close Associate for First Contact	−.73	.37	.40	83.0
Party and Public Affairs	.59		.29	46.8
Relative Factor Contribution	1.83	1.23	1.26	
% of Original Total Communality	22.80	15.40	15.70	53.9

*P ≤ .05
**Direction of non-significant loadings used in interpreting the meaning of the variate

The first variate (SEMOT) reflects an individual's independent motivation to join. Among its key aspects are a positive score for volunteering, a negative score for having a close relationship with the first contact person in the party, and positive scores for indications that the person would have joined even if facilitating factors had not been present, and for allusions to specific public and party events occurring at the time. The second component (EXPERT) is a profile of specialist recruitment. People recruited to perform specific and prestigious tasks in high level positions by those already occupying such positions receive the highest scores on this variate. The third and final variate (COOPT) indicates that a quality of co-option characterized the role of personal contact in initial recruitment. The loading pattern suggests that when relevant public and party events are occurring some people are

Table 5.2
Means for Components of Joining for Officials
of Each Party

Component	New Democratic	Liberal	Conservative	Social Credit	All Officials
Age	28.4	29.4	30.8	36.0	30.5
Self-Motivation	.19	−.16	−.01	−.02	−.00
Expertise	−.14	.01	.09	.10	−.00
Cooption	.04	.07	−.05	−.14	.00

quite vulnerable to appeals from those close to them and, in response, volunteer to perform various party tasks. The positive loading on volunteering suggests that people who are drafted in this way neither resist nor resent being approached.

Aside from age and having one's first party contact with an official in a high position, none of the eight items has most of its variance exhausted by only a single canonical variate. Elements of "volunteering" and "close association with first party contact" are reflected in all three variates and each of the other five items loads on two. The multiple loadings indicate that there are ambiguities in the manifest meanings of the individual variables, a problem that is alleviated by analyzing the canonical variate scores.

The procedure for generating canonical variate scores for each person sets the mean of the scores for each variate to zero and each standard deviation to one (age has been left in raw form). The average scores for each party's cohort of officials tend to diverge (see Table 5.2). Liberals have the lowest average self-motivation and experience the most co-option. Conservative and Social Credit officials tend to have been recruited for expertise. Socreds are distinctly older than any of the others, a fact that has considerable import in explaining how they join. (Differences of approximately one year are significant statistically.) NDP officials are youngest and have both the highest self-motivation and the lowest level of expertise when they join. Apparently, they affiliate to give of themselves and they bring more energy than experience to their party. These party profiles fit well with their popular public images.

Joining Parties

For reasons just reviewed, results of the analysis of each separate component will be merged and discussed as if joining were an undifferentiated

Table 5.3
Explained Variance (R^2) for Components of Joining
in Each Party
(in Percent)

	Maximum Adjusted, Full or Partial Model				
	New Democratic	Liberal	Conser-vative	Social Credit	All Officials
Age	44.6b	41.0b	23.4b	25.3b	32.5b
Self-Motivation	14.2b (4)	0.5 (4)	16.2b	11.5c (4)	10.6b
Expertise	0.8	−0.2 (2)	2.9 (2)	11.7c	2.6c
Cooption	0.9 (2)	2.7c (1)	9.2c	1.6 (3)	0.4
Total Variance Explained	60.5	44.0	51.7	50.1	46.1

	Percent of Total Variance Explained Accounted for by Explanation of Each Component of Joining				
	New Democratic	Liberal	Conser-vative	Social Credit	All Officials
Age	73.7	93.2	45.3	50.5	70.5
Self-Motivation	23.5	1.1	31.3	23.0	23.0
Expertise	1.5	−0.5	5.6	23.4	5.6
Cooption	1.5	6.1	17.8	3.2	0.9
Total	100.2	99.9	100.0	100.1	100.0

b - significant at .01 level.
c - significant at .05 level.

phenomenon. In addition, separate analyses were conducted for each party.[15] It is likely that there are basic general processes in joining common to all four parties. After all, they operate in the same governmental system and political and social environments. Moreover, their leadership cadres tend to come from a relatively restricted higher social stratum. However, it also is likely that the parties differ in some aspects of how people enter them. Perhaps most important are differences in their competitive situations that create different organizational needs. Joining a party is a two-way street. Parties seek and receive new members somewhat independently of the interests and desires of potential affiliates. Indeed, co-option as a component of joining implies as much. Unfortunately, measures of party needs at various times and

Table 5.4

Explained Variance (R²), Adjusted for Differences in Group Size, for Each Stage and Total Model

Increment in R² with Inclusion of Stage

Party and Component	1	2	3	4	5	R² Total Model	% of Final Total R²
Liberal:							
Age	.007	.036b	.140b	-.010	.236b	.409b	97.4
Self-Motivation	.004	-.005	-.012	.017	-.011	-.007	-1.7
Expertise	-.007	.005	-.011	.007	-.001	-.007	-1.7
Cooption	.027c	-.009	.002	.002	.003	.025	6.0
Total	.031	.027	.119	.016	.227	.420	100.0
Conservative							
Age	.011	.032c	.060b	.010	.121b	.234b	48.2
Self-Motivation	-.016	-.009	.084b	.092b	.012	.163b	33.6
Expertise	.011	.018	.000	-.020	-.013	-.004	-0.8
Cooption	-.015	.015	-.008	-.017	.117c	.092c	19.0
Total	-.009	.056	.136	.065	.237	.485	100.0

Social Credit:							
Age	-.013	.087b	.073c	.087b	.019	.253b	57.4
Self-Motivation	.033	-.020	.003	.100b	-.028	.088	20.0
Expertise	-.021	.017	.098b	.023	-.031	.086	19.5
Cooption	.013	-.020	.023	-.033	.031	.014	3.2
Total	.012	.064	.197	.177	-.009	.441	100.1
NDP:							
Age	.024	.091b	.029	-.004	.305b	.445b	78.1
Self-Motivation	-.017	-.003	.053b	.109b	-.021	.121b	21.2
Expertise	-.005	-.011	-.018	.027	.016	.009	1.6
Cooption	-.012	.021	-.010	.007	-.011	-.005	-0.9
Total	-.010	.098	.054	.139	.289	.570	100.0
Total:							
Age	.010	.060b	.085b	.002	.168b	.325b	70.5
Self-Motivation	-.001	-.003	.036b	.067b	.008	.107b	23.0
Expertise	-.001	.010c	.003	.010	.004	.026c	5.6
Cooption	-.003	.004	-.006	.004	.004	.003	.9
Total	.005	.071	.118	.083	.184	.461	100.0

b - significant at the .01 level
c - significant at the .05 level

of tastes and prejudices of recruiters in different constituencies are unavailable. The problem is alleviated partially because the weights of the variables that coincide with joining (fifth stage measures) reflect the sort of person who may have been perceived as an attractive member by those already in an organization. Hence, the roles of these variables in joining may vary by party and reflect any such differences among them.

The first question is how well the model explains initial joining. In this regard the multiple correlation coefficients for both the total sample and each party are statistically significant, and, in each case, the fit between the model and the data is quite good considering the numerous constraints on this analysis.[16] However, the fit of the data to the model does vary considerably among the parties, suggesting that different estimates be assembled. The upper half of Table 5.3 presents the results obtained when a downward adjustment in R^2 for differences in sample size is made.[17] Since earlier stages of the model sometimes fit relatively better than the full model, the stages at which the best ones occur are indicated in parentheses.[18] The size adjusted estimates suggest that in whole or part the model can explain approximately 44% to 60% of the variance in joining. It applies best to the NDP (60.5%) and least well to the Liberals (44.0%).

The model for each party, other than Social Credit, explains age best when all stages are included. Generally, however, motivation, expertise, and co-option are explained better without the last stage. Because of the unknown degree of overlap among the components, it is not clear whether the apparent general irrelevance of the last stage of the model (i.e., the proximate status attributes) for these latter aspects of joining is real or a product of the procedures. If real, by itself it would indicate that one's status at the time of joining a party is much more pertinent to when (i.e., at what age) than to how (i.e., under what circumstances of self-motivation, expertise, and co-optive strategies) one joins. This is a matter of considerable interest. If, however, the results are statistical artifacts, it would mean that although coincidental status attributes *are* somehow relevant to all aspects of joining, the extent and nature of their role in influencing motivation, expertise, and co-option is absorbed in and hidden by their role in explaining age of joining. Inability to establish component overlap also obscures the meaning of the fact that the distribution of R^2 by size among the components is quite different in each party. This is indicated in the lower panel of Table 5.3, which presents by party the proportion of the explanation of joining (i.e., the sum of the R^2s for each of the four components for a party) provided by the explanation of each component.[19]

The analysis in Table 5.4 reveals how adding each stage affects the model's performance. These changes come from the role of a stage (e.g., proximate social status) in explaining one or more of the components, but, again, it is not clear which components, because of the possible masking. Nonetheless, the larger an increment, the more likely is it that there are direct paths from measures at that stage to one or more of the components of joining. Neither for the total group of officials nor for any party cadre do first stage measures of origins make much of a direct contribution to the explanation of joining. However, the importance of subsequent stages varies considerably by party. Approximately three-quarters of the fit of the Liberal model derives from fifth stage coincidental status measures and from third stage youthful political activity and interest measures, both relating primarily to age of joining. No other party group has this pattern of development, but then for no other party is the explanation of age tantamount to an explanation of joining. Unlike the others, the pattern of increments for Social Crediters does not increase at the last stage. Indeed, adding proximate status measures adds nothing and lowers the levels of significance previously attained. The negligible role of proximate status may well reflect the fact that Social Crediters first affiliate later in life than do other party officials. Thus, proximate measures chosen for their particular pertinence to younger adults may be inappropriate for the typically older neophyte Social Crediter.[20] Even if this is not the reason for the irrelevance of these measures for the Social Credit group, it is the three middle stages, particularly one's political activities and interests at a relatively youthful age (CLUBS and INTER) that have the main roles in explanation. Also, for Social Credit, co-option is the only component of joining for which the model has no independent explanatory power.

Joining by Conservative and NDP officials is explained directly, albeit differently, by each stage of the model after the first. Among the Conservatives, expertise is the only component of joining that is not independently explainable. For them, as for Social Crediters and Liberals, youthful political activities and interests (stage 3) as well as coincidental status are particularly salient. In addition, for NDP officials both the political qualities of the childhood social environment (stage 2) and more immediate sociopsychological and environmental variables (stage 4) have major roles.

Paths to Joining

Although the model fits each party's officials, its applicability to different components, the roles of components relative to each other, and the unknown patterns of overlap among them certainly vary among the parties. Accordingly, the impacts and roles of the various causative agents included in the several

Table 5.5

Statistically Significant* Standardized Regression Coefficients in Path Model for Joining a Party (All Officials)

	PENCH	NIGHPTY	INTER	CLUBS	IMPORT	STABPTY	POLCY	PRESR	ENCOR	EDUC	CHILD5	BSEXC	BLUEC	PROF	Age	Self-Motivation	Exper-tise	Co-option
DSESF	—	—	—	.12	—	—	—	—	—	.26	—	—	—	.11	—	—	—	—
RFSES	—	—	—	—	—	—	—	—	—	.10	—	—	−.10	—	—	—	—	—
RESTAB	—	—	—	—	—	—	—	—	—	—	—	—	−.10	—	—	—	—	—
PENCH	—	—	.13	—	.26	—	—	.19	—	—	−.14	—	—	−.14	.12	—	—	—
NIGHPTY	—	—	—	—	.09	.21	—	−.09	—	—	—	—	—	−.12	—	—	.09	—
INTER	—	—	—	—	—	—	—	.12	—	—	−.14	−.14	—	—	−.15	—	—	—
CLUBS	—	—	—	—	—	—	—	—	—	.26	−.17	−.10	—	—	—	.19	—	—
IMPORT	—	—	—	—	—	—	—	—	—	—	—	—	—	—	—	—	—	—
STABPTY	—	—	—	—	—	—	—	—	.09	—	—	.09	—	—	—	—	—	—
POLCY	—	—	—	—	—	—	—	—	—	—	—	—	—	—	—	—	—	—
PRESR	—	—	—	—	—	—	—	—	—	—	—	—	—	—	—	−.21	—	—
ENCOR	—	—	—	—	—	—	—	—	—	—	—	—	—	.08	—	.15	.10	—
EDUC	—	—	—	—	—	—	—	—	—	—	—	—	—	—	−.26	−.13	—	—
CHILD5	—	—	—	—	—	—	—	—	—	—	—	—	—	—	.24	—	—	—
BSEXC	—	—	—	—	—	—	—	—	—	—	—	—	—	—	.20	—	—	—
BLUEC	—	—	—	—	—	—	—	—	—	—	—	—	—	—	—	—	—	−.11
PROF	—	—	—	—	—	—	—	—	—	—	—	—	—	—	.18	—	—	—
R^2	.013*	.003	.025†	.019*	.077†	.052†	.020	.088†	.015	.191†	.112†	.077*	.038	.046	.343†	.131†	.052†	.031
Adjusted R^2	.008	−.002	.017	.011	.069	.045	.006	.075	.001	.176	.099	.059	.019	.028	.325	.106	.026	.004

*P ≤ .05
†P ≤ .01

stages of the model also vary.[21] These conclusions, however, pertain only to *direct* effects of the independent variables on joining. They do not reflect any important *indirect* effects of a stage. Path analysis is an analytic technique that separates and identifies direct and indirect effects, and identifies the role of each individual variable of a model rather than just the collective relevance of a stage.[22] It does this by showing the actual linkages (or paths) among the proposed explanatory elements in a model and it can be employed when there is a reasonable basis for arranging these elements in a sequence of influence. If, on the one hand, everything at each stage were to influence the components of joining both directly and indirectly, paths would connect each measure to all others at later stages and to the components. On the other hand, if the model and the theory it represents really did not apply to the problem being studied, there would be no paths whatsoever.[23] The truth, of course, lies somewhere in between. Because what is "true" for one party is not necessarily so for others, each party's path model will be considered separately. And, since a preliminary examination of the individual party models disclosed a number of common features to the causal flow, we also shall comment on the party officials as a single group. Table 5.5 summarizes all the links in the model for the entire group. The four diagrams in Figure 5.3[24] depict how the forces represented by various measures in the model shape the experience of joining a particular party. In singling out features for discussion we are guided by the frequency with which they occur in the party models as well as the magnitudes of their weights.

Considering the general model from the first stage, we may note that there are no connections between any measures of (stage one) childhood family status and (stage two) early environmental politicization. Essentially, class and residential stability do not affect the politicization of the child's environment in any manner pertinent to the particulars of how that person eventually joins a party.[25] The forces represented by the two stages influence joining differently. The status measures primarily operate as in classic status attainment models for Canada and the United States; they tend to exert an influence on later status, specifically that at the time of joining. They also influence prejoining participation in paraparty organizations and nonparty political groups, the only third stage measure not·linked to political environment variables. The explanation for this pattern may be that paraparty participation is strongly and positively tied to level of schooling.[26]

The political environment variables, in contrast, not only are associated with political interest, viewing politics as important, and changing partisan identification, but those relationships frequently recur as initiating links in important indirect paths. Their influence extends to the fourth stage, for, in addition to promoting political interest and partisan change, they motivate

Figure 5.3(a)
Path Model of Components of Joining for Liberal Party Officials

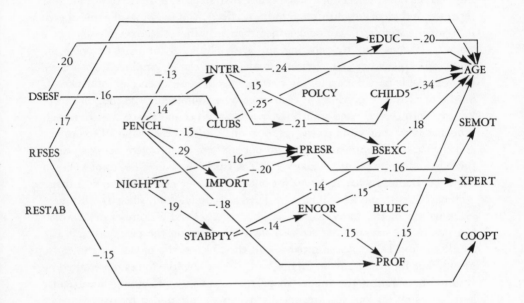

Figure 5.3(b)
Path Model of Components of Joining for Conservative Party Officials

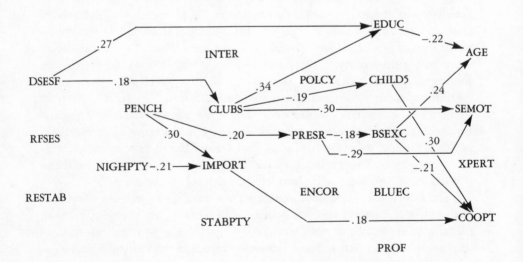

Figure 5.3(c)
Path Model of Components of Joining for New Democratic Party Officials

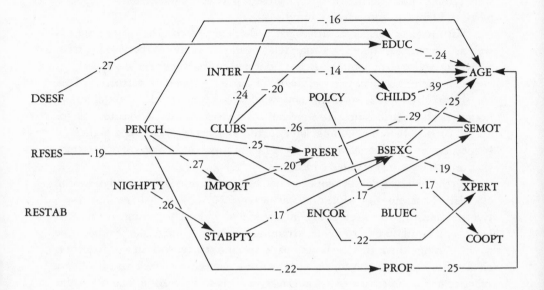

Figure 5.3(d)
Path Model of Components of Joining for Social Credit Party Officials

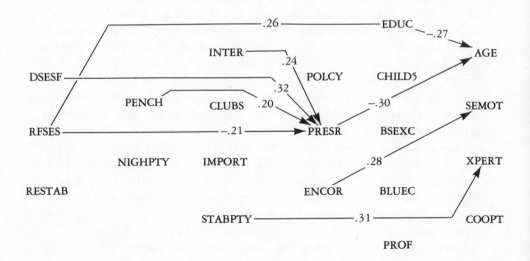

respondents and make them susceptible to pressures and forces that produce different joining styles. Further, officials who lived in neighborhoods that were strongholds of other than their present parties are likely to have changed partisan identification before joining.[27]

With respect to specific direct paths that characterize the entire group as well as the parties, there is a strong relationship in every case between years of schooling and age of joining. Better educated officials join earlier, reflecting, perhaps, the presence of party-affiliated clubs in Canadian universities.[28] That the school situation as such and not social status conferred by years of school underlies the relationships is suggested by the strong associations (except for Social Credit) between joining later in life and having been in a household headed either by a professional or by a businessman or executive, occupations that tend to require extended educations.

Further evidence of the workings of education is provided by analyses using alternative measures of educational achievement.[29] These analyses show positive relationships between being in law school and early joining, on the one hand, and being in other graduate training and later joining, on the other. The act of joining, then, may be functionally specific. Party work in a university is an accepted pattern through which aspiring lawyers can seek to establish a practice and to initiate a political career, so it is to their advantage to involve themselves in a party organization. Combining politics and a career is not a conventional pattern for those heading toward other high status occupations and they may defer joining. In summary, although type of degree sought as well as educational level *per se* are both relevant considerations, there are enough respondents for whom it was advantageous to join early to produce a net negative relationship between educational level and age of joining.

In addition to the very important roles of education and occupation, pertinent features of the model for age of joining for all officials may be summarized as follows. Facilitative socialization experiences and conditions generally lead to early joining. Without those advantages people tend to embark on work and family careers that delay joining.[30] Thus, the factor score measuring politicization of the childhood environment also is strongly and positively related to earlier joining. This relationship holds for each party but Social Credit. Since Social Credit officials tend to come from less politicized environments and since they join later in life, the absence of a relationship is not unexpected. More generally, among officials whose education continues beyond the average, personal political exposure and development have no impact on when they initiate party work. How party work meshes with their school and ultimate career interests is what primarily influences the timing of their joining.

Motivational levels also are susceptible to the complex flow of forces from class of origin, level of education, and participation in political activities prior to affiliating. Not surprisingly, those who do not have these facilitating advantages have compensating higher levels of motivation. Being the target of the suggestions and encouragement of others relates strongly to lower levels of self-motivation.[31] The highly motivated joiners are more likely to have acted purposively and not through accident or drift, probably as a result of having placed greater importance on politics early in life, and, in turn, having come from a more politicized environment and a neighborhood that was a stronghold of some "other" party. In summary, then, motivation is personal, active, and sustained from earlier political interests and activities. It seems to affect joining most when social class and school-related nonparty political activities do not contribute to early joining.

To the extent that expertise is a factor, it reflects both active reinforced entry and having been reared as a child in a neighborhood environment with different political leanings. Those leaders who score high on expertise come from environments that lead them to place great importance on politics and, perhaps, to see the attractions of working in a different party. Finally, with regard to co-option, the one direct path indicates that those who belong to households whose heads hold low status white-collar occupations or are not in the labor force are most likely to join through co-optive processes. In the remainder of this discussion we shall review any special and noteworthy features of the analyses for individual parties and compare the profiles of joining suggested by their various models.

Liberal Party: The fit of the general model (Figure 5.2) to the data for Liberal party officials is depicted in Figure 5.3a. As might be expected from material already examined, most of the direct paths to joining converge on age. Variables at all but the proximate stage of the model are involved directly or indirectly with every aspect of joining. Proximate status bears only on age and recapitulates the previously discussed patterns. Furthermore, as in each party's model, all significant proximate measures are tied to earlier stages. Liberal officials from higher social class backgrounds are more likely to have affiliated initially at a somewhat later age than are their lower status party colleagues and they also are less likely than the latter to have been co-opted. The indirect paths also recapitulate the patterns of the total model, although the presence of a strong link from a youthful unstable party identification to active pursuit of affiliation with the encouragement of others does clarify how certain older experts come into the Liberal party.

Conservative Party: The general model adapts to the joining experiences of Conservative officials in a relatively simple fashion. The basic strands of the class-school-prejoining activity, and politicized environment-importance of politics patterns are present (see Figure 5.3b). The seven direct paths go to three different components of joining. Only variations in expertise are not explained by the model. Co-option is more adequately explained for Conservative officials than for those of any other party. The paths indicate quite clearly that co-option brings into the party people who are politically inclined despite having had familial and occupational situations which are not facilitative. Since material presented in Chapter 2 indicated that Conservative officials are more likely to be lawyers than are their counterparts in other parties, some aspects of the parallel analyses using an alternative educational variable for law school bear mentioning. Conservative officials who join younger are more likely to have law degrees, and to have come from families whose fathers enjoyed high status occupations. Lawyers also are more likely to have been influenced by their awareness of and interest in party and public affairs in the year preceding affiliation. In addition, some of the lawyers who join at younger than average ages placed strong importance on politics earlier, an emphasis that eventually is manifested in an active interest in affiliating. Lawyers from higher status families also tend to join the party organization proper only after having been involved in other nonparty or paraparty political groups.

New Democratic Party: By and large, patterns for the NDP (See Figure 5.3c) are much like those encountered in considering all party officials. They repeat all but two of the fourteen direct paths. Despite the party's ideological appearance and appeal, the NDP model includes the network of paths that suggests that it, too, recruits as experts older persons who may have been prevailed upon to switch partisan allegiances. Also not in accord with conventional expectations, distinctive recruitment patterns for those from blue-collar headed households are not evident for the New Democrats. Overall, except for a path from sensitivity to party and public affairs to more co-option, nothing in the model suggests any very different influences than those already noted for other parties' officials.

Social Credit Party: There is very little overlap among the explanatory patterns for the different components among Social Credit officials (see Figure 5.3d). Expertise and motivation are represented by rudimentary models. When expertise is a factor, shifts in party loyalty are involved; the higher the self-motivation, the more active and purposive is the move to affiliate. As for age, the model is more complex. The typical path from upper status to more schooling to younger affiliation is apparent. Additionally, however, social class, being raised in a politicized environment, and having had a sustained and increasing interest in politics all relate to early joining, but only through some catalytic action by other people. For Social Crediters, apparently recruitment in its most classic sense of the "recruiting officer" is central. In addition, the two class measures for family of origin have opposite effects on the intervening recruitment measure (PRESR) for reasons that are not clear. Although undoubtedly there are numerous permutations, primarily, either party agents recruited some politically interested younger people who affiliated to continue their previous nonparty or paraparty political activities, or previous supporters of other parties were recruited for their special talents. Since Social Credit officials, on the average, are six years older than officials entering other parties, the term "younger" may actually describe joining at an age above the averages of the other parties. It also may explain why there are no proximate status influences, for these were included for their potential relevance to variations in joining during a younger age range.

Party Similarities and Differences: As previously suggested, the modes of joining can reflect party styles and needs as much as the personal predilections and choices that arise from the individual backgrounds of joiners. This is most obvious with regard to the Social Credit and New Democratic party groups. For their officials, the processes of joining depicted by both the distribution of direct paths to the components and indirect paths among the explanatory factors conform to certain elements of their parties' popular images. The NDP model suggests a group of relatively young, ideologically committed activists with a small brain trust of individuals with considerable political expertise. The Social Credit model reflects the experiences of older groups of politically uncommitted expert technicians on the one hand, and ideologues on the other. These judgments regarding the fit of the recruitment model to organizational styles and needs are easier to render for the New Democrats and Social Crediters because they are members of parties that happen to be well-organized and electorally successful in the areas where the data were collected: New Democrats in both provinces, Social Credit in British Columbia.

Whether popular images of the national parties apply to their local organizations in Vancouver and Winnipeg is difficult to establish. Nonetheless, inasmuch as age is the predominant component in the Liberal joining pattern, the results reflect what could be expected of a long-established, nationally successful party. It would seem that most Liberal officials join when they are "ready" and the organization is "ready" for them and that is what the model explains—joining patterns of older and younger people for whom party needs and perceived personal opportunities coincide. The Conservatives, in contrast, have fewer officials and probably cannot afford to sit back and pick and choose new members by processes that appear to express free choices on the recruits' part. There is a considerable bloc of Conservative party loyalists who appear to have joined as soon as they were able. However, to meet its organizational needs, the Conservative party must have had to recruit others, sometimes by co-opting those with weak or unstable attachments to other parties. In this

Table 5.6

Direct and Indirect Paths to Joining for Measures with a Total Net Relationship (.05 Level of Significance)

	Age of Joining			Self-Motivation			Expertise			Cooption		
	Direct	Indirect	Total	Direct	Indirect	Total	Direct	Indirect	Total	Direct	Indirect	Total
Stage 1												
DSESF	—	-.13	-.13	—	—	—	—	—	—	—	—	—
RFSES	.12	-.12	—*	—	—	—	—	—	—	—	—	—
RESTAB	—	—	—	—	—	—	—	—	—	—	—	—
Stage 2												
PENCH	-.12	-.13	-.25	—	—	—	.09	.02	.11	—	.08	.08
NIGHPTY	—	—	—	—	—	—	—	—	—	—	—	—
Stage 3												
INTER	-.15	-.08	-.23	—	—	—	—	—	—	—	—	—
CLUBS	-.14	—	-.14	.19	-.03**	.16	—	—	—	—	—	—
IMPORT	—	—	—	—	.13	.13	—	—	—	—	—	—
STABPTY	—	—	—	—	—	—	—	.09	.09	—	—	—
Stage 4												
POLCY	—	—	—	—	—	—	—	—	—	—	—	—
PRESR	—	—	—	-.21	—	-.21	—	—	—	—	—	—
ENCOR	—	-.08	-.08	.15	-.01*	.14	.10	.01	.11	—	—	—
Stage 5												
EDUC	-.26	—	-.26	.13	—	-.13	—	—	—	—	—	—
CHILD5	.24	—	.24	—	—	—	—	—	—	—	—	—
BSEXC	.20	—	.20	—	—	—	—	—	—	-.11	—	-.11
BLUEC	—	—	—	—	—	—	—	—	—	—	—	—
PROF	.18	—	.18	—	—	—	—	—	—	—	—	—

*Suppression, revealed by Stages 3 and 5   **Suppression, revealed by Stage 5.

regard, co-option is a relatively more important component of joining for the Conservatives than for officials of any other party (see Table 5.3). More generally, co-option, though the last variate of joining, is sufficiently independent (for all but the Social Credit) to manifest at least one statistically significant linkage in each of the path analyses.

With respect to the structures of the four party models, there are certain uniformities. Early socialization factors clearly are important for each. Moreover, in no case is either residential stabilty or being a member of a blue-collar headed household related to how respondents join, and in no case do social structural aspects of the early environment operate (first stage) through its political qualities (second stage). The major increments in explanation added by coincidental status measures (see Table 5.4) always reflect the impact of earlier socialization. However, they undoubtedly also influence the nature of joining in and of themselves. This is particularly true of age, where repeatedly the achievement of certain educational, familial, and occupational statuses accounts for older joining. These relationships hold despite the fact that the average ages of first entry differ significantly from party to party.

Direct and indirect paths to the various components of joining tie together every stage of the model but the first two. Family of origin's social class, politicization of the childhood environment, consistency between the dominant party of the childhood neighborhood and the official's present affiliation, an unstable partisan attachment, experiencing a pattern of consistently developing political interest, and placing a high importance on political matters are the most frequently recurring variables. Indeed, the model for all officials, regardless of party, cannot be comprehended without knowing about these features of early life. Finally, several paths recur in the party models. People from households headed by business proprietors and executives join at older ages. Persons from more politicized childhood environments or who have developed their political interests in an orderly fashion join younger. Those who participated in political but not party groups join with more self-motivation and those who join as experts are likelier to have switched from the party supported in their neighborhoods of origin. Among repeated indirect paths, two bear mention: the path between politicization of childhood environment and importance placed on politics prior to joining, and that between growing up in a neighborhood not dominated by one's current party and subsequently switching loyalties. Both are positive. It is revealing to note that the latter path relates not to the motivated joining that might characterize persons who had some sort of ideologically based or emotionally related conversion experience, but rather to the joining of what appear to be older experts recruited through co-optive techniques.

Finally, one other striking aspect of these analyses deserves special note. As

Chart 5.2

Summary of Direct and Indirect Effects of Stages of Model on Components of Joining a Party*

Component of Joining by Party	Direct Effects of Stages					Indirect Effects of Stages				
	1	2	3	4	5	1	2	3	4	5
Age										
NDP		some	some		considerable	considerable	considerable	some		
Liberal	some	some	some		considerable	some	considerable	considerable	some	
Conservative					considerable	considerable	some	some	some	
Social Credit				some	some	considerable	some	some		
All	some	some	some		considerable	considerable	considerable	considerable		
Self-Motivation										
NDP			some	considerable			considerable	some		
Liberal			some	some		some	considerable	some		
Conservative			some	some	some	some	some			
Social Credit				some		some	considerable	considerable		
All			some	considerable	some					
Expertise				some	some	some	some	some		
NDP				some	some	some	some	some		
Liberal				some			some	some		
Conservative										
Social Credit		some	some				some	some		
All				some						
Cooption										
NDP	some			some						
Liberal			some			some				
Conservative					considerable	some	considerable	some	some	
Social Credit										
All					some		considerable	considerable		

*The absence of any designation indicates no significant path.

the results of the path analyses were first transcribed it was observed repeatedly that factors from early life environments and experiences initially were important, but that their impact then was absorbed by measures of later environments and experiences. These patterns are reflected clearly in Table 5.6. This is a strategic observation with respect to questions concerning the role of socialization in explaining later life political behavior. It means that early life socialization measures are unlikely to appear important when they are included in explanatory models with more proximate measures. Indeed, often they are not as likely as more proximate measures to show strong relationships, given the corroding effects of the passage of time and the relation of these early events to intervening events (e.g., the kind and amount of education one secures, when and who one marries) which then more directly determine subsequent phenomena. In our analyses sometimes this even meant that roles of early life factors were suppressed until later factors were introduced into the model. This is the way things are in real life. Regardless of the launching most people receive, whether they reach their likely targets is strongly influenced by experiences and events along the way. From this perspective, it is perhaps surprising that our observations have detected as much early life influence as they have.

Summary

The isolation by canonical correlation of age, self-motivation, expertise, and co-option as components of joining specified and confirmed themes that were suggested in Chapter 4. The canonical procedure dictated that each component of joining be statistically independent of the others and that as a set they could be taken to represent the entire initial affiliation phenomenon. By using a causal model of joining incorporating a highly reduced subset of seventeen measures of attributes of party officials—starting with earliest life socioeconomic environment and progressing, in order, to the political climate of that environment during early childhood, adolescent political experiences and development, social and psychological forces perceived as present during the year preceding first joining, and the social and economic status of the respondents at the time of first affiliating—it was possible to explain substantial proportions of the variance in the officials' recruitment experiences. A summary of direct and indirect effects of the several stages of the model is presented in Chart 5.2.

The chart emphasizes that factors leading to different patterns of initial affiliation should be assessed separately for different parties. The outcomes are particularly satisfactory in view of constraints implicit in the procedures, measurement imprecision, and sharp restrictions on the composite set of explanatory variables included in the model. Factors at every stage of personal development contribute to separate components of the joining experience. With regard to the age component, coincidental status characteristics absorb and divert much of the effect of earlier factors. And, even though they are of less direct weight, political socialization events and experiences are important. Both directly and indirectly they help sort out individual variations in an experience that is shared by every one of the 625 officials. Particularly salient for future party leaders are the effects of a politicized childhood environment. Being raised in such an environment has strong indirect effects on mode of entry into party work for Social Credit and Conservative leaders and strong or discernible direct and indirect effects for Liberals and New Democrats. A politicized early life environment influences not only who becomes a party official, but also the diverse patterns of how initial entry into party organizations occurs. Having considered entry, we turn in the next section to the placement and careers of these entrants in their respective party organizations.

NOTES

1. Abraham Kaplan, *The Conduct of Inquiry* (San Francisco: Chandler, 1964), pp.55-57.

2. See, for example, Maurice Duverger, *Political Parties*, 2nd ed., trans. Barbara and Robert North (London: Methuen, 1964), chap. 2; Leon D. Epstein, *Political Parties in Western Democracies* (New York: Praeger, 1967), chaps. 5 and 6.

3. Canonical correlation as a statistical technique is discussed in T. W. Anderson, *Introduction to Multivariate Statistical Analysis* (New York: Wiley, 1958), chap. 12; W. W. Cooley and P. R. Lohnes, *Multivariate Procedures for the Behavioral Sciences* (New York: Wiley, 1962), chap. 3; and T. Hirschi and H. Selvin, *Delinquency Research* (New York: The Free Press, 1967), p. 100. For a useful nontechnical discussion of the technique see Paul Vincent Warwick, "Canonical Correlation Analysis," in N.H. Nie, William R. Klecka, C. H. Hull, eds., *Statistical Package for the Social Sciences,* 2nd ed. (Toronto: McGraw-Hill, 1975), pp. 515-519.

4. Despite its explanatory potential, because of the stringent demands the canonical model places on data, until recently the technique has been employed only infrequently. Hirschi and Selvin, *Delinquency Research*, pp. 170-171.

5. Hubert Blalock, *Social Statistics*, 2nd ed. (Toronto: McGraw-Hill, 1972), chap. 19.

6. On path analysis see Sewall Wright, "Path Coefficients and Path Regressions: Alternative or Complementary Concepts?" *Biometrics*, 16 (1960): 189-202; O. Dudley Duncan, "Path Analysis: Sociological Examples," *American Journal of Sociology*, 72 (1966):1-16; Kenneth C. Land, "Principles of Path Analysis," in E. F. Borgatta, ed., *Sociological Methodology: 1969* (San Franscisco: Jossey-Bass, 1969), chap. 1. See also Jae-On Kim and Frank J. Kahout, "Special Topics in General Linear Models," Nie, *et al., Statistical Package for the Social Sciences*, pp. 383-397.

7. "Path analysis is not a procedure for demonstrating causality . . . it is a method for tracing out the implications of a set of causal assumptions which the

researcher is willing to impose upon a system of relationships," Kim and Kahout, *Ibid.*, p. 389. In recursive systems where the relationships between variables are assumed to be linear, additive, and causal, path coefficients are normally estimated using Beta weights, *Ibid.*, p. 387. Verbally, path coefficients measure the proportion of a standard unit of change in a dependent variable associated with a standard unit of change in an independent variable, controlling for the influence of all other variables in the explanatory system. For a more precise definition see Land, "Principles of Path Analysis," pp. 8-10. As Land notes: "The *squared path coefficient* measures the proportion of the variance of the dependent variable for which the determining variable is *directly* responsible." "Principles of Path Analysis," p. 10. An excellent illustration of the combination of canonical correlation and path analysis is provided in James R. Lincoln, "Power Mobilization in the Urban Community: Reconsidering the Ecological Approach," *American Sociological Review*, 41 (1976): 1-15. The main difference in our approach is that we analyze four canonical variates and Lincoln analyzes only one.

8. Warwick, "Canonical Correlation Analysis," p.517.

9. The magnitude of each circle indicates the proportion of covariance accounted for by that variate. Necessarily, each succeeding variate is smaller than those that preceded it. Comparisons of the series indicate the relative salience of each as an aspect of the whole.

10 In essence, the absent part of each circle shifts the weights for each variate to bring the correlations among variates to zero.

11 Because the features of joining are represented as a set of scores on variates whose measurements may overlap, explanatory items are included in the model for their possible relevance to any one or more of these variates, and the model is a composite intended to explain joining as a whole.

12. Presumably, higher social class affords advantages of both access and know-how, and—if it facilitates interest through its impact on education—may result in earlier joining. Stability, in contrast, may enhance one's familiarity and concern with a local situation, and from a local party's perspective, increase a person's visibility and attractiveness as a recruit.

13 For example, such measures as the ages of first awareness and of first psychological identification with a party have partially tautological relationships with the age of first joining. Respondents who reported these as occurring early in life necessarily could have joined during a broader range of subsequent ages than could those who reported much later ages.

14. The table contains the loadings of each item on each of the three variates, the proportion of covariance among the original eight items accounted for by the three variates (note the bottom row of Table 5.1), and the proportion of the variance in each item accounted for by the variates (final column of Table 5.1).

15. If there are differences among the parties, they should influence the patterns of relationships among the joining components in each party. Moreover, if the predictor variables relate to the components differently in each party, a composite explanation of joining for all parties will differ from that for a particular party. In statistical language, there will be interaction between party as a variable and other independent variables. In fact, this is the case; the average values of the independent variables employed and the zero-order correlations do vary among the parties.

16. These constraints include missing material (i.e., uninterviewed officials); normal mechanical mistakes in recording and processing information; indexing imprecisions; and the exclusion of one or more salient features of joining which may not have been subsumed in the components identified by the four variates.

17. In deflating the coefficients, the adjustment makes some of them negative.

18. The decrease in significance for the full model, when it occurs, happens because of a greater loss in degrees of freedom than additional gain in explanation with the added measures.

19. Inter-party differences in the ability of the model to explain each component of joining may reflect variations in the degree of overlap among the components. If so, it would seem that for the Liberals the correlations are exceedingly high, and, therefore, that age masks almost everything else.

20. The other party groups do join at younger ages, and, by and large, for them coincidental status measures account for the largest increments in explanation, primarily through their roles in explaining age of joining.

21 Thus, we find that the number of direct paths to the components decrease in the order in which the latter were extracted and identified. Seven go to age, four to self-motivation, two to expertise, and one to co-option. This mirrors the decreased ability to explain each component as summarized in Tables 5.3 and 5.4. As Table 5.4 also suggests, the direct paths from proximate status variables tend to go to age. Of the fourteen direct paths, six are from these fifth stage measures and four go to age, whereas the other eight originate at each of the other stages and five go to the other three components.

22. The model included more than one item at each stage because, under certain conditions, each item was expected to have an independent role.

23. Depending on the nature of the data and the investigator's goals, the relationships among variables at the same stage, reciprocal relationships among variables, and sources of unexplained variance, also can be estimated and included. We have not done so here, being interested primarily in how these measures affect joining.

24. Direct paths are signified by arrows that terminate at the four components of joining on the right of the diagrams. All other arrows signify the existence of indirect paths that eventually terminate with one or the other of the aspects of joining. Many of the measures are connected to aspects of joining both directly and indirectly, the sum of the two being their total causal effect.

25. Indeed, of the six correlations among these first and second stage measures for all officials and for each party group—thirty in all—only one is significant (the relationship between family's relative social class and PENCH for Liberals is .14).

26. In this instance, the model may be distorting reality by inverting influence. Even though the placement of measures is correct in terms of timing (i.e., the participation occurred before joining and the educational level is at joining), the educational level also covers an earlier period in school. Since much of this nonparty political activity occurs in school-based organizations, the longer respondents stay in school, the greater their opportunities to participate in the activities of these groups. Years of school completed is a measure with a number of meanings—in this case, at least, possible exposure to paraparty groups, skill development, and prestige—and there is no way to separate them.

27. Although the paths in the total model suggest that the unstable partisans were businessmen who were co-opted at above average ages of affiliation, in fact, the party diagrams suggest that this is an averaging effect, and that switchers tend to be NDP officials who were recruited as experts.

28. The relationship also may reflect the exigencies of making a living if one is not in school.

29. The alternative form of educational achievement consists of three "dummy"

variables: a) respondent's highest degree is a B.A. or B.Sc.; b) respondent holds a non-law graduate degree; and c) respondent holds a law degree.

30. By and large the fifth stage occupational and family measures are correlated with older joining because they are negatively related to background measures that are clearly and obviously associated with younger joining (e.g., coming from a more politicized childhood environment, having experienced an orderly pattern of development of interest in politics, placing high importance on politics early, and never having changed one's partisan identification).

31. This need not have been the case. The relationship could well have been reinforcing and complementary since those who are the targets of others are also more likely to have come from more politicized environments and to have had a sustained and increasing interest in politics.

Chapter Six

A Typology of
Party Officials

> The democratic external form which characterizes the life of political parties may readily veil from superficial observers the tendency towards aristocracy, or rather towards oligarchy, which is inherent in all party organization.

Roberto Michels, *Political Parties,* p. 50.

Three Types of Party Leaders

Samuel J. Eldersveld characterized a political party as being like any other formal social group in consisting of "a set of individuals populating specific roles and behaving as member-actors of a boundaried and identifiable social unit."[1] He contended that parties are hierarchically organized but in Western democracies they are of a special type he calls "stratarchies." "The general characteristics of stratarchies are the proliferation of the ruling group and the diffusion of power prerogatives and power exercise."[42] As do all structures, parties contain "multiple-elites" who, lacking effective sanctions, interact with one another on the basis of "reciprocal deference." Moreover, since parties in a free, competitive society are "clientele-oriented," they also tend to be "alliances of sub-coalitions."[3]

Canada local parties we would argue also are all of these things. They are alliances of sub-coalitions that bring together in a sometimes uneasy union individuals of different ages, ethnic groups, and occupations.[4] They are clientele-oriented in that they constantly seek to expand the support their candidates receive. And, although anecdotal evidence suggests that influence generally is ascribed to higher rather than lower echelon position-holders, the relationship between formal position and individual influence is far from perfect. Parties also have what Joseph Schlesinger has termed "associational" and "public" leaders who could qualify for the label multiple-elites.[5] Finally, although activities are coordinated and directed toward the attainment of organizational goals, something akin to reciprocal deference does characterize many aspects of the relationship of party officials with one another. Since almost all of them are unpaid volunteers, it could hardly be otherwise.

If we pursuing a conventional descriptive approach, we would review each local party unit in very particular terms: when it was founded, its history, changes in the boundaries of the electoral district in which it operates, the extent to which it may fit the several models of party organization proposed by Eldersveld, and so forth. We shall not take this approach for a number of reasons. It would be impossible to describe each of the local party units exactly because there is no limit to the detail that might be covered, the features of the organization are subject to virtually continuous change, and the leaders themselves frequently are unaware of the exact structure of the organization at any time. This last attribute follows from the fact that the extent to which the real and paper tables of organization are congruent also varies. Although individuals often occupy specific roles, there can be considerable overlap and disjuncture. For example, a single person may occupy the same position in both the provincial and federal constituency organizations, one individual may occupy different positions in both, or more than one person can occupy the same position, or, at least believe they do. Further, although these local parties are, as Eldersveld contends, "boundaried and identifiable social units," their boundaries are anything but clear. As was indicated in the first chapter, a few individuals appear to exercise substantial influence in party affairs although they hold no position in a formal party hierarchy.

Even if the amorphousness and variability of their structures and activity levels did not pose difficulties, the task of describing party units explicity is compounded by a wide range of interparty and intraparty stylistic differences. For example, Frederick C. Engelmann has described the relatively democratic character of member participation in the CCF-NDP.[6] The Social Credit party appears to have the opposite orientation, and the two major parties generally fall somewhere in between. The electoral success of the New Democratic party generally is predicated upon a strategy of "working the riding," intensive face-to-face canvassing and recanvassing of virtually every household and building in a particular constituency. This canvassing is carried on by leaders and rank and file alike. The Social Credit party, in contrast, offers its electoral messages to the pubic principally through the media. Canvassing, to the extent that there is any, is carried out primarily by the party's "little old ladies in tennis shoes." The two major parties rely on both methods with upper echelon party functionaries probably preferring to let others canvass while they plan media campaigns.

The parties also differ with respect to their attitudes toward the modern technology of electioneering. The two major parties and the leadership of the British Columbia Social Credit organization are attracted to and make extensive use of newspapers, radio, and television, of sample surveys and "media experts." Liberal and Conservative party leaders, in particular, are very much attuned to the latest developments in American campaign technology.[7] (It will be recalled that the subject of one of our vignettes, Susan Spillman, had negotiated with a well-known firm of American campaign specialists to run her husband's campaign for the Conservative party leadership.) The NDP organization, while not eschewing the technology of the new politics, continues to place its emphasis on the tried-and-true (for them) methods of the old politics. Thus, if forced to choose, New Democratic party organization leaders prefer their personal impressions of the distribution of public political attitudes, impressions based upon intensive personal canvassing, to data on voter opinions generated by professional survey research firms.[8]

Yet another interparty difference involves the attitudes of current party leaders toward what may be termed the academic-intellectual communities. The Liberal and New Democratic party organizations include a considerable number of university professors, high school teachers and administrators, creative writers, and an assortment of other people who legitimately could be called "intellectuals."[9] Moreover, at least some of the ideas that emanate from this academic-intellectual cohort receive a sympathetic hearing in party councils. This is less often the case in the Conservative party and particularly not so in the Social Credit party.[10] Finally, as a caveat regarding these observations, it may not be too much of an exaggeration to state that there sometimes are as many intraparty stylistic differences among units of the same party as there are among parties. One only has to make a cursory comparison of either the Liberal or Conservative organizations in Vancouver East and Vancouver Quadra, or of the Conservative or New Democratic party organizations in Winnipeg North Centre and Winnipeg South, to understand the validity of this statement. Add to this the fact that our respondents may have been members of a number of these local organizations—some outside the areas of study—in their party careers, and the enormity of the task of treating all organizations descriptively is dramatized.

Still another reason for not adopting a descriptive approach is our interest in the questions of why people join and stay in parties and why a relatively small number of an already minute fraction of the population either become contenders for public office, or the powers behind these people. These two questions transcend any particular case, for candidates and power brokers are to be found in all party organizations. With respect to the second of these questions, our reading of the works of students of parties together with our own experiences led us to assume that the achievement of what we feel is a local party's principal organizational goal, filling public offices with its candidates, is facilitated by the fact that a group of men and women, frequently of upper-middle class status, primarily professionals and members of the business community, are willing to engage without pay in a variety of mundane, prestige-lacking, but critically important activities. Many of them work expecting that they can either secure public offices for themselves or be in a position to participate in determining who will hold them. We have termed such people Elites and Insiders. Equally important, from the perspectives of organizational maintenance and goal attainment, is an even larger group of people who may have no personal ambitions for public office or no desire to be kingmakers, but who also are willing to engage in these activities for a variety of other social, political, and psychological reasons.[11] We have labeled these people Stalwarts, and have suggested in our introductory chapter that although the distribution of Stalwarts, Insiders, and Elites within a particular party unit may vary because of a party's competitive position or the idiosyncratic preferences of current party leaders, all local party units contain these three types.

Organizational Features and Activity Types

In the following discussion we shall explain and clarify the considerations and assumptions that underlie the criteria used to classify types of party officials. Essentially our choices are grounded in perceptions of key features of parties *qua* political organizations. Parties are seen as usually seeking the highest status individuals available to fill their personnel needs. This preference should also influence the assignment of workers within a party hierarchy. We shall consider more specific expectations of each of the designated types from Stalwart to Insider to Elite in that order.

Although it has been demonstrated in Chapters 2 through 4 that, as a group, party officials are a social and political elite, the Stalwarts probably are less so than their colleagues. By way of illustration, given the prejudices that have existed against women in political organizations and the conventional belief that they simply do not make attractive candidates, one would expect a disproportionate number of the officials who are women to be found in the Stalwart category. Another substantial proportion of Stalwarts is likely to be composed of "just plain folks" who may go along for years working and enjoying their occasional interactions with other members of a party of which they feel a part. Intermittent party work can be fun, even exciting, and they may regard their co-workers as pleasant people whose company they enjoy.

Most Stalwarts probably have no ambitions for public or highest level party offices and most of them are not paid for what they do. Since the Elites and Insiders have no effective sanctions to induce Stalwarts to work in a vigorous and efficient manner, and since Stalwarts presumably have other demands upon their time, party organizational work is likely to be very much an avocation.

In contrast, party politics for the typical Insider are a fairly serious business. Insiders can be expected to hold higher echelon positions, and there are likely to be proportionately fewer women and lower status white- and blue-collar workers among them. Given the already demonstrated positive relationship between socioeconomic status and politicization levels, we may expect Insiders to come from more politicized backgrounds and to be more involved in and committed to their parties than are Stalwarts. Higher levels of commitment to a party, a longer and more continuous involvement in party affairs, the occupancy of higher echelon positions, and the enjoyment of influence in party decision making are probably the political attributes that distinguish Insiders from Stalwarts. Another distinguishing feature may be the Insiders' expectations that they will receive higher party offices and serious consideration as contenders for public office. Even for the Samuel Neilsens among them who cannot expect realistically to become candidates, the status of Insider can be used to secure favored treatment for themselves and others. A Samuel Neilsen can take advantage of the reciprocal deference established with a party colleague who is a MLA to secure summer employment for a favorite nephew or niece or to speed his own claim to reimbursement for a hospital stay through a provincial health insurance bureaucracy.

Many other Insiders, usually younger men who are business executives or professionals, probably do expect to be contenders for a public office. With very little encouragement they can see themselves as city councilmen, MLAs, MPs, lower and appeal court judges, and as well-paid members of prestigious boards and commissions. They may feel that people no more knowledgeable or gifted than themselves are currently occupying these positions. However, they also probably believe that in order to become serious contenders for office they must demonstrate that they are deserving. In a local party organization there is no better way to demonstrate one's worth and responsibility than by working assiduously to help others to attain office.[12] The younger Insider's own opportunity for public office candidacy will come in due time, or so he or she may believe.

In a very real sense, Elites are the Insiders' "Insiders." They possess all of their status attributes and already have attained the political goals that Insiders seek. Many currently are or formerly were public officials, members of school boards, city councils, provincial legislative assemblies, even members of parliament. Those who have not attained federal or provincial elective public office may have "shown the flag" for their parties in previous contests. Losing an election in a constituency in which a party is weak is no sin and such a loss does not necessarily diminish one's personal influence. Although we expect the majority of a party's Elite cohort of officials to have a long history of party office holding, influence in a party also may be ascribed to non-officeholders who have special skills and politically useful contacts. It will be recalled that the subject of another one of our vignettes, Pat Robertson, said she had been approached a number of times to affiliate with the Liberal and Conservative parties. Mrs. Robertson had special skills; she was an expert in advertising and survey research. Another highly prized skill is the ability to raise money. Party organizations are skeletal and relatively somnolent in the period between elections; around election time they must quickly expand their structures and scope of activities. This requires money and effective money raisers. For this reason, "bagmen" normally are people who have a great deal of influence ascribed to them even if they do not hold or have not held formal party positions. Finally, because of a longer history of involvement in party affairs, it is assumed that Elites will have acquired a large stock of valuable information about "who's who" and "what's what."

The suggestion that party officials can be typed as Stalwarts, Insiders, or Elites reflects a conceptualization of parties as political institutions with three significant dimensions. The first is essentially internal and consists of what scholars usually refer to as the extraparliamentary party. These resemble squat truncated pyramids with constituency level associations forming the broad base and provincial and federal level executive committees a very narrow apex. The majority of party members spend their entire careers working in these organizations and, if they hold a party office, it is likely to be at or below the consitituency level of federal or provincial party organizations.

The second dimension of parties is public and is comprised of the small cohort of public officeholders or aspirants for such offices. Although these two dimensions can be distinguished analytically, it is important to emphasize that both participants in extraparliamentary parties and candidates and public officeholders are part of the same political organization. To borrow Schlesinger's metaphor, parties resemble atoms, with public officeholders and candidates as nuclei around which coalesce the individual activities and interaction patterns which collectively consitute the local party organizations.[13]

The third dimension is influence in party affairs. The fact that political parties are amorphous and protean, characterized by long periods of relative quiescence and sporadic bursts of activity on behalf of candidates for federal and

Table 6.1
Highest Current Positions of Respondents by Party

Detailed Categories	NDP	Liberal	Conser-vative	Social Credit	Total
Present Federal and Provincial Public Officeholders and Candidates*	7.1%	3.8%	2.0%	6.1%	4.6%
Local Public Officeholders and Candidates	1.2	.5	0.0	0.0	.5
Federal and Provincial Level Executive*	9.5	12.4	14.3	6.1	11.0
Federal and Provincial Constituency Executive	37.3	39.5	36.7	49.5	39.9
Full-time Professional and Miscellaneous High Level Positions*	3.5	5.2	1.4	1.0	3.2
Poll Captain and Miscellaneous Low Level Positions	30.8	26.7	27.2	20.2	27.1
Paraparty—Federal or Provincial Level*	.6	1.9	4.8	4.0	2.6
Paraparty—Constituency or University Level	1.2	1.9	4.1	4.0	2.6
Not Ascertainable	8.9	8.1	9.5	9.1	8.4
Total	100.1	100.0	100.0	100.0	99.9
Summary Categories					
High	20.7%	23.3%	22.4%	17.2%	21.4%
Low	79.3	76.7	77.6	82.8	78.6
Total	100.0	100.0	100.0	100.0	100.0
(N =)	(169)	(210)	(147)	(99)	(625)

*Considered high level positions.

lower offices, should not be taken to imply that they are without a continuing influence structure. Such students of parties in Western democracies as Michels, Eldersveld, and Barnes, have demonstrated that although parties differ structurally from many other political organizations (e.g., parliaments, administrations), they do have established and ascertainable intra-organizational patterns of influence which vary from one party or one political milieu to the next.[14] In some instances, the occupants of the top positions in extraparliamentary parties monopolize intraparty decision making, whereas in others, all or some of the elected public officeholders dominate. In still others, there is a diffusion of influence throughout the organization and, in some cases, influence is exercised by those who hold neither internal nor public office.[15] However, as Eldersveld has argued, in order to understand parties as organizations we must comprehend the patterns of influence within them.

Categorizing Party Leaders

As the first step in delineating how parties differentiate their leadership groups, party officials will be distinguished in terms of their: a) formal position in the extraparliamentary party organization, b) public office candidacy, and c) degree of informal personal influence within the party as a functioning group. Using these three criteria, it is possible to classify the Vancouver and Winnipeg officials into the three types described above—Stalwarts, Insiders, and Elites. Before discussing the results of this classification, we shall examine the distribution of the respondents on the three dimensions, and the relationships among them.

Table 6.1 presents the distribution of party officials in terms of their reports of the highest position[16] they currently hold in their organizations. Only small minorities in each party indicate that they hold office above the constituency level in the extraparliamentary party. Similarly, less then 5% of all party workers indicate they currently are candidates for or incumbents of the federal parliament or the legislatures of British Columbia and Manitoba. Nearly two-fifths of the officials report holding their highest party office at the federal and/or provincial constituency level, and aproximately one-fourth mention that they hold positions below the riding level, such as poll captain or campaign worker.

Two other features of the distribution of self-attributed party positions are worth noting. First, 5.2% state that their highest current position is in a paraparty organization such as a woman's auxiliary or university or youth club. Some indicate that their positions in these paraparty groups are at the local level, for example, in a particular riding or university, whereas others mention that they hold federal or provincial level office.[17] Second, 8.4% either state explicitly that they do not have a formal position or we could not ascertain what these positions were. This is not unexpected since the lists of workers interviewed were constructed to include all those who were influential members of the real as opposed to the paper party organizations.

Table 6.2

History of Respondents' Elective and Appointive Public Office
Candidacy by Party

Candidacy: Highest Office Sought	NDP	Liberal	Conser-vative	Social Credit	Total
			Frequencies		
None	91	136	84	57	368
Local	26	27	10	6	69
Provincial (MLA)	32	35	36	18	121
Federal (MP)	20	12	17	18	67
Total	169	210	147	99	625
			Percentages		
None	53.8	64.8	57.1	57.6	58.9
Local	15.4	12.9	6.8	6.1	11.0
Provincial (MLA)	18.9	16.7	24.5	18.2	19.4
Federal (MP)	11.8	5.7	11.6	18.2	10.7
Total	99.9	100.1	100.0	100.1	100.0

For purposes of classifying respondents, "high" party positions essentially are those above the constituency level, federal and provincial paraparty executive positions, plus current federal and provincial public officials and candidates.[18] All other positions, "no position" and "position not ascertainable" are in the "low" category. This identifies slightly more than 20% of the officials as occupants of high party positions, with the proportions varying only modestly among parties.

The second dimension used to categorize party leaders is candidacy for federal and provincial elective and appointive offices. To tap this dimension of party organizations, the officials were asked if they had *ever* been candidates for public elective office or on the "short lists" prepared for appointive offices at the federal and provincial levels. The responses contained in Table 6.2 reveal that fully 30% had been contestants for or holders of public office at these levels. Since they were asked about public office candidacies over their entire lives, it is to be expected that the percentage would be considerably larger than the 4.6% who indicate current elective office candidate status. The highest percentages of current or ex-candidates are found in the NDP and Social Credit and the lowest percentage in the Liberal party. The former pattern is congruent with the conventional wisdom that the largest proportion of highly committed officials are found among the "third" parties where

Table 6.3
Influence Nominations Received by Respondents

Nominations Received	NDP	Liberal	Conser-vative	Social Credit	Total
0	52.7%	60.0%	52.4%	61.6%	56.5%
1–4	25.4	21.9	29.3	28.3	25.6
5–9	8.9	7.1	9.5	6.1	8.0
10–14	3.6	5.2	4.1	2.0	4.0
15 or more	9.5	5.7	4.8	2.0	5.9
Mean	4.3	3.6	3.2	1.7	3.4
Standard Deviation	10.0	10.3	8.4	4.8	9.1
(N =)	(169)	(210)	(147)	(98)	(624)
Gini Coefficients of Inequality of Distributions of Influence Nominations	.83	.86	.81	.84	.85

ideological or other impersonal and altruistic motivations more frequently bulk large. The Liberal party's control of the national government may account for the lower Liberal percentage. Some of the defeated Liberal candidates may have been appointed to public offices such as judgeships or received patronage appointments that would have made it awkward or impossible for them to remain active in their organizations.[19] For classifying the respondents, the public office candidacy data are used to divide the officials into two groups, current and past contenders for federal or provincial office, and others.

Regardless of the analytic distinction that can be drawn between extra-parliamentary and parliamentary party organizations, they are part of a single political group possessing an ascertainable structure of influence. The many problems of measuring influence either within particular political organizations or in larger political systems are not easily resolved but we considered the reputational approach appropriate for our purposes.[20] Each respondent was asked to nominate colleagues in the party who were particularly influential in the organization.[21] The number of nominations received by each person is summarized in Table 6.3. The distribution of influence within the four parties is highly skewed. Over half the officials of each party receive no influence nominations at all, and less than 10% are nominated by ten or more of their colleagues, a pattern that is hardly surprising. Unequal influence is a characteristic feature of political parties in Western democracies. Although inquiries concerning American and Italian parties have disputed the universality of Michel's "iron law of oligarchy,"[22] not a single investigation that we are aware of has delineated a pattern of influence which Lasswell and Kaplan designated so felicitously as "coarchal"[23] (perfectly equal). A number of reasons for skewed patterns of influence within political parties can be suggested. Differences in material, informational, and psychological resources among officials, coupled with demands on parties as institutions operating in competitive political settings where an overriding goal is to elect public officeholders, militate against the development or maintenance of even roughly egalitarian influence structures.[24] As Michels observed in his classic study of the German Social Democratic Party, the strength of such forces is so great that even a party with a strong ideological commitment to internal democracy will find it impossible to avoid developing oligarchic influence patterns.

The question is which officials are most likely to be ascribed disproportionate amounts of influence. In parties that are basically electorally-oriented organizations, strong correlations between public office candidacy and intraorganizational influence may be expected. To the extent that extraparliamentary parties provide a variety of structural, informational, and other advantages to those holding high level party positions, influence also should correlate with occupancy of such positions. When the mean number of influence nominations are analyzed according to highest current party positions these expectations are confirmed. Considering all party officials as a single group, candidates or incumbents receive a disproportionately high number of influence nominations ($\overline{X} = 17.9$). Individual party analyses reveal, however, that the tendency for public officeholders and candidates to receive a large number of nominations varies sharply from a high of 31.4 for the Liberals to 18.4 for the NDP to 6.7 and 4.7 for the Conservatives and Socreds, respectively. The large number of influence nominations received by officials holding national or provincial executive office also was anticipated ($\overline{X}$ for all parties $= 11.7$). Although the level of influence ascribed to them is significantly less than that ascribed to the public officeholder-candidate groups, as with the latter, there is considerable interparty variance (Liberal, 15.7; NDP, 10.7; Conservative, 10.4; and Social Credit, 6.0). Except for NDPers not holding formal positions or for whom current party positions are not ascertainible ($\overline{X} = 7.1$), none of the remaining four groups in any party has a mean level of ascribed influence (maximum $\overline{X} = 2.6$) approximating those of the public officeholder-candidate and highest organizational echelon groups.

Since the typology is three-dimensional, we wanted to ascertain the relationships among public office candidacy, party position holding, and ascribed

Table 6.4
Mean Number of Influence Nominations Received by Current Position and Candidacy Status of Respondents

Public Office Candidate		NDP	Liberal	Conser-vative	Social Credit	Total
Yes		10.3	10.6	5.3	2.2	7.5
No		1.6	1.5	2.0	1.5	1.6
Current Position						
High		11.9	11.5	7.4	4.2	9.7
Low		2.3	1.2	2.0	1.3	1.7
Public Office Candidate	Current Position					
Yes	High	16.6	21.8	7.2	5.3	13.8
Yes	Low	6.4	2.7	4.4	0.8	3.8
No	High	5.5	4.4	7.7	1.8	5.2
No	Low	1.0	0.9	0.9	1.5	1.0
Total		4.3	3.6	3.2	1.7	3.4

influence. For this purpose we computed the mean number of influence nominations ascribed to 1) party officials who were *both* candidates and high officeholders; 2) candidates who were not officeholders; 3) officeholders who were not candidates; and 4) those who were neither high officeholders nor candidates. The results, presented in Table 6.4, are interesting for a number of reasons. First, they illustrate the value of using all three dimensions in constructing a typology of party officials. Second, they reveal the effects that the confluence of high position holding and public office candidacy can have on the influence ascribed local party officials. The importance of the latter is most dramatically illustrated in the distributions of influence among Liberals and New Democrats. The average twice-blessed Liberal official is attributed eight times as much influence as a colleague who is or had been a public office candidate but is not currently an occupant of a high party office, and is accorded five times as much influence, on the average, as a colleague who currently holds a high party office but is not a candidate. In the New Democratic party the average official who is both a high party officeholder currently and a present or former candidate has approximately three times as much influence as colleagues who are either only one or the other. Third, the late V.O. Key's admonition[25] regarding the possible disjuncture between formal position and real influence notwithstanding, very few people are ascribed influence if they are without either a public or a party office. Indeed, only a handful (four

Liberals, two New Democrats, and two Social Crediters) of the respondents in the no high office-no candidate category could be described with any accuracy as "informal influentials." As noted previously, their influence likely rested on the highly prized ability to raise funds. Fourth, the data also reflect elements of the rich diversity that exists in party organizations. Although in the Liberal and New Democratic parties officials who held both high party offices and who are current or former candidates have very substantial influence, in the Social Credit party this type of official has considerably less. In the Conservative party such a person actually has slightly less influence, on the average, than a colleague who currently holds only a high party office.

We were intrigued by these differences and reasoned that the Social Credit and Conservative patterns of influence might have been distorted by their very different competitive statuses within the two provinces. When these interviews were taken the Conservative party formed the provincial government of Manitoba and was a force to be reckoned with in federal elections. In contrast, in British Columbia they were weak both federally and provincially. The Social Credit party had formed the provincial government in British Columbia for years, but, apart from a single seat the party held in the provincial legislature, they were extremely weak in Manitoba. We assumed that if the data were disaggregated into city-party units the differences in the Social Credit patterns of influence between candidate-officeholders and every-one else might be considerably sharpened (no one in our Social Credit sample in Winnipeg actually was or had been a public officeholder although some had been unsuccessful candidates). We further assumed that the distribution of influence among Winnipeg Conservatives might approximate that which existed in the New Democratic and Liberal parties, organizations which were politically competitive at the federal or provincial levels in the two provinces.

An examination of the disaggregated data reveals very modest support for these expectations. The average influence ascribed to Social Credit officials who are candidates and high party officeholders and those who only had been candidates does increase, but only marginally (from an average of 5.3 to 5.9 for the first group and from .8 to 1.5 nominations for the second group). In addition, the pattern of influence among Conservative officials in Winnipeg approximates more closely that found in the Liberal and New Democratic parties.[26] As for the Liberal and New Democratic parties, patterns of influence among their officials in both cities are relatively similar. Among Liberals the average number of influence nominations received by Vancouver and Winnipeg officials in each of the four categories is virtually the same. The principal effect of disaggregating the New Democratic party data is the sharpening of the difference in the Winnipeg sample between high party officeholder-candidates

Chart 6.1
Initial Allocation of Attribute Combinations
to Party Leader Types

Number of Influence Nominations	Present Position in Party			
	Low		High	
	Contested for Provincial or Federal Public Office		Contested for Provincial or Federal Public Office	
	No	Yes	No	Yes
Under 10	Stalwart (N=362)	Insider (N=108)	Insider (N=54)	Elite (N=39)
10–14	Insider (N=4)	Insider (N=5)	Insider (N=5)	Elite (N=11)
15 or more	Elite (N=5)	Elite (N=7)	Elite (N=6)	Elite (N=19)

on the one hand and all other officials on the other. The latter pattern, of course, is hardly in keeping with the image of greater democracy in the NDP. Nor is the fact that the Conservative and Liberal organizations have somewhat different influence structures in keeping with their "tweedledum-tweedledee" image.

Despite these departures, what is most impressive about the data is the strength of the observed associations, regardless of party or city, between candidacy and office holding on the one hand and influence ascription on the other. This increases our confidence that the relative positions of Stalwarts, Insiders, and Elites within party organizations can be thought of in terms of the analogue to Prewitt's "Chinese box" model of political recruitment outlined in Chapter 1. The actual application of the principles utilized to create the three types is summarized in Chart 6.1. Officials who possessed none of the attributes associated with intraparty influence (i.e., holding high party office and being a candidate) and who received fewer than ten influence nominations were designated Stalwarts. Conversely, officials who were the recipients of a great deal of peer recognition (i.e., they were nominated as influentials fifteen or more times) were placed in the Elite category regardless of what formal positions they held. Everyone else initially was designated an Insider. Of these, officials who had been selected to contest for federal or provincial public office and were now occupying a high party position were included in the Elite group. The latter assignment reflects our view of the importance of the confluence of candidacy and high party office in local organizations. To validate

Table 6.5
Distributions of Respondents by Type
and Party

	NDP	Liberal	Conservative	Social Credit	Total
Stalwart	58.6%	60.0%	50.3%	55.6%	56.6%
	(99)	(126)	(74)	(55)	(354)
Insider	24.3	27.1	34.0	31.3	28.6
	(41)	(57)	(50)	(31)	(179)
Elite	17.2	12.9	15.6	13.1	14.7
	(29)	(27)	(23)	(13)	(92)
Total	100.1	100.0	99.9	100.0	99.9
(N =)	(169)	(210)	(147)	(99)	(625)

the judgments implicit in this procedure, informed observers of the local parties were asked to evaluate the lists of those designated as Stalwarts, Insiders, and Elites. On the basis of these supplementary data a total of thirteen of the 625 respondents were recategorized.

The adjusted distribution of types of officials by party is presented in Table 6.5. The proportions of party officials decline markedly across the Stalwart, Insider, and Elite categories. This supports the earlier contention that influence and public office candidacies are relatively rare commodites in parties. The fact that no more than 17.9% of the officials in any of the parties can be classified as Elites further suggests there is validity to the "squat and truncated pyramid" metaphor for local parties. This point gains added force when it is recalled that the party officials do not constitute random samples from the entire structures. Had such samples been drawn, undoubtedly the percentage of Elites would have been considerably smaller. The relative similarity of distributions in each party, despite their differing historical origins, ideologies, and competitive statuses in federal and provincial politics, suggests the universality of these aspects of organizational structure and the general validity of categorizing party officials as Elites, Insiders, and Stalwarts.

Summary

This chapter has described how a typology of local party leaders was implemented. Three dimensions of local parties were identified: a) the extra-parliamentary or internal dimension; b) the public dimension (i.e., public office candidates and incumbents); and c) the influence dimension. Categorizing the party officials into three types yielded a distribution consistent with the notion that local party organizations resemble "squat and truncated pyramids." Specifically, 14.7%, 28.6%, and 56.6% of the party officials were designated Elites, Insiders, and Stalwarts respectively. The small differences in the proportions of types in each party are congruent with the assumption that local party organizations, regardless of historical origins, ideological proclivities, or competitive statuses, are primarily public office-seeking organizations. In the next chapter we shall examine the utility of the typology by considering whether there are real and predictable differences of a kind that might be expected in the backgrounds, affiliation experiences, and careers of Stalwarts, Insiders, and Elites.

NOTES

1. Eldersveld, *Political Parties: A Behaviorial Analysis*, p. 1.
2. *Ibid.*, p. 9.
3. *Ibid.*, pp. 5-7.
4. Concerning support patterns for Canadian parties see Clarke, *et al.*, *Political Choice in Canada*, chap. 4; and Meisel, *Working Papers on Canadian Politics*, chap. 1.
5. Schlesinger, "Political Party Organizations," in March, ed., *Handbook of Organizations*, pp. 775-801.
6. See Frederick C. Engelmann, "Membership Participation in Policy-Making in the CCF," *Canadian Journal of Economics and Political Science*, 22 (1956): 161-173. See also, David Hoffman, "Intra-Party Democracy: A Case Study," *Canadian Journal of Economics and Political Science*, 27 (1961): 223-235.
7. See Stephen Clarkson, "Pierre Trudeau and the Liberal Party: The Jockey and the Horse," in Howard R. Penniman, ed., *Canada at the Polls* (Washington, D.C.: American Enterprise Institute for Public Policy Research, 1975), chap. 3; George Perlin, "The Progressive Conservative Party in the Election of 1974," in Penniman, ed., *Canada at the Polls*, chap. 4. See also John Meisel, *The Canadian Election of 1957* (Toronto: University of Toronto Press, 1962), chaps. 8-10; and Richard Gwyn, "Ad-Men and Scientists Run This Election," in Hugh G. Thorburn, ed., *Party Politics in Canada*, 2nd ed. (Scarborough, Ont.: Prentice-Hall, 1967), pp. 121-123.
8. See Jo Surich, "Purists and Pragmatists: Canadian Democratic Socialism at the Crossroads," in Penniman, ed., *Canada at the Polls*, chap. 5.
9. Regarding the Liberal Party's linkages with the academic-intellectual communities see the insightful essay by John Meisel, "Howe, Hubris and '72: An Essay on Political Elitism," in Meisel, *Working Papers on Canadian Politics*, 2nd ed., chap. 5. The ties between the NDP and Canadian intellectuals were developed in the 1930's at the time of the formation of the NDP's predecessor, the CCF. See, for example, Young, *The Anatomy of a Party: The National CCF*, chaps. 2,4.

10. On anti-intellectual tendencies in the Social Credit party see MacPherson, *Democracy in Alberta: Social Credit and the Party System*, pp. 111-112, 119; John A. Irving, *The Social Credit Movement in Alberta* (Toronto: University of Toronto Press, 1959), pp. 339-340; and Stein, *The Dyamics of Right-Wing Protest*, pp. 34-36, 168.

11. On the importance of "social" motives for sustaining party work see Clarke, *et al.*, "Motivational Patterns and Differential Participation," 137-139.

12. A summary of the reports of 165 members of parliament on how they became candidates in a parliamentary election indicates that, "Apparently, there were three ways in which a local party position could be used to obtain a nomination. First, one could be 'personally chosen' (in the words of a number of respondents) by the former MP in the event of the latter's retirement or defeat, if one had been president or chairman of the constituency organization and had worked to elect or re-elect the former MP. Such nominations were rarely contested. A second route to candidacy was to work one's way up in the organization and to establish a wide claim as one deserving of the nomination. Such nominations were also rarely contested. A third springboard to the nomination was to use the position of local party leader to promote one's own candidacy or to have it promoted by one's friends. Such . . . candidacies were the ones most likely to be contested." Kornberg, *Canadian Legislative Behavior*, p. 65. The significance of party work in the processes by which MPs and MLAs were selected also is suggested by the facts that 83.1% of the MPs studied by Kornberg and Mishler and 79% of the MLAs studied by Clarke, *et al.*, had been party workers prior to being nominated to run for federal or provincial legislative office. See Kornberg and Mishler, *Influence in Parliament*, pp. 70-71, Table 2.3; Clarke, *et al.*, "Backbenchers," p. 219.

13. Schlesinger, "Political Party Organization," pp. 774-775.

14. Michels, *Political Parties*, *passim*; Eldersveld, *Political Parties*, chap. 5; and Barnes, *Party Democracy*, chaps. 1, 5, 13, 14.

15. An interesting case of this latter circumstance is provided by John Meisel's examples of senior civil servants playing a major policy-making role for the Liberal party in the post-World War II period. See Meisel, "Howe, Hubris, and '72." in Meisel, ed., *Working Papers*, pp. 231-232; and John Meisel, "The Formulation of Liberal and Conservative Programmes in the 1957 General Election," *Canadian Journal of Economics and Political Science*, 26 (1960): 571. See also J.E. Hodgetts, "The Liberal and the Bureaucrat," *Queen's Quarterly*, 62 (1955): 176-183.

16. Some respondents indicated that they currently held more than one position in their respective organizations.

17. In their consitutions Canadian parties traditionally have allocated a certain proportion of federal and provincial executive positions to those occupying corresponding positions in paraparty organizational hierarchies. See McMenemy, *et al.*, *Political Parties in Canada*, chap. 10.

18. The reason that current federal and provincial officials and candidates for these offices are classified as high party officeholders is that in their minds candidacy and incumbency in a legislature were party positions. In response to the question on what their current party positions were, they replied "MLA" or "candidate for MLA" or "candidate for parliament." When they were probed they insisted these *were* their party positions. The fact that they considered candidacy or incumbency in a public elective office as a party position provides an interesting insight into the nature of party and legislative politics in a parliamentary system of the British model.

19. There are other possible explanations of the interparty differences in the numerical and percentage distributions of candidacies. 1) A candidate might be able to move up in terms of level of office sought in some but not in other parties. This

would influence the distribution of frequencies differentially. 2) Candidates affiliated with each party may not contest each office. This appears to be the case for Conservative and Social Credit officials in Winnipeg and Vancouver. 3) Conservative and Socred candidates may have started at lower levels and moved up. 4) Others who were successful at these levels may have moved out. Although we were unable to select among these alternatives, the frequencies do suggest that the number of candidates in each of the parties largely is a function of the number of elections contested and the appointive opportunities available to them.

20. On the merits and deficiencies of using reputational techniques for delineating holders of political power or influence see, for example, Robert A. Dahl, "A Critique of the Ruling Elite Model," *American Political Science Review*, 52 (1950): 463-469; Nelson W. Polsby, "The Sociology of Community Power: A Reassessment," *Social Forces*, 37 (1959): 232-236; Raymond E. Wolfinger, "Reputation and Reality in the Study of 'Community Power,'" *American Sociological Review*, 25 (1960): 636-644; William V. D'Antonio and Eugene C. Erickson, "The Reputational Technique as a Measure of Community Power: An Evaluation Based on Comparative and Longitudinal Studies"; Raymond E. Wolfinger, "A Plea for a Decent Burial"; William V. D'Antonio, Howard S. Ehrlich, and Eugene C. Erickson, "Further Notes on the Study of Community Power," all in *American Sociological Review*, 27 (1962): 362-376, 838-854; and Thomas J. Anton, "Power, Pluralism and Local Politics," *Administrative Science Quarterly*, 7 (1961): 425-457.

21. The following question was used:

"Who would you say are the most important people in the ————— party organization in ————— constituency? We mean important in terms of what things happen and how things happen and not necessarity just in terms of the titles people may have. (If one or more names mentioned) Anyone else?"

22. Eldersveld, *Political Parties*, chap. 5; Barnes, *Party Democracy*, chap. 13.

23. Harold Lasswell and Abraham Kaplan, *Power and Society* (New Haven: Yale University Press, 1950), pp. 204-205.

24. See Barnes, *Party Democracy*, chaps. 13, 14.

25. V.O. Key, Jr., *Politics, Parties and Pressure Groups*, 4th ed. (New York: Crowell, 1964), p. 369.

26. Winnipeg Conservatives who were both candidates and high party officeholders received an average of 7.6 influence nominations. Those who were only high officeholders received 4.0 nominations, whereas those who only were candidates received 2.2 nominations.

Chapter Seven

Elites, Insiders, and Stalwarts

Even when academic degrees, scientific training, special aptitudes as tested by examinations and competitions open the way to public office, there is no eliminating that special advantage in favor of certain individuals which the French call the advantage of *positions dèja prises*.

Gaetano Mosca, *The Ruling Class,* p. 50.

A CCOUNTING for the differential status and prestige of people in the small organized groups that comprise a large institutional system is no easy task. For one thing, the individuals in such units usually are relatively alike, marked by similarities in background, current status, values and attitudes, and even life style. But despite these similarities, they also differ in a variety of subtle and not so subtle ways that can have significant effects on both their placement within the strata of an organization and the success and prestige those within a particular stratum enjoy.

Faculty members of universities in countries like Canada and the United States provide a good example of the difficulties entailed. They are very homogeneous with respect to attributes such as sex, race, social origins, and current status. The great majority has earned doctorates in one of the several disciplines. An individual faculty member normally enters a university as an instructor or assistant professor and proceeds through associate to full professor status. In any university, irrespective of discipline, full professors generally have longer tenures and are better paid than their lower ranking colleagues. But faculty members also differ in various ways. Some receive their early educations in public schools whereas others attend exclusive preparatory schools, and this difference may have affected their opportunities as undergraduates. In Canada, graduates of exclusive preparatory schools, such as Upper Canada College, rarely experience any difficulty being accepted at prestigious universities. Attendance at a prestigious undergraduate institution facilitates acceptance at an equally prestigious graduate school. These factors as well as performance considerations such as how quickly they finish their graduate studies and how many and what kinds of awards and distinctions they achieve while doing so are important because they affect not only initial faculty appointments but also the development of professional careers. They influence such matters as what colleagues expect of new appointees, and what facilities, opportunities, rewards, and other perquisites are offered with the appointment. These perquisites, in turn, further affect young scholars' chances of being judged successful by peers and superiors. Although it may be difficult for initially advantaged academicians who fail to meet the high expectations held for them to disabuse their colleagues of their favorable preconceptions, it may be an even harder task to change unfavorable initial assessments by repeated demonstrations of competence. Nonetheless, reassessments eventually must be made, at least some of the time, if a university is to survive. Accordingly, if we were trying to account for differences in the status attainments of faculty members, we would have to examine their backgrounds because early advantages can cumulate and influence conditions of initial employment and subsequent success within a university system. We also would want to examine the conditions of their initial appointments and their performances since then, because these affect prestige levels attained within both a university and a discipline.

The difficulties involved in accounting for which officials are Elites, Insiders, and Stalwarts in political parties are far greater because parties' procedures are less rational and predictable than those of universities. By way of illustration, although ordinarily the initial appointment of a fledgling Ph.D. is to an instructorship or an assistant professorship, individuals can and do enter parties at the middle, and, at times, the top, as well as the bottom of their hierarches.[1] Nonetheless, in trying to account for which party officials are in which group, we shall start with the same approach we would use if we were trying to explain differences in the status and prestige of members of a homogeneous group such as a university faculty.

Membership in Elite, Insider, and Stalwart categories is expected to be a function of both "what you do" and "who you are." Regarding the former, local parties, striving to maximize popular support, require the services of individuals who are willing and able to expend considerable time and energy in the pursuit of electoral victory. *Ceteris paribus*, the most important positions within these organizations probably will go to persons who make recognizably great efforts on their behalf. In some instances, particularly when a party is in a state of disarray and chances of electoral success appear slim, someone who is devoting long hours to party service simply may assume a position of influence or become a party's token candidate by virtue of being the only one willing to do so.

The *ceteris paribus* assumption is seldom met/however, ~~because~~ social structural characteristics and political socialization experiences also influence the
development of party careers in several ways. As argued throughout this book,
possession of certain social, economic and psychological resources facilitates
political participation. Those who possess such resources are ~~likelier~~ *more likely* than
others to initiate and to continue party work./In addition, these resources
enhance the effective conduct of various tasks on behalf of party organizations.
This, in turn, increases the probability of achieving elite status within instrumental organizations, however inefficient they may be. Moreover, it is prob-
able that certain social and economic characteristics give those who have them
an aura of effectiveness as party functionaries and attractiveness as potential
public officials. Regardless of their validity, these "halo" assessments of prior
or anticipated performance enhance opportunities to attain elite status.

In order to assess the relevance of these various factors for understanding
which party officials become Elites, Insiders, and Stalwarts, we first shall compare the statuses of the three types when they joined their parties, contrasting
their modes of entry, the reasons they gave for joining, and their initial reactions
to party work. Then we shall examine their social origins and political socialization experiences, factors that may have influenced the conditions under which
they entered a party. The latter, in turn, may have affected their subsequent
performance and the recognition they have received from party colleagues. We
next shall compare the experiences of the three groups of leaders in the period
between the time they joined and the time they were interviewed. Our concern
will be with such aspects of their careers as the number of party positions they
have held, what proportion of these positions were in the upper echelons of their
respective hierarchies, and what proportions of their time they have been willing
to commit to party work over the years. These factors should shed light on the
distribution of officials among the types. Various aspects of the respondents'
behavior, attitudes, and expectations also will be examined to determine whether
the hierarchy reflected in the types has meaningful consequences. In pursuing
these matters the discussion often will proceed without regard to party, but
when there are notable interparty differences we shall comment on them.

Beginning Party Work

Social Status at Joining. An examination of a variety of social and economic
status characteristics of the officials at the time they joined their respective
parties reveals a consistent upward progression as one moves across the
hierarchy from Stalwart to Insider to Elite (see the upper section of Table 7.1).
The most striking difference among the three types is the possession of a law
degree. Despite the fact that only a minority (15%) of party officials held a law

Table 7.1

Measures of Social and Economic Status and Variations in Modes
of Entry into Party Organizations by Stalwarts,
Insiders, and Elites

	Stalwarts	Insiders	Elites
Status When Joining			
% Living in same community as at age 6	9.9	11.7	18.5
% Who attended university in city of birth	29.9	41.9	53.3
% Who were married	66.7	57.5	48.9
$\overline{X}$ Number of children among married respondents	1.3	.77	.55
% Heads of respondents' households not in labor force	20.3	26.8	38.0
$\overline{X}$ SES of head of household's occupation	53.2	55.1	60.7
% Holding a law degree	9.6	17.3	31.5
% With baccalaureate or better	23.0	32.4	48.9
Variations in Modes of Entry			
$\overline{X}$ Age of first joining	31.8	29.7	27.4
$\overline{X}$ Years between first psychological identification with a party and first joining	17.4	13.4	12.7
$\overline{X}$ Years between first contemplating and actually joining	2.1	1.7	1.6
% Whose first party contact held high party office	40.4	41.9	47.8
% Who knew first party contact personally	55.1	55.9	56.6
% Whose first party work included glamorous tasks	20.6	26.8	28.3
% Whose first party position was high level	13.8	24.6	28.3
% Who joined to perform specific tasks	33.1	37.4	44.6
% Approached to join and do general work	18.1	11.7	8.7
% Approached to join and work at specific tasks	24.6	25.7	34.8
% Reporting joining was personal positive act	38.7	37.4	30.4

degree at the time of joining, the proportion increases sharply with the progression from Stalwart to Elite and can be observed in all parties except the Social Credit, where the only two law degree holders are a Stalwart and an Insider. More generally, levels of education attained at the time of entry increase sharply from Stalwarts to Insiders to Elites.

Perhaps reflecting this increased level of education, higher party leadership status invariably is related to the likelihood that respondents had not established their own families at the time of first affiliation. Elites are less likely to have been married and, if married, less likely to have been the parents of young children. Not having family responsibilities is consistent with the increased probability that respondents were single individuals still securing an education and, in fact, the proportion not in the labor force at the time of initial affiliation with a party increases steadily from Stalwart to Elite. Despite this, among those who were working, Elites also have the highest proportion from professionally-headed households. For all the other occupational categories of head of household at the time, the progression is reversed. Moreover, the lower the occupational status, the greater the extent of Stalwart dominance.[2]

Modes of Entry. If launching one's party career under auspicious circumstances increases the likelihood that one will occupy Elite status, then Stalwarts would be expected to report the least and Elites the most favorable circumstances of entry. With respect to the timing of entry, if early affiliation affords a head start in the competition for accomplishment and recognition, then the data indicate that the Elites have had the greatest advantage and the Stalwarts the least (see lower section of Table 7.1). Elites, on the average, join at an age almost two-and-a-half years younger than do Insiders and four-and-a-half years younger than do Stalwarts. Moreover, the average number of years between first psychological identification with a party and joining declines, and the average number of years of identification with the present party increases, from Stalwart to Insider to Elite. One result of the more sustained identification with a party that characterizes Elites is an apparent eagerness to join. The time between seriously contemplating and actually establishing membership increases steadily across the progression form Elite to Stalwart.

Analyses presented in Chapter 4 suggested that officials who, when interviewed, were more important in their organizations, affiliated with the express purpose of performing specific tasks for their new parties. It is not surprising, therefore, that the proportion of leaders reporting that they joined to do specific tasks increases sharply from Stalwart to Insider to Elite, and the proportion approached to do general work decreases. Surprisingly, the proportions interpreting their affiliation as a conscious and positive rather than incidental act on their part decreases with the Stalwart-Insider-Elite hierarchy.

Perhaps, potential Elites were sought after and inducted into party positions quickly, whereas many Stalwarts may have come unbid and, therefore, had to present themselves to party leaders. The validity of this speculation is suggested by the larger proportion of Elites who had their first party contacts with people in high ranking party offices—people whom Elites were slightly more likely to have known personally. Elites also were more likely initially to have held high level organizational positions and to have performed interesting and glamorous tasks. In short, the data on joining a party suggest that Elites more often than the other two leader types joined their respective parties under propitious circumstances (see Table 7.1, lower section).

Reasons for Joining. As explained in Chapter 4, respondents were asked which of the various reasons people give for joining political parties applied to them and which was the most important. By a substantial margin they most frequently select improve government reasons as being both relevant and most important. Smaller proportions of officials report political or personal reasons, and relatively few cite pressures from a variety of others as the most important reason they joined their parties. When the sample is disaggregated by types, although similar proportions report that political reasons generally were most important in getting them to join, more Elites (7.6%) than Insiders (2.8%) or Stalwarts (2.5%) cite personal political career reasons as most important. Elites more often report a desire to improve government as most important in moving them into a party whereas pressure from others is less often cited by them than by the others.[3] Personal considerations are cited by relatively similar proportions of all three groups. The only substantial interparty differences are: 1) the greater tendency of NDP Elites to cite political reasons as most important (by a margin of about two to one compared to the Elites of other parties); 2) the greater frequency with which Elites of the major as opposed to minor parties refer to the importance of personal reasons; and 3) the much greater frequency with which Social Credit party officials, regardless of type, report a desire to improve government as the most important reason they joined.

It was demonstrated earlier that the several aspects of joining could be reduced to age, self-motivation, expertise, and co-option. The scores on the latter three components do not vary substantially or in a fixed order with the hierarchy of types, but this is not surprising in view of both their tendency to cluster at zero and the nature of the composite score. Nonetheless, relatively, the highest score for Stalwarts is on co-option, for Insiders, self-motivation, and for Elites, expertise.[4] For each of the three types of leaders, regression and path analyses were performed to test the model used in Chapter 5, but the results are inconclusive. When the data are disaggregated by party, the

Table 7.2

Initial Reactions to Party Work by Stalwarts, Insiders, and Elites

	Stalwarts	Insiders	Elites
% Reporting more time and work required than expected	52.0	54.0	44.6
% Reporting feeling other party workers largely effective	68.1	60.3	57.6
% Reporting feeling party organizations frustrating and ineffective	43.2	44.1	51.1
% Reporting an initial sense of personal accomplishment	89.8	92.7	93.5

number of Elites in each is so small that any relationships between variables must be quite large to be statistically significant. Consequently, each of the four Elite models is skeletal whereas those for the Stalwart groups are extremely complex and difficult to interpret because the groups are so large that relatively small coefficients are statistically significant. However, both the regresssions and the actual flows of influence from stage to stage in the path models do conform to the patterns noted in Chapter 5.

One has the impression that when they began working in a party, the Elites were a more realistic group of people than were their colleagues. They are least likely to report that more time and effort were required by party work than they had anticipated (see Table 7.2). They also are more likely to have perceived the relative ineffectiveness of their co-workers and any hampering effects of the organizational structure itself. Their greater ability to view their co-workers and organizations with a somewhat jaundiced eye and to carry out their tasks despite any constraints they may have imposed may help explain why the Elites report having derived a greater sense of accomplishment from their first efforts. That very large percentages of all three types report an initial sense of accomplishment probably reflects the fact that the party officials are "survivors." That is, regardless of leader type, all have remained in their party organizations.

Background Differences. The ability of individuals to enter an organization under favorable circumstances may be explained not only by the status and skills they have at the time but also by earlier social backgrounds and experience. Taking university faculty members as an example, we argued that the effects of earlier favorable conditions tended to cumulate over time. Assuming this is also the case with party officers, we should find that the Elites derive from the highest socioeconomic status backgrounds and were reared in the most politicized environments. The opposite should be true of the Stalwarts, and the Insiders should be in intermediate positions. However, since a person's social status tends to remain fairly stable and affords a more obvious and immediate resource to a party, status measures should differentiate the three types more consistently and sharply than political socialization measures. A perusal of the several social background and political socialization variables indicates, however, that *both* clearly distinguish the three types of officials.

Three aspects of social background—nativity, class, and occupational status—were examined (see upper section of Table 7.3). We anticipated that native-born Canadians would have a status advantage over the foreign-born, and that those who not only are native but whose parents also are, might have had an even greater advantage. It was also expected that Elites would be more likely to have been born and reared in the community in which they joined a party since this would have given them the double advantage of knowing and being known by important others. The data on nativity generally confirm these expectations. Although they do not reflect a simple linear progression, the Elites are most "Canadian." The results are similar with respect to community of birth. Stalwarts are more likely than Insiders or Elites to have been born somewhere other than in the community in which they first affiliated.

Patterns with respect to the family of origin's position in terms of local community standards of the time are more clear-cut and are present in each party cadre. Level of class background increases from Stalwart to Insider to Elite. This pattern occurs even in the NDP, despite the public image of the party as that of the blue-collar worker. The status of the family, as indicated by the Duncan score for occupation of head of household, differs from the social class index in being based on national rather than local standards. Nonetheless, the measures of head of household's occupation and socioeconomic status repeat the patterns observed for class. Average scores progress upward from Stalwart to Elite. Professional-headed households are increasingly the rule, with the relatively small proportion of blue-collar headed households among Elites being especially striking.

Regarding political backgrounds, Elites report having become aware of politics at an earlier age than do Insiders and Stalwarts (see lower section of Table 7.3). In addition, they perceive the experience as having been more overtly and unequivocally political. Elites more often had parents who supported political parties other than the ones with which they are affiliated. This is due to the tendency of the parents of Social Credit and New Democratic officials to have been supporters of other parties when the Elites were children —a pattern consistent with the fact that the two parties did not come into existence until the mid-'30's.

Table 7.3
Socioeconomic and Political Background Characteristics
of Stalwarts, Insiders, and Elites

Social Background	Stalwarts	Insiders	Elites
% With both parents born in Canada	23.7	23.5	35.9
% Not born in community in which they first joined a party	63.6	49.7	48.9
% Judging their economic well being above average relative to standards of the time	32.5	34.6	40.2
X̄ SES scores of fathers	41.3	44.6	51.6
% Whose fathers were professionals	12.1	16.2	17.4
% Whose fathers were skilled laborers	20.3	18.4	10.9
Political Background			
X̄ Age of political awareness	11.4	11.2	10.4
% Reporting first political experience was overtly political	38.4	37.4	41.3
% With both parents active in political work	12.7	10.6	16.4
% Whose parents supported a different party than respondent's current one	27.7	29.1	33.7
% With relatives and close friends who held public offices	27.1	28.5	38.0
% With close associates, friends, and relatives who were electoral candidates and party workers	38.7	39.2	45.7
X̄ Factor scores of politicized childhood environments	.10	.07	.24
% With university age friends who were interested in politics	20.6	32.4	43.5
% With post-university age friends interested in politics	9.9	19.6	28.3
% Who did paraparty work prior to joining a party	37.9	40.7	44.6
X̄ Number of political club memberships prior to joining	.10	.17	.24
% Who followed politics closely from first political awareness to joining	33.3	40.8	42.4
% Who between first awareness and joining were politically better informed than average	55.9	67.0	71.7
% Whose interest in politics developed steadily	72.6	74.9	80.4

Aside from partisanship, political action clearly was a model more available in the home environments of those who now are Elites than in the homes of Insiders and Stalwarts. With the exception of the Liberals, Elite officials more frequently report that both their parents were active in party work. In addition, relatives and close friends of their families are more likely to have been public officeholders, candidates for office, or party officials. Counting all the various sorts of political role models, including both political activists and those who were simply very interested in politics, Elites report having known a larger average number of such persons when of grade school age than do Stalwarts or Insiders. This pattern holds for all the parties but Social Credit. Elites had followed politics more closely; they felt they possessed superior information; and they more often had been involved in nonparty and paraparty political activities than either Insiders or Stalwarts. The expected pattern also is reflected in reports of how interest in politics and public affairs developed. Considering the age periods from early childhood to affiliation, Elites more than Insiders more than Stalwarts report their interest as either increasing or being sustained in intensity. The sequence is reversed for those with more volatile patterns marked by declines or interruptions in interest.

In summary, the political socialization experiences of the three types of officials indicate that the Elite leaders were more predisposed to party work than the Insiders and that both were more predisposed than the Stalwarts. Although the progressions are somewhat less orderly than those observed for the various socioeconomic status measures, on balance, the data clearly reveal significant socialization differences among the three types.

Varying Career Patterns

The fact, then, is that Elites, more frequently than Insiders or Stalwarts, began their careers in party organizations by occupying high party positions and performing interesting tasks such as writing speeches and collecting campaign funds. It was anticipated that their careers also would differ; Elites should have enjoyed the most successful and Stalwarts the least successful careers. Insiders could be expected to have enjoyed considerably more success than Stalwarts but not quite as much as Elites. Although easily stated, these expectations are not easily tested because it is difficult to assess the success of careers within local political party organizations. It would not be difficult, for example, to measure the success of careers of members of university faculties. There are a plethora of measures that could be employed for this purpose: time within rank; magnitude of salary relative to rank; number of students enrolled in classes; number of doctoral dissertations directed relative to rank and teaching experience; number and location of professional publications; frequency with which published research is cited; number and magnitudes of research grants and contracts awarded; number of offices held in professional associations; and so forth. These several indicators of success within a university are a function and a reflection of both the effectiveness of individual effort and of the judgments made of this effort by peers and superiors. Assuming that placements and prestige within party units are analogous to and affected by similar considerations, we attempted to generate several measures of career success that would reflect both individual effort and the judgment of peers and superiors within parties.[5]

Because there really are no equivalent or equitable output measures for the unpaid officials of parties operating in environments in which both their competitive statuses and periods of intense activity vary considerably, and because parties are rational entities that can not indefinitely tolerate extensive activity from an ineffective participant, one very revealing indicator of the quality of individual effort, it was assumed, might be the amount of time respondents commit to their party work. A related indicator might be the proportion of their leisure time they would be willing to give to this endeavor. Yet another indicator might be the number of years of service within a party. Peer judgments of competency and effectiveness might be reflected in the number of organizational positions respondents had held and the proportions of these positions that were at higher levels of a party's hierarchy.

Unfortunately, attempts to utilize even such seemingly simple indicators can be complicated by a variety of factors. Number of years of party service may be a good indicator of the quality of individual effort, but it is affected by respondents' ages. Similarly, the number of high level organization positions held may reflect peer judgments of competency very well, but these judgments also are affected by seniority claims and by specific organizational needs. For example, at times a party may need to fill a low level position with an especially effective person. Further, even measures of work on behalf of a party are affected by the fact that organizational roles carry with them particular expectations; candidates for public office may expect and be expected by others to work harder than other colleagues. Given these considerations, it was decided that pertinent aspects of the careers of the three leader types would be measured in terms of four individual effort items: number of years of party service relative to the average of their age cohort; number of hours worked each week in the periods between electoral campaigns; number of weeks in which party work took up virtually all of an official's free time, normally the period around election time; and the proportion of one's leisure time allocated to party work. More direct judgments of the effectiveness of individual efforts on behalf of a party would be measured by: a) the number of party positions held controlling for years of party service; and b) the number

Table 7.4

Average Number of Organizational Positions and Higher Level
Positions Held by Stalwarts, Insiders, and Elites

Mean Number of Party and/or Paraparty Positions Held		Stalwarts	Insiders	Elites
Total		4.5	5.9	6.3
Party:	NDP	4.4	6.6	5.4
	Liberal	4.5	6.2	6.7
	Conservative	4.8	6.2	8.3
	Social Credit	4.0	4.3	3.9
Years in Party:	0–5	3.2	3.6	3.2
	6–10	5.1	5.5	5.1
	11–15	5.6	7.0	8.1
	16 or more	5.8	7.7	8.4
Mean Number of High Party Positions				
Total		0.3	1.8	2.7
Party:	NDP	0.4	2.1	2.9
	Liberal	0.4	2.2	2.7
	Conservative	0.3	1.6	3.3
	Social Credit	0.1	1.1	1.4
Years in Party:	0–5	0.1	1.1	1.9
	6–10	0.4	1.6	2.6
	11–15	0.4	2.2	2.6
	16 or more	0.6	2.3	3.5

of high level organizational positions held controlling for years of party
service.

Table 7.4 presents data on the distributions of Stalwarts, Insiders, and
Elites on the latter two measures. For all officials, as well as for those of the
two major parties, Elites tend to have held more party positions than have
Insiders who, in turn, have held more positions than Stalwarts. In the two
minor parties the average Insider has held the most positions. Controlling for
years of party service reveals that the anticipated relationship between the
level of position held and leader type is affected by seniority, but that this
relationship does not operate during the first decade of the respondents' party

Table 7.5
Differential Participation in Party Work by Stalwarts,
Insiders, and Elites

Mean Number of Years of Party Work		Stalwarts	Insiders	Elites
Total		9.2	12.5	13.4
Party:	NDP	9.6	14.1	15.2
	Liberal	8.1	12.0	11.6
	Conservative	11.3	12.8	15.7
	Social Credit	8.5	10.5	9.4
Age Cohort:	Under 35	4.5	5.6	6.7
	35–44	7.4	10.1	10.7
	45–54	9.5	11.3	14.3
	55 and over	16.3	21.5	22.8
Percentage of Respondents with Number of Years of Party Work Above Cohort Median				
Total		33.0	49.7	58.7
Party:	NDP	34.3	51.2	62.1
	Liberal	29.4	54.4	51.9
	Conservative	40.3	54.0	73.9
	Social Credit	29.1	32.3	38.5
Mean Number of Hours Devoted to Party Work during Non-Campaign Periods				
Total		4.2	5.4	10.1
Party:	NDP	6.2	4.2	12.9
	Liberal	2.9	5.1	13.2
	Conservative	3.4	7.1	5.6
	Social Credit	5.0	4.8	6.1

service. However, the anticipated relationship between leader type and the holding of a high level organizational position occurs in every party and in every length of party service category.[6]

Regarding efforts on behalf of party organizations, on the average, Elites have served their parties longer than have Insiders who, in turn, have been party members longer than have Stalwarts (see Table 7.5). This pattern is not apparent in the Liberal and the Social Credit parties where Insiders have slightly longer party careers than their Elite colleagues. The latter deviations, however, seem only to reflect differences in the age structure of party cadres, for within age cohorts mean years of service consistently are related to

(Table 7.5 continued)

Mean Number of Weeks Where Party Work Required All of Respondent's "Free Time"

Total		8.5	8.1	17.5
Party:	NDP	12.3	13.4	29.0
	Liberal	8.3	8.8	10.5
	Conservative	5.5	5.1	9.2
	Social Credit	5.9	4.7	19.5

% of Party Officials Devoting at Least 1/4 of Their Leisure Time to Party Work

Total		41.4	49.8	67.8
Party:	NDP	56.7	69.6	88.9
	Liberal	23.8	38.5	68.4
	Conservative	39.5	50.0	50.0
	Social Credit	51.2	44.0	50.0

Mean Factor Score for Participation in Party Work

Total		−.311	−.243	.348
Party:	NDP	.044	−.169	.899
	Liberal	−.489	−.297	.309
	Conservative	−.463	−.170	−.234
	Social Credit	−.216	−.315	.094

leadership type. Futher light is shed on the possible influence of age on the relationship between leader type and length of party career by the fact that in every party but the Liberal the proportion of officials with careers greater than the median length for their age cohort increases from Stalwart to Insider to Elite.

In addition to having worked for a party for several years, the average official, regardless of type, devotes substantial amounts of time to party work. For the entire sample, the average number of hours worked each week during the period between elections is 5.4, and the mean number of weeks in which virtually all of the respondent's free time was required is 9.7. Further, 17.8% of the officials state that they gave over one-half of their leisure time to party activities and an additional 29.6% report having given one quarter of their leisure time to party work.[7]

Elites are considerably more active in party affairs than are either the Insiders or the Stalwarts, spending an average of 10.1 hours per week on

Table 7.6

Differential Participation in Party Work by Dimensions
of Party Leader Typology

	Party Position		Public Office Candidacy		Influence Nominations	
	High	Low	Yes	No	10+	0–9
Mean Number of Hours Devoted to Party Work during Non-Campaign Periods	9.5	6.2	6.7	4.9	12.2	4.7
Mean Number of Weeks Where Party Work Required All of Respondent's Free Time	13.7	8.6	11.9	8.7	19.7	8.6
% of Party Officials Devoting at Least 1/4 of Their Leisure Time to Party Work	62.5	42.8	54.8	44.2	75.0	44.8
Mean Score on Summary Index of Differential Participation	.137	−.286	−.048	−.261	.496	−.270

party work as compared to 5.4 hours for the Insiders and 4.2 hours for the
Stalwarts. Elites work more hours per week in every party but the Conservative; in the latter party the highest average is reported by the Insiders.
Elites also report more weeks in which party work required virtually all of
their leisure time: 17.5 as opposed to 8.1 for Insiders and Stalwarts respectively. The tendency for Elites to devote more time to party work also is
reflected in the relative allocation of their leisure time. In all but the Social
Credit, Elites devote as high or higher a proportion of their leisure to party
work as do other officials. For the entire sample, as well as for the Liberals
and New Democrats, there is a steady increase from Stalwarts to Insiders to
Elites in reports of proportions of leisure time given to party work. Finally,
the tendency for the three types of party officials to allocate different amounts
of time is reflected in a summary measure of such commitment.[8] Using this
summary measure, Elites, other than in the Conservative party, have the
highest party work commitment scores. The Stalwarts have the lowest mean
scores when all officials are considered as a group. In the NDP, Insiders have
slightly lower scores than Stalwarts.

Conceivably, intraparty work levels might have been affected by role expectations; individuals who were or who hoped to be public officials also might have expected and have been expected by others to commit more time to party work than nonaspirants for public office. To assess this possibility we cross-tabulated the several measures of commitment to party with the components making up the types: candidacy, level of party position, and ascribed influence. The results indicate that current higher level party office holding, public office candidacy, and ascribed influence all are related to the measures of intraparty activity. Differential participation is most strongly related to ascribed influence. It is less strongly associated with currently being a high party officeholder[9] and least strongly correlated with being a current or former candidate for a public office or being a public officeholder.[10] In each instance, however, there is a very definite relationship, and one that generally persists, regardless of party. Overall, the data are in accord with the expectation that Elites have had more effective and presumably successful careers than have Insiders who, in turn, have enjoyed more success than Stalwarts. They also indicate that career success, even in organizations as amorphous as political parties, is a joint function of individual effort and the evaluations of that effort by colleagues. Since, with only a few exceptions, the patterns observed persist when the data are disaggregated by party, there is additional support for the view that the categorization of party officials into Elites, Insiders, and Stalwarts is applicable beyond the parties studied.

Current Statuses and Perspectives

There are other ways of illustrating the manner in which the use of the Stalwart-Insider-Elite typology enhances understanding of the structure and function of local party organizations. One way is to demonstrate that the officials who have enjoyed the most successful careers within their parties (i.e., Elites and Insiders) also are most successful in the outside world.[11] Another way of illustrating the utility of the typology is to show that it has consequences for the ways in which the three types of officials view themselves and others.

With reference to their current socioeconomic status, Elites are considerably more likely than Insiders or Stalwarts to be members of the business and professional communities (Table 7.7). The mean occupational prestige scores of Elites, Insiders, and Stalwarts are 70.5, 66.9, and 59.9 respectively. Indeed, work itself is directly related to status in a party. Status differences among types also are reflected in levels of formal education and income. The absence of substantial age differences among the three types of party officials indicate that these differences are real and not simply artifacts of age variations. Elites are twice as likely to be university graduates as are

Table 7.7

Current Social and Demographic Characteristics of Stalwarts,
Insiders and Elites

	Stalwarts	Insiders	Elites
Occupation			
% Who Are Professionals	28.0	37.4	46.7
% Who Are Businessmen, Proprietors or Executives	23.7	26.8	31.5
% Not in Labor Force	20.7	12.9	6.6
Mean Socioeconomic Index Score for Head of Household's Occupation	59.9	66.9	70.5
Education			
% With at Least a Baccalaureate Degree	27.4	40.2	55.4
% With High School Diploma or Less	64.7	54.2	34.8
Mean Number of Years of School Completed	12.5	13.9	15.4
Income			
Mean Annual Family Income	$21,375	$25,330	$31,905
Age			
Mean Age	44.9	46.5	45.4
Sex			
% Female	23.2	16.2	6.5
Voluntary Associational Memberships			
Mean Number of Memberships	1.9	2.5	3.0

Stalwarts; and Insiders are approximately one and one-half times as likely as Stalwarts to hold at least a baccalaureate degree. Annual income differences among types are equally, if not more, impressive, ranging from an average of $21,375 for Stalwarts to $25,330 for Insiders to $31,905 for Elites. The sharpest income differences between Insiders and Stalwarts occur among Conservatives ($29,936 vs. $20,689) and the smallest ($17,675 vs. $16,508) among New Democrats. Additional interparty comparisons indicate that the sharpest income differences between Elites and Insiders exist in the Liberal and Social Credit parties, $8,718 in the former and $8,532 in the latter. Again, the narrowest differences in income between these types occur among New Democrats, $5,362 on the average. Regardless of the ideologies their parties profess, there is a perfectly orderly progression of income levels among leader types in each organization.

One other aspect of the data in Table 7.7 suggests there may be class as well as socioeconomic status differences among the three types. The average number of nonpolitical, voluntary association memberships increases from Stalwart to Insider to Elite. Since Elites most often have the kinds of occupations that require more than the proverbial forty hour week, and since they also report devoting more time and a higher proportion of their leisure to party work, the evidence of higher participation in nonpolitical spheres suggests a difference in the perceptions of the three types regarding their own capacities and obligations. Such differences in perspective reflect what social scientists have described as a fundamental aspect of class in Western societies. [12]

Regarding possible differences in the way the three types view their party organizations and their own careers, it seemed reasonable to expect, given generally longer periods of service and hard work on behalf of their respective parties, that Elites would have the most favorable views of their organizations. Moreover, greater success as a party functionary should be associated with both feelings of enhanced gratification and optimism about future political career opportunities. Additionally, one would anticipate that the reasons Elites and Insiders give for maintaining a party career as opposed to their reasons for joining might differ from those offered by Stalwarts. Assuming that whatever political ambitions Stalwarts might have had initially have been dampened over time by a lack of significant achievement, they should refer to political considerations less often and more frequently offer social reasons for remaining in their parties. [13] In contrast, Insiders and Elites should have had initial political ambitions maintained or sharpened by the passage of time. Consequently, they should more often cite political, particularly career, considerations for remaining in their parties. Finally, for a variety of reinforcing reasons —longer periods of party service, more intensive effort on behalf of their parties, greater success, and so forth—politics should constitute a more salient dimension of the personal identity of Elites and Insiders than of Stalwarts. By this is meant that the first two types of officials should be more likely than Stalwarts to think of themselves in "political" terms and, therefore, to include "politics" in their expressed conceptions of self.

The data generally support these expectations. [14] An exception is the failure of Elites and Insiders to offer political reasons for remaining active more than Stalwarts and for the latter to offer social gratification reasons more than the former. Improve government reasons continue to be the most frequently cited. These are followed by political considerations, personal considerations, and pressure from others. It is true that career considerations are more important for Elites than for Insiders and Stalwarts. Specifically, 20.7% of the Elites, 18.5% of the Insiders, and 10.4% of the Stalwarts cite political career reasons for continuing party work, and 6.5%, 4.5%, and 2.5% of the same groups

Table 7.8
Perspectives on Party Work and Political Career Expectations of
Leadership Types

	Stalwarts	Insiders	Elites
% Reporting Increased Sense of Enjoyment of Party Work Since Initial Period of Membership	48.0	54.2	55.4
% Reporting Party Organization More Effective Since Initial Period of Membership	56.2	55.9	65.2
% Reporting Increased Sense of Accomplishment Since Initial Period of Membership	53.7	64.8	67.4
% Finding Party Work Increasingly Enjoyable	31.1	32.4	41.3
% Finding Party Work Rewarding and Enjoyable	39.5	41.9	59.8
% Expecting to Receive Public Office Nomination	44.6	67.0	67.4
% Expecting to Hold Higher Party Office	41.0	39.7	42.4

state that they are most important. However, other differences in motives are not particularly sharp. Nor are they consistently patterned in an Elite-Insider-Stalwart order.

Since comparisons of gross differences in overall rates could mask turnover at the level of the individual, we also examined the extent of *individual* changes in reasons given by the three types of officials for joining as opposed to staying in politics. As anticipated, the proportions of Elites and Insiders expressing career aspirations increase more over time than does that of Stalwarts (i.e., 16.3% for the Elites, 12.3% for the Insiders, and 4.2% for the Stalwarts). Overall, the reasons the three types of officials give for staying in as opposed to joining a party make clear that in all cases "motivational pluralism" is the rule. Moreover, the patterns within parties are neither sufficiently sharp nor consistent to support *a priori* expectations that there are strong associations between: a) leadership type and motivational change over time; or b) leadership type and variations in motivations for continuing party work.

A second anticipated finding that received no confirmation is that leader type would be related to expectations of holding higher party offices in the

Table 7.9
Self-Concepts of Party Leadership Types

Proportions with Political Components in Self-Concepts

	Stalwarts	Insiders	Elites
All Parties	26.3	33.5	47.5
Party: NDP	32.3	36.6	55.2
Liberal	22.2	36.8	44.4
Conservative	27.0	32.0	39.1
Social Credit	23.6	25.8	53.8

Proportions with "Narrow and Constricted" Self-Concepts

	Stalwarts	Insiders	Elites
All Parties	39.5	31.8	26.1
Party: NDP	34.9	28.1	18.5
Liberal	35.1	22.0	26.1
Conservative	45.5	45.2	38.5
Social Credit	45.5	39.0	27.6

future. Almost equal proportions of Elites, Insiders, and Stalwarts expect to hold such offices.[15] However, there is confirmation for our other expectations. In every instance favorable evaluations of party careers increase in an orderly fashion as one moves from Stalwarts to Insiders to Elites (Table 7.8). Elites also are the most likely to expect that in the future they will represent the party as contestants for public offices. The principal difference in this regard is between Elites and Insiders on the one hand and Stalwarts on the other. However, the minute differences between the Elites and Insiders is in accord with an earlier speculation that Insiders include a sizable group of younger party officials who perceive party activity as a stepping stone to the attainment of public office.

Two aspects of party officials' self-concepts[16] ought to be especially sensitive to what we have assumed are real differences in their political orientation, commitment, and effectiveness. The first of these is the presence of a narrow and constricted self-concept, one lacking in both topical variety and detail. Since such a concept of self (which is given by 36% of the respondents) suggests relative ineffectiveness and a resultant lack of esteem from others, we expected such self-concepts to increase in frequency in moving from Elite to Insider to Stalwart. The data support this with the proportions of party officials with narrow and constricted self-concepts rising from a low of 26.1% for Elites to 31.8% for Insiders to 39.5% for Stalwarts. Additionally, it was anticipated that the proportions mentioning some aspect of politics (32% of all party officials) would increase from Stalwarts to Elites because the latter, much more than the former, presumably have had the high quality and effectiveness of their performance reinforced by being recognized and ratified by others. Therefore, according to most theories of social identity formation, this dimension of their activities should be more often incorporated in their self-concepts.[17] This expectation is supported, the relevant percentages increasing in the predicted sequence from 26.3% to 33.5% to 47.5%. Party variations from this pattern are minimal. There seems little doubt, then, that the threefold typology reflects both significant aspects of the reality experienced by the three types and of the judgments of them by others.

Attributes of Types: An Overview

A large array of information has been scrutinized for differences among Elites, Insiders, and Stalwarts. Since so many differences are present, we judged it would be useful to evaluate their importance in distinguishing among the different types of officials. Accordingly, twenty-one variables reflecting differences among types were evaluated in a multiple discriminant function analysis, a statistical procedure that permits an assessment of the relative discriminatory power of a number of variables for separating accurately two or more groups that have been defined *a priori*.[18] After assessing the relative discriminating power of the variables, those having statistically significant effects were then applied to each of the party units.

The twenty-one predictor variables are quite effective in distinguishing among the groups that we had defined prior to any of these analyses. Indeed, 63.4% of the respondents were placed correctly by the predictors into the groups to which we initially had assigned them (Table 7.10). A substantial number of social structural, political socialization, and party career measures play a significant role in these classifications. The strongest discriminating variable is educational level, and another socioeconomic status measure, income, ranks fifth. Both party career and intraparty participation variables also discriminate leader types; differential commitment to party work is the second strongest predictor and two career variables, number of party positions held and number of years of party work, rank third and eighth respectively. What might be called "subjective" career variables,[19] namely, politics in the self-concept and expectations of future public office holding, rank fourth and seventh. Finally, three political socialization measures, age of first party identification, stability of party identification, and partisanship of the neighborhood in which one was reared as compared to one's present affiliation, enter the analysis, sixth, eighth, and eleventh.

Table 7.10
Multiple Discriminant Analysis of Membership in Elite, Insider and Stalwart Groups

Statistically Significant Predictors	Relative Predictive Power (rank order)
Education	1
Level of Participation in Party Work	2
Number of Party Positions Held	3
Politics in Self-Concept	4
Income	5
Age of First Party Identification	6
Expectation of Holding Public Office	7
Number of Years of Party Work	8
Partisanship of Neighborhood	9
Sex	10
Stability of Party Identification	11

Summary of Results of Multiple Discriminant Analyses by Party

	NDP	Liberal	Conservative	Social Credit	All Officials**
% correctly grouped*	66.3	65.2	68.7	60.6	63.4
% of variance in predictor variables explained by discriminant functions	42.9	30.8	46.7	24.7	26.1
% increase in predictive power over chance levels	23.6	19.9	36.8	18.2	20.6

* adjusted for group N's
** classification based on all twenty-one variables

Analyses of individual parties confirm the importance of education (an indicator of both ascribed and achieved status) as a discriminator of types. Income, which also appears as a discriminator for all parties, is an especially salient predictor of types among New Democrats and Social Crediters. Similarly, party career and intraparty participation variables are significant predictors of types, regardless of party, as are measures of political socialization. Overall, the several predictor variables are able to place correctly between 60% to 70% of the members of each party (see Table 7.10). In short, the multiple discriminant analyses support our general hypothesis that although "who you are" factors (the social structural and political socialization attributes and advantages that individuals bring to a political party) affect initial placements, opportunities for advancement and the acquisition of prestige and influence, so also do performance factors (the "what you do" variables). Regardless, therefore, of whether the organization in question is highly structured, rational, and efficient, or a relatively amorphous and inefficient political party, it appears that demonstrated competence as well as ascribed and achieved status all play a role in determining the career opportunities and achievement of their individual members.

Summary

The material discussed has demonstrated that Elites, Insiders, and Stalwarts vary with regard to a variety of social structural and political socialization characteristics presumed to be of theoretical significance for understanding recruitment and activity within local party organizations. Elites more frequently than Insiders or Stalwarts come from higher status backgrounds. These initial socioeconomic status advantages are maintained and even enhanced over time. Their strength and persistence consistently suggest that social structural variables not only help explain who joins local parties, but also how political careers within these organizations develop.

Political socialization differences also characterize the three types. Elites more often than Insiders or Stalwarts report that they were reared in politicized childhood and adolescent environments; having had parents who were politically active and having come into contact with other politically involved individuals. Also, Elites tend most frequently to report steadily increasing political interest and involvement prior to joining a party. Although socialization differences among the three types are not as consistent as are the social structural, overall the data do indicate the relevance of political socialization for explaining who achieves Elite status.

The three types of party officials further are differentiated by varying levels of commitment to party work and by their attitudes toward their organizations and themselves. As anticipated, Elites tend to report doing more work, having worked longer for their parties than Insiders or Stalwarts, and having held both more positions generally and more high level positions in particular. Such objective differences also are reflected in the subjective reactions of the three types to their experiences. Elites and Insiders more frequently than Stalwarts derive a sense of accomplishment from their party activities and are more likely to view party work as leading to public office opportunities. Again consonant with objective career differences, the three groups vary in their conceptions of self, with Elites being the most and Stalwarts the least likely to think of themselves in political terms. The ability of social structural, socialization, and career factors to distinguish the three types of officials was summarized with a multiple discriminant analysis. As in other types of organizations, "what you do" as well as "who you are" both play a role in determining top leadership. The principal exception to this generalization are the women in parties, who are the focus of discussion in the following chapter.

NOTES

1. For a more detailed discussion of the difficulties of studying the organizational careers of party officials see Allan Kornberg, Joel Smith, and Harold D. Clarke, "Semi-Careers in Political Work: The Dilemma of Party Organizations," *Sage Professional Papers in Comparative Politics*, Harry Eckstein and Ted Robert Gurr, eds. (Beverly Hills: Sage Publications, 1970).

2. For example, at the time they initiated party work 20.3% of the Stalwarts, 18.4% of the Insiders, and 10.9% of the Elites were members of households where the head was a skilled laborer.

3. Specifically, 50.0%, 43.6%, and 49.2% of the Elites, Insiders, and Stalwarts mention improve government reasons as being most important for initiating party work; 8.8% of the Elites, 13.4% of the Insiders, and 10.3% of the Stalwarts cite pressure from others as the most important initiating reasons.

4. The mean canonical variate scores for the three types are as follows:

	Self-Motivation	Expertise	Co-option
Elites	.034	.187	-.109
Insiders	-.009	-.018	-.067
Stalwarts	-.004	-.040	.062

5. Career success is, of course, also measured by the Elite-Insider-Stalwart typology itself. The measures of success considered here are *not* the same as those used to *define* these types.

6. That these distributions are not simply an artifact of the criteria used to define the three types of party officials is reflected in the fact that not only are the means for the Insiders and Elites considerably greater than 1.0, the minimum value given the criteria used in constructing the typology, but also that the Insider and Elite means are different in all parties.

7. Even more impressive figures are reported by members of particular parties. The New Democrats, for example, state they work an average of 6.9 hours per week and have devoted virtually all of their free time to party work for 15.5 weeks a year during the past two years. Nor are such reports especially surprising, for despite their protean nature, the local parties are real organizations and the individuals studied here comprise their key personnel.

8. The summary measure is a factor score for each individual for the three variables analyzed above; that is, average number of hours worked, number of weeks of intense work, and proportion of leisure time spent on party work. The method used to compute factor scores can be found in Harry H. Harman, *Modern Factor*

Analysis, 2nd ed. (Chicago: University of Chicago Press, 1967), p. 348. The weights were derived from factors obtained by using the method of principal axis factoring with iteration, and varimax rotation of the factor matrix.

9. On the relationship between party office holding and differential participation in Canadian parties see Harold D. Clarke, Allan Kornberg and James Lee, "Ontario Student Party Activists: A Note on Differential Participation in a Voluntary Organization," *Canadian Review of Sociology and Anthropology*, 12 (1975): 213-220; and Clarke, *et al.*, "Motivational Patterns and Differential Participation," (1978): 130-151.

10. Although there may be a variety of reasons for the relative weakness of the latter association, two may be particularly pertinent. First, some of the officials classified as public office candidates were *incumbents*, and the demands of public office may have curtailed the amount of time they were able to devote to local party activities *per se*. Second, some of the individuals in the candidate category were ex-candidates and one can speculate that the level of interest in and commitment to party affairs may not be as great among ex-candidates as it is among active and aspiring ones.

11. If worldly success can be measured by the current socioeconomic status of the three types of officials, then the data already presented in the upper sections of Tables 7.1 and 7.3 indicate that Elites more than Insiders more than Stalwarts derive from favored socioeconomic backgrounds and that initial advantages have persisted and, indeed, even widened by the time of affiliation.

12. See, for example, Verba and Nie, *Participation in America*, pp. 176-208. For Canadian data see James Curtis, "Voluntary Association Joining: A Cross-National Comparative Note," *American Sociological Review*, 36 (1971): 872-880.

13. On the significance of "social" motives for sustaining party work see Eldersveld, *Political Parties: A Behavorial Analysis*, chap. 11; Conway and Feigert, "Motivation, Incentive Systems, and the Political Party Organization," *passim*; Tom Gavin, "Local Party Activists in Dublin: Socialization, Recruitment and Incentives," *British Journal of Political Science*, 6 (1976): 369-380; Clarke, *et al.*, *op. cit.*, (1978): 137-139.

14. It might be noted, however, that 41.5% of the Stalwarts as compared to 36.9% of the Insiders and 29.4% of the Elites cite loyalty to other party officials or public office candidates and incumbents as reasons for sustaining their party careers. This is consistent with the notion that personal loyalties, a type of social motive, may be a particularly important reason for officials such as Stalwarts continuing party work since they have little realistic opportunity to develop political careers through this activity, and are unlikely to obtain meaningful material rewards for continued service.

15. One is tempted to attribute this to the fact that fairly large proportions of Elites and Insiders already have held such offices and, given the relative paucity of provincial and national level party offices, the assumption that they might not hold such offices again in the future is not unrealistic. Although this is a plausible explanation, if it were entirely valid it also should apply to expectations of being a candidate for a public office in the future. Substantial proportions of Elites and Insiders had been candidates in the past or currently were candidates for either a local, provincial, or national public office, and these offices also are scarce.

16. Self-concepts were measured by asking respondents "What would you say about yourself in three sentences in answer to the question, 'Who am I?'"

17. For a discussion of relevant literature see Allan Kornberg and Joel Smith, "Self-Concepts of American and Canadian Party Officials;" Joel Smith and Allan Kornberg, "Self-Concepts of American and Canadian Party Officials: Their Development and Consequences."

18. A concise nontechnical description of multiple discriminant analysis is contained in William R. Klecka, "Discriminant Analysis," *Statistical Package for the Social Sciences*, pp. 434-467.

19. Concerning the distinction between "objective" vs. "subjective" political careers see Harold D. Clarke, "Political Socialization, Political Recruitment and Party Careers: An Exploratory Study," (Unpublished Ph.D. dissertation, Duke University, 1971), chap. 1.

Chapter Eight

Women in Parties:
The Disadvantaged Majority

> . . . the most important and interesting question about women's
> political role is why that role is so insignificant. The most impor-
> tant and interesting question about women's political behavior is
> why so few seek and wield power.
>
> Jeane Kirkpatrick, *Political Woman*, p. 3.

IF there is one aspect of conventional wisdom that has been widely accepted
by social scientists, no less than by practicing politicians and average
citizens, it is the old saw that "politics is a man's game." In a review of the
literature on political elites, Robert Putnam concluded that:

> In statistical terms, women are the most underrepresented group in the
> political elites of the world. The world of high politics is almost univers-
> ally a man's world. The extent of this underrepresentation varies surpris-
> ingly little from country to country. . . .There is, it seems, an 'iron law of
> andarchy.'[1]

There is ample support in our data for Putnam's assertion. Women
comprise over one-half of the general population of Vancouver and Winnipeg
but only 19% of the parties' organizations in these two cities. As shown in
the last chapter, women are significantly overrepresented in the Stalwart
category and underrepresented in both the Insider and especially in the Elite
categories. At the time this study was undertaken, almost three times as
many men as women were members of their respective parties' national or
provincial executive committees and almost six times as many men as women
were public officials or contenders for a public office. And, although influence
was very unequally distributed in every organization, the average male official, nonetheless, was ascribed almost three times as much influence over the
conduct of party affairs as was the average woman official.

Male dominance in politics generally and in elite political institutions in
particular is an established fact.[2] The feminist movements have challenged

the underlying normative assumptions on which this dominance rests by taking the position not only that politics does not need to be a man's game but that it should not be. As individuals most social scientists probably agree with this position, but as scholars they have confined themselves largely to the study of males in politics and to explaining why their domination continues. Although these explanations appear in various permutations and combinations, they can be subsumed basically under four categories: 1) those pertinent to the unequal statuses and resources men and women are able to bring to politics; 2) those focusing on the socialization of men into political roles and the socialization of women into culturally approved wife-mother roles; 3) those structured in terms of a male conspiracy to keep women out of politics and out of positions of political influence in particular; and 4) those arguing the existence of political behavioral consequences of physiological differences between the sexes.[3] We have previously noted that for convenience and simplicity the first two may be termed social structural and socialization explanations. Let us suggest some of the ways in which they can help illuminate the concerns of this chapter.

Some Theoretical Expectations

Social structural theories have particular relevance for the question of why women comprise less than 20% of the party organizations of Vancouver and Winnipeg. If (as one version of social structural explanation contends) women are underrepresented in party organizations because they generally lack or do not control the necessary high status attributes and resources of men, we ought to find that women who *are* officials do possess these resources (e.g., good occupations, above average incomes) and attributes (e.g., middle class backgrounds). Indeed, in order to overcome the culturally generated "handicap" of being women they may have to have even more of them.

Socialization theory also is relevant to the question. If both men and women are inculcated very early in life with cultural values that suggest politics are a man's game and women do not belong in it, we should find sharp and systematic differences between the early political socialization experiences of women party officials and women in the general and nigh-dweller samples of the public, but no such differences between men and women officials since the latter group of women, after all, are participants in the political game. Indeed, if, as some investigators have contended, women have to be like men but more so to attain political positions,[4] then we may find that women party functionaries derive from more politicized milieux than either the two samples of nonparty men or their male party colleagues. Additionally, if socialization theory can help explain a relatively exotic type of political behavior like becoming a political party official then it also ought to bear on the question of who participates in more general kinds of political activity. Materials presented in Chapter 3 have indicated that the social status and level of politicization of people affect both the frequency with which they are asked by party representatives to engage in activities going beyond voting and their willingness to do so. If there are substantial differences in early socialization experiences of the sexes,[5] it may be anticipated that party representatives will not solicit the assistance of women, regardless of their social status, as often as they will men. More important, perhaps, women may not respond positively to any such requests as often as men. If this proves to be the case, how does one account for the fact that some women *are* party officials?

The obvious explanations are that women constitute more than one-half of the adult population, they vote, and the officials of political institutions purporting to be both open and representative would be less than rational if they did not try to include at least some women in their number. Even so, we may find that men and women enter party organizations in different ways and at different age periods. With respect to the latter possibility, one variant of a social structural explanation would contend that women are deprived of the leisure time men are able to allocate to politics because the burdens of homemaking, childbearing, and childrearing fall upon them more heavily than upon their spouses. Thus, we may find that the average woman party official who had married and had children may have had to postpone joining a party until her children no longer needed her more or less constant attention. Conversely, one reason she may have joined a party whereas her nigh-dweller match did not may be that she is less likely to have been married, but if married, likelier to have had fewer children than her match at a similar stage in life. Whatever the actual facts, comparisons of the statuses of women officials with their nigh-dweller matches at that same time may clarify the conditions under which the men-politico and women-wife-mother associations hold.

We shall examine and compare the career patterns of men and women in parties, for the maldistribution of women among the three leadership types also might be accounted for by social structural and socialization factors. For example, women may have been socialized to have different motives for staying in parties and to expect that, although they will help to put men in public offices, they themselves will not be contenders for these positions.[6] Social structural theory suggests that because of their wife-mother roles, women in political parties may have less time to devote to organizational affairs and may need to drop out of their parties more frequently and for longer periods of time than male colleagues. For similar reasons, women may not have held as many party positions, or at least may not have held as many

Table 8.1

Selected Social Background and Current Status Characteristics
of Women Party Officials and Women in the General Public

	Women In Parties	Women in the General Public
Social Background		
% Born in Canada	77.8	78.6
% Whose fathers were professionals or business proprietors and executives	40.5	25.7
$\overline{X}$ SES of fathers	40.7	32.8
% Perceiving family's economic status as above average relative to standards of time	33.3	23.6
% Attended a university	21.4	12.6
% With at least one university degree	12.0	5.0
Current Status		
% In work force	43.1	61.0
% In work force who are professionals or business proprietors or executives	41.5	25.8
% With annual family income over $34,200	11.7	7.4
$\overline{X}$ Number of years residing in community	33.2	22.9
% Home owners	82.9	58.5
% Affiliated with high status Protestant church	33.6	21.5
% Belonging to three or more non-church organizations	21.4	9.9
$\overline{X}$ Number of executive offices held in these organizations	1.3	0.5
% Reading two or more daily newspapers	39.3	15.5
$\overline{X}$ Age	50.6	42.1

high level positions in their party hierarchies as have men.[7] In sum, a number of tests of several aspects of social structural and political socialization explanations of political behavior can help clarify the extent to which, and conditions under which, men and women participate in local party organizations.

Social and Political Resources

We begin this examination by comparing the socioeconomic backgrounds and current statuses of the party women with those of women in the general population.[8] Even a cursory inspection indicates very marked differences between the two groups. By way of illustration, a larger proportion of party women were reared in middle and upper-middle class homes and, as a group, they are much better educated than average women. A substantially larger percentage of women in the general public are in the work force, but, given the fact that in the late 1960's the expectation that middle class Canadian women would work was not strong, this is not surprising. Of the women who are working, however, the proportion of party women who are engaged in professional or business occupations is 60% greater than for the general public. Other indicators of the higher statuses and resources of women in parties are their larger annual incomes, the larger proportion who are members of families that owned their own homes, the larger proportion who are joiners and officers of voluntary organizations other than their churches, and their conspicuously greater media consumption. These differences are particularly striking because party women, on the average, are eight-and-one-half years older than women in the general public. *Ceteris paribus*, they were more likely to have been children during the Depression, and thus the differences in status may be even greater, relatively, than the absolute numbers suggest. Moreover, although the data are not displayed, on virtually every one of these same indicators party women are more of a socioeconomic "elite" than are men in the general public.

This picture of status advantage is not as clear in comparisons of the women with their male party colleagues. Briefly, pertinent comparisons reveal that party women have less of an advantage over women in the public than party men have over men in the public. In a sense, party women stand in approximately the same relationship to their male counterparts with regard to status as do women members of the general public to them. The mean SES scores of the fathers of the male officials is significantly higher than those for the fathers of the women. More than twice as many men as women officials have attended a university and almost three times as many men have at least one university degree. Of those officials in the work force, almost twice as large a proportion of the men are professionals or business proprietors and executives and almost twice as large a group of male officials enjoy annual incomes over $34,200. The men also more often are joiners of other voluntary organizations and more avid readers of printed media.

More generally, however, these initial comparisons suggest that one reason the party women are in their organizations is that they are a part of the

Table 8.2
Percent of Women at Each Level of Childhood
Environment Politicization Index

Politicization Level	General Public		Nigh-Dwellers		Party Officials	
	Men	Women	Men	Women	Men	Women
0 (low)	42%	58%	81%	19%	81%	19%
1	41	59	80	20	80	20
2	44	56	84	16	85	15
3 (high)	40	60	86	14	77	23
Total	42	58	81	19	81	19
(N=)	(1187)		(625)		(625)	

Distribution of Women on Childhood Environment Politicization Index

Politicization Level	General Public	Nigh-Dwellers	Party Officials
0 (low)	42%	38%	21%
1	36	42	29
2	17	17	26
3 (high)	4	3	24
Total	99	100	100
(N=)	(691)	(117)	(117)

stratum of population from which political parties in liberal democracies disproportionately have recruited their functionaries. Although, contrary to initial expectations, they are less of an elite group than their male colleagues,[9] they clearly are a part of the middle class. But given that there are at least as many middle class women as men, this still does not explain why their male colleagues outnumber them by a margin of more than four to one. Socialization theories would contend that the imbalance in these rates is rooted in differences in early life experiences. Thus, a reasonable next step involves a comparison of pertinent aspects of the political solicalization of men and women party officials and the contrast of these, in turn, with socialization experiences of men and women in the nigh-dweller and general public groups.

The data in the upper half of Table 8.2 reflect the effects of normal demographic proceses. The sex ratio at birth is almost equal, and the politicization of home environments in no way determines the sex of children. Not surprisingly, then, we find that the proportions female (and male) at each

Table 8.3
Socialization Experiences at Each Level of Politicization
of the Childhood Environment for Men and Women in Each Sample

Politicization Level	General Public		Nigh-Dwellers		Party Officials	
	Men	Women	Men	Women	Men	Women
	$\overline{X}$ Age of First Political Awareness					
0	14.0	15.2	14.5	14.0	12.5	15.8
1	12.9	13.3	11.6	13.6	11.6	12.8
2	11.3	12.0	11.5	11.0	10.6	10.0
3	9.9	12.3	10.6	14.0	9.6	8.9
Total	13.0	13.7	12.6	13.3	11.1	11.7
(N=)	(475)	(650)	(501)	(116)	(508)	(116)
	$\overline{X}$ Age of First Partisan Identification					
0	20.1	21.2	19.6	19.6	18.1	18.4
1	12.9	19.1	17.4	18.8	15.7	17.3
2	14.8	16.5	15.6	14.2	13.9	14.9
3	14.3	15.7	14.8	20.0	11.6	12.4
Total	18.0	19.3	17.7	18.3	14.8	15.7
(N=)	(441)	(598)	(480)	(102)	(504)	(115)
	% Interested in Politics During High School (14–18)					
0	33.2%	20.6%	44.1%	26.7%	53.6%	36.0%
1	55.1	48.4	58.8	40.8	69.6	58.8
2	69.2	58.1	60.2	65.0	81.0	80.0
3	68.8	58.1	77.8	66.7	87.2	71.4
Total	48.8	39.0	54.3	40.2	73.2	62.4
(N=)	(496)	(691)	(508)	(117)	(508)	(117)

level of the politicized environment index (see Chapter 2) are not appreciably different. In the general public, the percentage of women at various points on the index ranges from 58% in the low politicization category (42% are men) to 60% in the high politicization category (40% are men). Equivalent percentages for nigh-dweller and party women are, respectively, 19% (81% men) and 14% (86% men), and 19% (81% men) and 23% (77% men). Given these relatively constant proportions, the differences along the index in the distribution of party women as compared to their nigh-dweller matches and the general public women are indeed impressive. Fully 24% of the party women as compared to only 3% and 4% of the latter two groups respectively are on the high end of the index (see the lower half of Table 8.2). Politicized environments, it will be recalled, may be pertinent for a number of reasons. It is presumed that they contribute to a child's early interest in politics and the early development of a strong positive affect for political parties and political actors. In addition, politically involved parents may serve as role models for young children. Childhood role models help explain adult political behavior. They are especially important in accounting for the involvement of women in what is supposed to be a man's game. With reference to women legislators, Means has argued:

> It would seem reasonable to expect a high incidence of political role models in the backgrounds of women legislators, on the basis of the reasoning that for women, even more than for men, political participation beyond the voting act is essentially 'deviant behavior.' The example of politically active relatives therefore appears particularly essential, as a compensation for the constraints inherent in traditional role expectations, and the very real difficulties women sometimes face when attempting to transcend these expectations.[10]

Table 8.3 suggests that the political socialization experiences of men and women begin to differ relatively early. Although the proportions of boys and girls reared in the same sorts of politicized settings are very similar, we find that the average woman became aware of politics and developed an initial partisan identification later than did the average man. Moreover, the proportions who had developed an interest in politics by high school age also are systematically lower among women (see Table 8.3). As a result of these differences, when all of the information is merged to create the political socialization index utilized in Chapter 3, sex-differentiated patterns emerge. These are summarized in Table 8.4.

Two aspects of these data are particularly striking. First, the average party woman was raised in a more politicized environment, became politically aware, first developed a partisan identification, and was more interested in politics earlier in life than the average man in either the general or the nigh-dweller samples of the public. In this regard it should be noted that although the average positions of nigh-dweller men and women on the socialization index differ in a statistically significant fashion and those of men and women in the general public almost do, the *observed differences between men and women party officials do not even come close to significance*. Second—Czudnowski's argument regarding the irrelevance of preadult socialization for political recruitment[11] notwithstanding—it would appear that variations in political socialization do make a difference. For, as compared with men, women in the group most

Table 8.4
Distribution on Political Socialization Index
of Men and Women in Different Samples

Political Socialization	General Public		Nigh-Dwellers		Party Officials	
	Men	Women	Men	Women	Men	Women
0	18%	22%	12%	16%	5%	8%
1	23	22	20	24	10	15
2	19	22	24	28	13	12
3	19	14	22	16	21	17
4	13	13	14	10	21	13
5	7	5	6	6	20	27
6	1	1	2	—	10	9
Total	100	99	100	100	100	101
% Highly Politicized (3–6)	40%	33%	44%	32%	72%	66%
Mean	2.07	1.89	2.28	1.98*	3.39	3.26
Mean of group	1.97		2.23		3.37	

*P ≤ .05

likely to supply party officials (i.e., the nigh-dwellers) do not have facilitating socialization experiences to the same degree as do men in the general public. Since the analysis in Chapter 3 already has shown that party officials appeal for assistance to people on the basis of their politicization as well as their social status, from an early age higher status women as a group do not comprise as "attractive" a recruitment pool as do men. This, in part, may help to account both for women's underrepresentation in political party organizations and the fact that those who are in them are not as elite a group as are their male colleagues.

Other data on the political attributes of party women and their nigh-dweller matches lend additional support to our contention that political socialization experiences do appear to matter in the lagging entry of women into party organizations. Despite the similarities in both their social backgrounds and current life statuses, party women differ from their nigh-dweller matches in having much stronger and longer partisan commitments and interests. By way of illustration, the party women's current partisan identifications more often (72% vs. 39%) are congruent with those of their parents[12] and have been maintained for a much longer period (29 years vs. 3½ years) than have those of their nigh-dweller matches. Further, from the time they became politically aware to the adult stage of life (i.e., age 26) more party than nigh-dweller women followed politics closely (26% vs. 4%). During this same period politics more often were salient (i.e., following politics "mattered") for the party women (68% vs. 31%) and they felt much better informed about political affairs (52% vs. 10%) than did their nigh-dweller matches.

It has been observed that politically active parents are much more likely to serve as positive role models if children have strong and positive feelings toward them. David Sears has stated (using pronouns that reflect the sex bias in the study of politics noted by McCormack):

> By all the several sociopsychological theories . . . adoption of family political norms ought to be closely related to the offspring's affective ties to his parents. If he feels positive toward them, he should adopt their attitudes (insofar as he knows them), whereas if he is strongly hostile toward them, he should reject their views, possibly even reverting or 'boomeranging' to an opposite political stance. [13]

Other scholarly observers have contended that the authority structure of a family and the relative involvement of parents and children in family decisions affect later life political participation. [14] The expectation is that children reared in families characterized by democratic patterns of decision making, families in which children feel they have some control over the outcomes of decisions that affect them personally, are more likely as adults to participate in politics and public affairs than are adults who were reared in more authoritarian families.

There is considerable support for these hypotheses in our data. Of those who were reared in homes with politically active fathers, 54.3% of the party women as compared to 24.2% of the nigh-dweller women felt "very close" to this parent. Comparable percentages for male party officials and nigh-dwellers are 30.5% and 14.0% respectively. Similarly, for those reared in families with politically active mothers, 64.0% of the party women but only 18.9% of the nigh-dweller women report having felt "very close to their mothers." For male party officials and nigh-dwellers the equivalent percentages are 52.6% and 6.1%. Further, as compared to nigh-dwellers, party officials also most often report having had "a lot to say" about their lives when they were growing up (28.2% vs. 18.0% for women; 36.7% vs. 16.4% for men). Finally, women officials most often report growing up in families in which their mothers were integrally involved in important family decision making (70.2% of officials vs. 53.9% of nigh-dwellers for women; 52.2% of officials vs. 50.3% of nigh-dwellers for men).

These data help explain why women who are currently party officials occupy these positions. However, since holding a position is but one type of political participation, albeit a very important and relatively unusual one, it was assumed that additional light could be shed on the more general question of political participation by women if the analyses in Chapter 3 were extended to assess the importance of sex differences. It will be recalled that the nigh-dwellers and members of the general public were presented with a list of various kinds of political actions, most of which were related to election campaigns, and asked if they ever had been approached by a party's representative to engage in one or more of these.

Very briefly, analysis revealed only minor sex-related differences in both electoral participation beyond voting and whether that participation had been invited. However, in each sample the small differences *always* showed more women *not participating* and *not being asked to participate* and this pattern remained even when differences in level of childhood politicization were controlled. The most salient difference between the sexes when the politicization control was applied was that 10% fewer women than men among the least politicized members of the nigh-dweller group ever had participated when asked to do so. Since the activities about which respondents were being questioned are pertinent to one of the two principal functions of parties, electing their candidates to public office, and since parties more frequently solicit the assistance of middle and upper-middle class people like the nigh-dwellers, this datum suggests a sex-related pattern that handicaps women as participants in party politics.

Other data examined fall into this same pattern. They reveal that women are generally less frequently asked for their political opinions and are less likely to have been asked for them recently. Moreover, nonparty groups which, nonetheless, ask people to engage in political activities (e.g., unions, civic clubs) less frequently ask women for assistance. It is true that the data in Table 8.5 indicate that the level of politicization affects who is asked about political matters, but so does the sex of the person. Thus, only the men in the general public who are low on the politicization index are less likely to have been asked about politics than are women in any group. Indeed, the *most* politicized women report being asked their opinions and advice only slightly more often than the *least* politicized men.

To recapitulate, women probably are less likely to be in political parties than men because: a) they are less socialized into politics from an early age; b) they are less able to participate to the same extent even when socialization effects are controlled; and c) either others do not expect them to participate at the same rates as men or they do not expect it of themselves. On this last point, the key factor probably is the receptiveness of others to the idea of women being politically involved, for when we consider answers to the question of whether one would work for a party if approached, taking into account all relevant controls (i.e., status, prior experience, level of politicization) there are

Table 8.5
Proportions of Men and Women Asked by Others for Their Political Opinions and to do Political Work by Levels of Politicization and Sample

	General Public		Nigh-Dwellers	
	Not Highly Politicized	Highly Politicized	Not Highly Politicized	Highly Politicized
% More likely to be asked for opinions, advice or information on politics and public affairs				
Men	15.3	27.1	21.9	38.3
Women	8.9	17.9	5.3	18.9
% Less likely to be asked				
Men	38.7	14.1	29.1	13.5
Women	50.8	32.6	53.3	32.4
% Recently were asked				
Men	27.1	48.4	40.4	54.3
Women	19.9	35.6	18.7	27.0
% Approached by non-party groups for political work				
Men	8.9	19.3	10.0	19.2
Women	6.2	8.7	4.0	8.1

no systematic or sizable differences between the proportions of men and women answering in the affirmative.[15] With respect to why they would not work, the answers suggest that it is because of established norms and the way they are reinforced. Whereas at every combination of politicization and prior experience in political work men are more likely than women to choose those reasons that include negative affect for politics and parties, women—even if they had been politically active previously—are likelier to choose reasons related to habit and a sense of inappropriateness. The latter difference is most sharp among the nigh-dwellers, members of the social strata most likely to supply party affiliates. There is nothing in the evidence to indicate that there is any widespread feeling of personal incompetence among women that leads them to participate less than men. Accordingly, we may infer that it is the impermeability of politics for women, the expectation of experiencing the uncomfortable consequences of being in an extreme minority, and a belief that such activities will violate social norms, that are likely to be important in explaining women's lower rates of political activity.[16]

Table 8.6
Statuses of Men and Women Officials and
Their Nigh-Dweller Matches atthe Time
Officials Joined Their Parties

| | Women | | Men | |
	Parties	Nigh-Dwellers	Parties	Nigh-Dwellers
$\bar{X}$ Age of joining	34.5	*	29.6	*
% Who were married when they joined	74.4	68.4	58.4	55.7
% Of those married when they joined and who had children at home	34.5	45.3	48.2	59.2
% In households headed by professional or executive at time of joining	26.5	34.1	41.3	29.3
% In households headed by a blue-collar worker at time of joining	23.1	28.2	17.5	28.7
% In households headed by a student at time of joining	7.7	2.6	16.1	9.2
$\bar{X}$ SES head of household at time of joining	47.8	44.6	56.1	39.9

*Not applicable

Women in Parties: Joining

Turning from sex differences in general political participation to their role in actually joining a party, we find that on average party women are fully five years older than their male colleagues when they join (see Table 8.6). This highly significant difference is consistent with that aspect of a social structural approach which suggests that during the period in life when men tend to become party activists, the rearing of children and responsibilities for maintaining a home deprive women of this opportunity. The data clearly show that if women do not invariably have to forego joining a party because of wife-mother obligations, at least they postpone the occasion. Although a larger proportion of married male officials have children under five at home at the time they join, this difference only may reflect the higher age of joining of the women officials.[17] Regarding differences in the matched pairs of women at the time of joining, we find that a somewhat higher proportion of the party officials than of the nigh-dwellers are married, but that they less often have young children (34.5% vs. 45.3%).

When women join, they less frequently are part of a household headed by a high status professional and more often are a part of a blue-collar family than their male colleagues. We find that party women also are less often a part of a family headed by a professional or business person than are their nigh-dweller matches. In addition, the patterns of marital status, children, and age of joining suggest that most women officials, whether through choice or necessity, delay affiliating until they have discharged their more demanding wife-mother responsibilities. Finally, perusal of standard census data and our own general sample material indicates that, as compared to men, Canadian women as a group have fewer of the status attributes—extended educations and higher status occupations—that appear to be a virtual *sine qua non* for contending for high level political positions in liberal democracies. It would seem, therefore, that as a result of the combination of initially having had lesser status resources and having had to take role-based deferments before being able to start participating, the pool of women potentially available to parties shrinks and selectively excludes those who might be the status equals of men—for example, their spouses or occupationally successful women like Pat Robertson.

The reasons men and women officials give for joining parties illustrate our contention that political socialization experiences are especially important in explaining the membership of women. We find that 58.1% of the women as opposed to 44.5% of the men cite party loyalty as one of their reasons for joining. Regarding personal loyalties, 37.6% of the women give loyalty to a public office candidate or incumbent as a reason for joining and 23.1% mention loyalty to someone already active in party work. Comparable percentages for men are 24.8% and 11.2% respectively. More significant, perhaps, is the fact that almost twice as high a proportion of women as men (34.2% vs. 18.1%) cite aspects of party or candidate loyalty as their *most important reason*[18] (see Table 8.7). Both men and women cite "improve government" most frequently as their most important reason (49.0% and 41.9% respectively). They differ in that although men cite "personal considerations" more than "pressure from others" by a margin of nearly two to one (18.5% and 10.7% respectively), almost similar proportions of women (9.4% and 12.8%) offer these as most important reasons. Finally, although great numbers of officials do not cite "launching a political career" among their reasons for beginning party work, men do so more frequently than women (13.6% vs. 3.4%).

Table 8.7

Party Official's Most Important Reasons for Joining a Party

	Men	Women
To Improve Government:		
At all levels	22.2%	21.4%
At a specific level	26.8	20.5
Sub-total	49.0	41.9
Response to Pressure From:		
Family	2.0	6.8
Friends, relatives, co-workers, etc.	8.7	6.0
Sub-total	10.7	12.8
Political Considerations:		
Loyalty to a party	11.0	24.8
Loyalty to candidate or party official	7.1	9.4
Launch a political career	3.7	1.7
Sub-total	21.8	35.9
Personal Considerations:		
Personal satisfaction	17.7	8.5
Enjoy expanded social life	.8	.9
Sub-total	18.5	9.4
Total	100.0	100.0
(N=)	(508)	(117)

The parties vary considerably in terms of the most important reasons their men and women cite for first having affiliated. In the New Democratic party, for example, women and men differ on all categories of reasons, the men being more committed to the improvement of government and the women being more responsive to pressure from others. Among the Liberals, men cite improvement of government at a rate almost twice that of the women. Indeed, Liberal women's rate of selecting such reasons is so low that, though it is the most popular of the alternatives for the women officials of the three other parties, in their case it is a distant second to partisan considerations (selected by more than half).

Other than differences in age, differences between men and women in other aspects of joining are rather small. However, this is not the case either within or among the parties. Regarding mode of entry, for example, the NDP and Liberal women most frequently report being approached to perform specific tasks whereas two-thirds of the Social Credit women and about one-half of the Conservative women report volunteering for general work. We find

Table 8.8

Selected Aspects of Joining a Party by Party and Sex

	NDP		Liberal		Conservative		Social Credit		Total	
	Men	Women	Men	Women	Men	Women	Men	Women	Men	Women
X̄ Age of joining a party	28.2	29.4	28.7	34.2	29.0	36.7	35.2	39.5	29.6	34.5
Mode of Entry										
% Approached—specific task	14.0	30.3	28.7	41.3	28.6	25.7	34.2	20.0	25.6	29.9
% Approached—general work	11.0	24.2	17.7	13.8	17.9	14.3	10.1	5.0	14.8	15.4
% Volunteered—specific task	12.5	6.1	8.3	—	10.7	11.4	10.1	10.0	10.2	6.8
% Volunteered—general work	62.5	39.4	45.3	44.8	42.9	48.6	45.6	65.0	49.4	47.9
% Whose first contact was in a high party position	36.0	42.4	43.6	41.4	42.0	57.1	44.3	30.0	41.3	44.4
% Whose first contact was a close personal associate	41.2	66.7	63.5	51.7	56.3	60.0	57.0	50.0	54.9	58.1
% Whose first party position was at a high level	20.6	12.1	14.4	27.6	25.9	11.4	19.0	30.0	19.3	18.8
% Whose first party activities included glamorous functions	25.0	30.3	13.8	24.1	25.9	20.0	41.8	10.0	23.8	22.2
(N=)	(136)	(33)	(181)	(29)	(112)	(35)	(79)	(20)	(508)	(117)

that the NDP and Liberal women, since they more frequently are approached to join for a specific purpose, also are more likely than either their male colleagues or women in the other two parties to have been offered interesting first jobs. The Liberal party women also are more likely than their male party colleagues to have received higher level first positions in their local party hierarchies. So, for that matter, are Social Credit women. However, the latter are less likely than women in the other three parties to have had an initial party contact in a high level organizational position or to have been acquainted personally with that contact (see Table 8.8).

In Chapter 5 we reduced aspects of joining to age and three canonical variates—degree of self-motivation, degree of expertise, and co-option. A comparison of scores on these variates indicates that in general the women are: a) less self-motivated to join; b) as likely as men to join for considerations of expertise; and c) less likely to be co-opted than their male colleagues.[19] This last observation may be unexpected, given that these party organizations appear to be male preserves that women do not enter easily, but which have a certain number of positions requiring female incumbents. Indeed, the average profile of joining for women seems to depict a process like co-option in which certain women have been prevailed upon by someone close to them to volunteer. In this regard, a comparison by party of the women's canonical scores suggests that party also is a factor. Thus, NDP women are the most likely to have been co-opted; Liberal party women the least. The Social Credit and Conservative women fall in between. The Social Credit women have the most and the Conservative women the least self-motivation to join. NDP women seem to have brought the most expertise to their organizations, Liberal women the least, a pattern that also would help explain why NDP women are the most and Liberal women the least likely to have been co-opted into their respective parties.

Party differences between men and women in modes of entry may be summarized as follows: The NDP men are almost as likely to have been co-opted as their women counterparts but were more self-motivated and brought less expertise to their first party tasks. Liberal party men are far more likely to have been co-opted, less self-motivated, and somewhat, albeit not appreciably, more expert than their female colleagues upon joining. Conservative men scored higher on self-motivation and expertise and were less likely to have been co-opted than women. Finally, the Social Credit men were not as self-motivated to join as the women. Nor were they as likely to be co-opted despite the fact that they seemingly brought more expertise than did their female counterparts.

In Chapter 5 the four principal elements of joining a party were related to pertinent explanatory factors in a model organized as a flow of influences and experiences over time that lead a hypothetical average official to affiliate. Although the small number of women in each of the parties make it impossible to generate four individual party models for them, we have examined separate identical models for all men and all women. Like the analyses conducted in Chapter 5, the models for both men and women are most successful in explaining age of joining. Specifically, they account for 36% of the variance in age of joining for men and 18% for women. For both sexes the percentages of variance in self-motivation, expertise, and co-option explained are considerably lower.[20] Overall, the models explain 54% of the variance in aspects of joining for men as opposed to 20% for women. Two factors could account for the relative explanatory weakness of the model for women. It may be that the model does not contain the appropriate variables for them since they are a far from average group. A more likely explanation, however, is that they are older than men when they join. This may make the model's variables less directly applicable to them, given the greater opportunity for additional intervening factors to operate (cf. the similar possibility applying to the model's lower efficiency for Social Credit in Chapter 5).

A comparison of the joining models for both sexes reveals a number of similarities. For both men and women, age of joining is related to the proximate status variables, respondent's education and occupation of head of household. In both instances, higher levels of formal education are associated with early joining, and being in a household that at the time was headed by a business or professional person is linked with later joining. The degree of self-motivation displayed in joining a party is positively associated with both political club membership prior to beginning party work, and with being encouraged to join. Not surprisingly, level of self-motivation is negatively related to reports of taking into consideration the views of family, relatives, or co-workers in deciding to become a party worker.

There also are some differences in the models. For women only, level of education is inversely related to degree of self-motivation. For men, co-option is negatively linked to business or managerial occupational status at the time of joining. The expertise dimension of initial recruitment is greatest for women whose current party identification is the same as the dominant party of the neighborhood in which they were reared, but the converse is true of men. Although being reared in a politicized milieu is associated with early joining for both sexes, this relationship is discernibly stronger for women. The zero-order correlations between the politicized milieu variable and age of joining are -.31 for women and -.24 for men and the unstandardized regression coefficients in the age analyses are -1.4 and -.6 for women and men respectively.

The greater importance of placement in a politicized setting for women is suggested by the links between variables at various stages in the model. Although politicization has statistically significant linkages with several variables in the models for both sexes, there are proportionately more such linkages in the women's model. Particularly interesting are the links for women between being reared in a politicized environment and both organizational activity prior to joining and perceptions that others were interested in one's affiliating. These latter variables, in turn, have statistically significant relationships with age of joining and self-motivation respectively. The paucity of other linkages in the women's model makes the impact of a politicized environment bulk relatively larger for women than for men and reinforces the possibility that the political socialization experiences of that small group of women who become party officials are especially important in leading them in the direction of party work. Materials still to be discussed suggest that these experiences also may help keep women in political parties even if they do not obtain many of the rewards their male colleagues receive for equal work.

Career Development: Initial Reactions

There are strong indications in the data that women react much more positively to their initial involvement in parties than do men. Although virtually similar proportions of men and women report that the time and effort required of them by their parties were greater than they had anticipated, two-thirds of the women, as opposed to slightly over one-half of the men, report they enjoyed their first experience in party work more than they had expected. Women also tend to have more favorable attitudes to both their party colleagues and their organizations; 72.6% report that the efforts of their party colleagues "largely were effective" and 63.3% say the same thing of their party organizations. The proportions of men making similar observations were 62.4% and 53.5%, respectively. With regard to interparty differences in initial reactions to party work, Liberal women are least likely to report enjoying it; Social Credit women most often report that it took more of their time and effort than they had anticipated; and, initially, Conservative women are somewhat less enthusiastic about the effectiveness of their party organizations and fellow workers than are women in other parties.

Patterns of Career Development

Contrary to expectations that women would have interrupted their party organizational work more than men, we find instead that virtually similar proportions (49.9% and 47.4%) of men and women have had unbroken careers as officials. Among those officials who had interrupted their work,

13.3% of the men and 11.4% of the women had dropped out of their parties once but had been active for over three-quarters of the period between first affiliating and being interviewed. An additional 16.7% of the men and 23.7% of the women either had dropped out only once but had been active less than three-quarters of that time, or had had two or more gaps in their careers but had remained active more than three-quarters of the time since joining. The remaining officials (20.0% of the men, 17.6% of the women) had interrupted their careers two or more times and also had been active less than three-quarters of the time since first affiliating. During the 12.3 years that the average woman official has been affiliated with her party she has held 4.7 positions. The average male official has been involved in party affairs for 10.4 years but has held 5.3 positions. Men have held slightly more positions in a shorter period than have women in all parties but Social Credit. In the latter, 60% of the women but only 10% of the men have held six or more positions. Despite this discrepancy, the Social Credit men have held more high level positions: twice as many, on the average. This also is the case in the Conservative and New Democratic parties. Only in the Liberal party have women held approximately the same number of such positions as men (see the first section of Table 8.9).

At the time the interviews were taken 10% of the men and 3% of the women were members of their parties' national and provincial executive committees, and another 5.5% of the men but less than 1% of the women were then public officials or candidates for public office. Relatively similar proportions of men and women were members of their constituency executive committees or held poll captain and miscellaneous lower level positions. The only other substantial difference in the current positions of men and women is the considerably greater percentage of women holding paraparty positions, without which perhaps even fewer women would have been in the organizations. By a margin of approximately two to one, women also are less likely to have contended for an appointive or an elective public office in the past. However, women in the two minor parties have fared better in this regard than have their counterparts in the major parties largely because some 20% of the NDP women have stood for a local office while the same proportion of Social Credit women have been candidates for the House of Commons.

Despite these differences, women seemingly are as committed, at least insofar as commitment may be measured by work, as are the men. For example, the average woman official reports devoting 6.0 hours per week to party work in the period between election campaigns whereas the comparable figure for men is 5.3 hours. Similarly, the average number of weeks during the past two years in which party work required all of an official's time is 8.9

Table 8.9

An Overview of the Party Careers of Men and Women Officials

Structure of Party Careers	NDP Men	NDP Women	Liberal Men	Liberal Women	Conservative Men	Conservative Women	Social Credit Men	Social Credit Women	Total Men	Total Women
X̄ Years of party activity	11.7	11.4	9.3	11.3	12.5	12.8	8.0	14.2	10.4	12.3
X̄ Number of party and para-party positions held	5.2	4.6	5.5	4.2	6.2	4.7	3.6	5.5	5.3	4.7
X̄ Number of high level positions held	1.4	.61	1.1	1.2	1.4	.43	.68	.30	1.2	.66
% Who report having been contenders for an elective or appointive office during their careers	50.0	30.3	39.6	13.8	50.0	20.0	45.6	30.0	45.6	23.1
% Who currently are public officeholders or candidates	8.0	3.0	4.4	—	2.7	—	7.6	—	5.5	*
% Who currently are members of national or provincial party executive committees	10.2	3.0	8.3	6.9	16.1	—	5.0	5.0	10.0	3.4
% Who currently hold a para-party position	—	6.0	1.6	17.2	4.5	22.8	3.8	25.0	2.4	17.1
Commitment and Ascribed Influence										
X̄ Number of hours devoted to party work between campaigns	6.5	8.4	4.9	3.9	4.7	5.8	4.9	5.7	5.3	6.0
X̄ Number of weeks party work required almost all free time	14.6	18.8	9.6	3.6	5.7	6.5	7.9	4.7	9.8	8.9
% Who received 15 or more nominations as influential	11.0	3.0	6.6	—	5.3	2.8	1.3	5.0	6.7	2.6
X̄ Number of influence nominations received	4.9	1.8	4.2	.14	3.5	2.1	1.6	2.2	3.8	1.6

Distribution of Party Types										
% Who are Stalwarts	53.7	78.8	59.1	65.5	44.6	68.6	53.2	65.0	53.5	70.1
% Who are Insiders	26.5	15.2	26.5	31.0	35.7	28.6	32.9	25.0	29.5	24.8
% Who are Elites	19.9	6.1	14.4	3.4	19.6	2.9	13.9	10.0	16.9	5.1
Current Attitudes and Perspectives										
% Who find party work more enjoyable than when joined	53.7	57.6	37.9	39.2	32.1	54.3	34.2	70.0	40.7	53.8
Importance ranking of party *vis a vis* occupation, family, etc. (1=high, 9=low)	5.3	5.2	7.0	6.4	6.9	6.3	7.2	5.5	6.5	5.9
% Who expect to hold a higher level party office	43.4	27.3	50.3	31.0	40.2	22.9	39.2	15.0	44.5	24.8
% Who expect to hold a public office	64.7	33.3	60.2	31.0	53.6	22.9	57.0	50.0	59.4	32.5
% Who report they would most miss personal, social, or psychological satisfaction if they stopped party work	39.0	51.5	42.5	41.4	46.4	60.0	27.8	55.0	40.2	52.1
% Who report they would most miss opportunity for public service, influence public policy, etc., if they stopped party work	30.8	18.2	24.3	24.1	25.0	5.7	35.4	10.0	27.8	14.5
% Whose interest in party work had increased steadily and who never had contemplated quitting	61.8	69.7	54.1	75.9	56.3	74.3	58.2	75.0	57.3	73.5

*Less than 1%

for women and 9.8 for men. NDP women commit the most and Liberal women the least amount of their time to party work either during a campaign or in the periods between elections. Perhaps because they work less than do the women in other parties, and perhaps because almost one in five holds a paraparty position rather than one in the organization proper, Liberal women are distinguished by the lack of influence (in party affairs) attributed to them by their party colleagues. Indeed, despite the auspicious beginning to their careers and the fact that on average they have held as many high level party positions as men, fully twenty-six of the twenty-nine Liberal women do not receive even a single nomination for being influential. In contrast, five of the NDP women receive five or more nominations as do two of the Social Credit women. Overall, however, men receive almost three times as many such nominations as do women (see the second section of Table 8.9).

Given both their overall lack of influence and access to either public offices or highest level party organizational positions, there are disproportionately more Stalwarts and fewer Elites among the women as compared with the men. The ratio of Stalwarts to Elites among women is almost fourteen to one whereas among men it is approximately three to one. Women are represented more equitably in the Insider category, but still there are almost three times as many women Stalwarts as there are Insiders whereas among men the ratio is less than two to one.

The lack of status and recognition have not disenchanted the women with their parties, at least in terms of the expression of negative feelings.[21] In fact, when interviewed, they appear to have had more favorable attitudes toward party work than their male co-workers. Women more often report that their sense of accomplishment is "greater" and the time and effort required of them is "less" than when they joined. All women, but particularly those in the NDP, have a somewhat more favorable opinion of the effectiveness of their party organizations and colleagues. They more often find their work very enjoyable and almost three-fourths of them report that their interest in party activities has increased steadily over the years and that they never have contemplated quitting. If forced to stop working, however, a larger proportion of the women say they would miss the social and psychological gratifications that derive from party work. Regardless of party affiliation, women rank their parties higher vis-à-vis their occupations, religions, and communities than do men. And, they appear to be quite realistic about what they can expect in the future. Only a quarter of them, as opposed to some 45% of the men, expect to hold a higher level party office while only one-third, as opposed to almost 60% of the men, expect eventually to hold a public office.[22]

Many of the same differences that characterize male Stalwarts, Insiders, and Elites also distinguish the women in these groups. Because such a small number of women are Insiders and only a mere handful are Elites, systematic male-female comparisons are hazardous. However, a few examples will show that the pattern of differences discussed in Chapter 7 generally applies to both men and women. 12.1% of male Stalwarts begin party work in positions at or above the constituency level, whereas 26.7% of the Insiders and 29.1% of the Elites begin in these positions. Equivalent percentages for the women are 13.8%, 19.5%, and 33.3%. Average years of party activity also increase across types; from 9.9 years for male Stalwarts to 13.3 years for Elites. For women the equivalent figures are 10.3 and 15.3 years. Since length of party career is related to age, we may note that these differences persist when age is controlled. Thus, 33.5% of the male Stalwarts, 48.0% of the Insiders, and 58.1% of the Elites have had above average length careers relative to their age cohorts. For the women equivalent percentages are 30.5%, 58.6%, and 67.6%. The number of positions held in a party organization also increases across types regardless of sex—from 4.6 to 5.9 to 6.3 for men and from 4.9 to 6.6 to 7.0 for women. Similarly, average scores on the composite measure of participation in party work increase across types from −.342 to −.270 to +.278 for men, and from −.207 to −.099 to +.300 for women. Even expectations of holding a public office in the future vary by type regardless of sex; 50.4% of the male Stalwarts expect to hold public office in comparison to 63.3% of the Insiders and 70.7% of the Elites. The figures for the women are 25.6% (Stalwarts), 48.3% (Insiders), and 50.0% (Elites).

The patterns of differences that distinguish Stalwarts, Insiders, and Elites, regardless of sex, extend to some of the social and economic indicators that have been employed. Thus, among men, current SES scores rise by ten points (from 62.8 to 72.2) across types from Stalwart to Elite. Among women, scores rise by approximately the same amount, from 49.6 to 58.7. Annual family incomes also rise across types, although not as sharply among women as among men—an average of approximately $9,800 for the latter but only $3,900 for the former. Finally, the average number of voluntary organizations to which they belong increases from 2.1 to 2.6 to 3.0 for men and from 1.3 to 2.0 to 2.5 for women.

If the three types of officials have different clusters of attributes which distinguish women as well as men, why, one may ask, do we not find a larger proportion of women in the Elite and Insider categories? The material suggests a number of reasons. Discrimination against women in politics is rooted in the culturally conditioned norms concerning the roles the sexes ought to play in

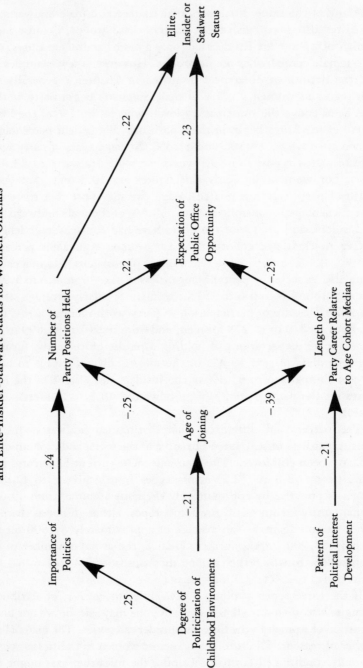

Figure 8.1
Path Model of Linkages Between Early Life Political Socialization Experiences
and Elite-Insider-Stalwart Status for Women Officials

society. In contemporary Western democracies both men and women are socialized to view politics as a set of activities that are far more appropriate for men than for women. In many countries even the franchise was extended to women only decades after it was enjoyed by men.[23] People also are socialized to believe that all men should work whereas the primary roles of women are those of wives and mothers. Thus, in preparation for their work, men more often have been extensively educated and consequently have held prestigious, high income-producing jobs. Conventional wisdom assumes and experience generally supports the assumption that a good education and a prestigious, well-paid position are conducive to effective political participation because they facilitate the development of necessary skills and resources, not to mention personal contacts with those active in politics. The principal consequences of these norms and conventional practices for the involvement of women in political parties are that: 1) from an early age women as a group are disadvantaged politically; 2) women, particularly upper status women, do not constitute as attractive a group of prospective party officials as do men, and so they are less frequently recruited for party work by the men who dominate parties; and 3) women, especially upper status women, are less frequently available for, or, for that matter, desirous of such work. Cultural norms, in brief, have reinforced a self-perpetuating process in most Western democracies, Canada included.[24]

If and when women do enter parties, they may be placed in paraparty or low level positions in the organization proper from which advancement is relatively difficult. Further, the often frivolous and menial activities that are associated with such positions tend to bore, frustrate, and anger women who have envisioned other types of party work and they look elsewhere for constructive and challenging activities. Pat Robertson's comment that, "the things they want you to do—telephoning, committee room work, typing, holding coffee parties—are not my idea of fun and excitement," exemplifies this response to men's ideas of what women ought to be doing for parties. That many well-educated women from the top of the status hierarchy either do not join parties or drop out of them as a consequence, may be inferred from the fact that the current socioeconomic status of women officials is considerably lower than that of male party colleagues. In this light, the women we studied may be regarded as "survivors" since they had attained the middle level organizational positions or achieved the degree of ascribed influence required to be included in this group of party officials. Even so, the pervasive influence of culturally rooted stereotypes regarding the appropriate political roles of men and women is manifest in the analysis which indicates that when all other factors (e.g., social status, structure of careers, commitment to party work) are controlled, sex remains a significant predictor of the placement of officials in Elite, Insider, and Stalwart positions (see Table 7.10).

The cultural stereotype that political activities are men's work probably operates most strongly in the area of candidate recruitment. Party selectors, perhaps acting on their own sex role conceptions or believing that the public will not vote for women, rarely select them as candidates for elective office. And, although precise data are unavailable, it would appear that when women are selected they usually are assigned hopeless constituencies to contest. Since they almost always are unable to win or even poll a substantial vote in hopeless races, the established belief that women are not attractive candidates is reinforced. Because so few women are recruited as candidates, even the career opportunities afforded a losing candidate, such as increased visibility or gratitude in the form of patronage for "showing the flag," are denied them.

The data, nonetheless, indicate that 30% of the women were able to move beyond Stalwart status. In our view, it is the political socialization experiences of the women Insiders and Elite that provide the psychological resources (e.g., attitudes, motivations, self-concepts) that enable them to overcome more general and pervasive sex roles stereotypes to which they also are exposed. Once in a party, these resources may sustain them—even if they are mired in low level positions for a time or assigned routine tasks to carry out—until they are able to rise to positions at or near the apexes of their organizations.

There is support for these assumptions in a path analysis that was conducted employing a model similar to the one used to explain joining a party (Chapter 5). The model was extended to encompass the period after joining and culminated in the assignment of women officials to Elite, Insider, and Stalwart positions. (The predictors included variables measuring attitudes toward party work, levels of commitment to party and extent of participation in party affairs.) Very briefly, analysis indicated that although early life political socialization experiences do not exert direct effects on whether women become Elites, Insiders, or Stalwarts, they do have several important indirect effects. By way of illustration, we found that being reared in a politicized environment is associated with the early joining of a party. The latter is linked to the number of party positions women hold and the number of years they have been active in their parties. Length of party service is linked to expectations of holding a public office which, in turn, have a direct effect on a career type. The number of party positions held also is linked to expectations of holding a public office. Moreover, it has an additional direct effect on whether women are Elites, Insiders, or Stalwarts (see Figure 8.1). In short, their political socialization experiences not only are important for bringing women into parties, but also have consequences for some of the factors that directly determine whether they will rise to Elite and Insider statuses within them, or remain Stalwarts during the course of their careers.

Summary

We have examined how social structure and political socialization help explain the presence of women in local party organizations. Since political roles tend to be thought of as male roles in Western democratic societies, it was suggested that those few women who do "make it" in political parties have to have many of the qualities that facilitate the political success of men. We find that the 117 women officials bring to their party organizations certain attributes and resources that not only vary markedly from those of women in the general public and nigh-dweller groups, but also, in many instances, from men.

An examination of their careers as party officials indicated that although the experiences and accomplishments of men and women are not markedly different, the ratio of Stalwarts to Elites among male officials is approximately three to one, while there are almost fourteen times as many Stalwarts as Elites among party women. Despite these distributional disparities, many of the differences that characterize Stalwarts, Insiders, and Elites who are men also apply to women. Path analysis suggests that the political socialization experiences of women officials indirectly affect whether they will rise to Insider and Elite statuses or remain Stalwarts. The political and social meaning of these and other aspects of party officials' careers, as well as their recruitment into party organizations, is the concern of our concluding chapter.

NOTES

1. Robert Putnam, *The Comparative Study of Political Elites*, pp. 32-33. In a study of two U.S. cities, Alan Booth reports that male dominance is most evident in instrumental organizations, a type that includes political parties. See "Sex and Social Participation," *American Sociological Review*, 37 (1972): 188-189.

2. The literature documenting low levels of female involvement in political activities other than voting is extensive. See, for example, Maurice Duverger, *The Political Role of Women* (Paris: UNESCO, 1955); Ingunn Nordeval Means, "Political Recruitment of Women in Norway," *Western Political Quarterly*, 25 (1972): 491-521, and "Women in Local Politics: The Norwegian Experience," *Canadian Journal of Political Science*, 5 (1972): 365-388; Edmond Costantini and Kenneth H. Craik, "Women as Politicians: The Social Background, Personality, and Political Careers of Female Party Leaders," in Marianne Githens and Jewel L. Prestage, eds., *A Portrait of Marginality: The Political Behavior of the American Woman* (New York: David McKay, 1977), pp. 221-240; Jeane J. Kirkpatrick, *Political Woman;* Gail Warshofsky Lapidus, "Political Mobilization, Participation, and Leadership: Women in Soviet Politics," *Comparative Politics*, 8 (1975): 90-118. See also Putnam,

The Comparative Study of Political Elites, p. 34. For data on female participation in Canadian politics see Van Loon, "Political Participation in Canada," 388-389; Clarke, et al., "Backbenchers," p. 217; Bird, et al., *Report of the Royal Commission on the Status of Women in Canada*, pp. 340-343.

3. For specific studies using various combinations of these types of explanations see, for example, Means, "Women in Local Politics;" and Kirkpatrick, *Political Woman*. See also Thelma McCormack, "Toward a Non-sexist Perspective on Social and Political Change," in Marcia Millman and Rosabeth Moss Kanter, eds., *Another Voice* (Garden City, N.Y.: Anchor Press/Doubleday, 1975), pp. 1-33; and the several essays in Githens and Prestage, *A Portrait of Marginality*. In focussing on socialization and social structural factors, we are not suggesting that conspiratorial or unequal inherent resources explanations do not deserve serious consideration. We simply are not able to assess their explanatory importance with only the data available.

4. Means, for example, argues that ". . . since politics has traditionally been defined as a masculine pursuit, one might argue that environmental stimuli must be stronger to penetrate the female's perceptual screen than that of the male, and that politically active women probably will be found to have a particularly high incidence of political role models in their backgrounds." "Women in Local Politics," p. 379.

5. For evidence of differences in the childhood political socialization of men and women see Herbert Hyman, *Political Socialization*, pp. 22-23, 80-81; Fred I. Greenstein, *Children and Politics* (New Haven: Yale University Press, 1965), pp. 107-127; Robert D. Hess and Judith V. Torney, *The Development of Political Attitudes in Children* (Garden City, N.Y.: Doubleday, 1968), pp. 199-222. Not all studies, however, disclose substantial sex differences. See, for example, David Easton and Jack Dennis, *Children in the Political System* (Toronto: McGraw-Hill, 1969), pp. 335-343; and Anthony M. Orum, et al., "Sex, Socialization and Politics," in Githens and Prestage, eds., *A Portrait of Marginality*, pp. 17-37.

6. Costantini and Craik, for example, in their study of California party officials, conclude that, "Politics for the male leader is evidently more likely to be a vehicle for personal enhancement and career advancement. but for the woman leader it is more likely to be a 'labor of love,' one where a concern for the party, its candidates, and its programs assume relatively greater importance." Costantini and Craik, "Women as Politicians," p. 238. See also Ralph H. Turner, "Some Aspects of Women's Ambition," *American Journal of Sociology*, 70 (1964): 271-285.

7. An even more sophisticated application of a structural analysis that would account for such patterns is offered in an essay by Rosabeth Kanter. Her analysis refers to the internal structure of organizations in which an identifiable group such as women can be present in variable proportions. In organizations in which they constitute less than 20% of the membership, she contends, women become "tokens." Their token status has specific consequences (of the type we shall examine) for both their roles and behavior in the organization. "Skewed Sex Ratios and Responses to Token Women," *American Journal of Sociology*, 82 (1977): 965-990. A report of research by Spangler, et al. tends to support Kanter's assumptions regarding the consequences of tokenism. See Eve Spangler, Marsha A. Gordon, and Ronald M. Pipkin, "Token Women: An Empirical Test of Kanter's Hypothesis," *American Journal of Sociology*, 84 (1978): 160-170.

8. Since there is such a relatively small number of women party officials we shall not report the results of significance tests.

9. Contrary to these findings Costantini and Craik report (p. 225) that the women party officials they studied derived from more prestigious social backgrounds

than did their male counterparts. However, despite their less favored origins, the men in the parties had achieved higher current statuses than the women (p. 224).

10. Means, "Political Recruitment of Women in Norway," 510-511.

11. Moshe Czudnowski, "Political Recruitment," pp. 204-205.

12. The parents of the party women more often than their nigh-dweller matches (85.5% vs. 65.0%) had partisan identifications.

13. David O. Sears, "Political Socialization," in Fred I. Greenstein and Nelson W. Polsby, eds., *Handbook of Political Science*, V. 4, p. 126.

14. Gabriel Almond and Sidney Verba, *The Civic Culture* (Princeton: Princeton University Press, 1963), chap. 12.

15. Among those who say they would work, if asked, women in the general public are more likely than men (21.4% compared to 11.3% for the highly politicized, and 16.8% versus 9.4% for the less politicized) to indicate they would do so for the enjoyment and pleasure. The women among the nigh-dwellers more often said they would work because it is a citizen's duty (43.8% of the women versus 26.5% of the men among the highly politicized, and 40.0% versus 29.2% among the less politicized). Men, in contrast, more often cite party loyalty and acting out of a personal interest in politics as reasons for working, if asked.

16. The tenor of the argument that is indicated by our data is also in accord with a variety of material in such sources as Kanter, "Skewed Sex Ratios," *passim*; and, Githens and Prestage, "Introduction," *A Portrait of Marginality*, pp. 3-10.

17. A comparison of men and women who joined at approximately the same ages shows that among people who join young (up to age 35) women are more likely than men to be married, whereas they are less likely to be married among those who join when they are older. Similarly, among those people who are married, the proportion with young children shifts increasingly in favor of men as age of joining increases. Both these trends accord well with the facts that in Canada: 1) women are younger than men when they marry and have their children, and 2) men die younger than women, leaving increasing surpluses of unmarried women in the higher age groups. These demographic patterns combined with the much earlier age of joining of men than of women go far in accounting for the gross differences observed.

18. By a margin of approximately two to one the women officials also give party-related reasons for remaining in a party (21.4% vs. 12.7% for the men) and for both joining and remaining in it (11.1% vs. 6.8%). Consistent with these data is the fact that the mean rankings of importance of party to the respondent on a nine point scale (1=highest, 9=lowest) are 5.9 for the party women, 6.5 for the party men, 7.5 for the nigh-dweller women, and 7.8 for the nigh-dweller men.

19. The mean canonical variate scores are:

	Men	Women
Self-motivation	.029	-.026
Expertise	.005	.000
Co-option	-.033	-.598

20. Possible substantive and methodological reasons for this pattern have been discussed in Chapter 5 and will not be reiterated here.

21. In interpreting these data it should be remembered that these women do not constitute a sample of all women who have joined party organizations at any level. If they did, it is likely that we would have found higher levels of disaffection.

22. This pattern of response is consistent with the assertion that women tend to sublimate their ambitions and to derive intrinsic rewards from activities in which

they engage. Men, in contrast, aggressively pursue material and status rewards. This and related arguments are developed more extensively in Turner, *passim*, and Costantini and Craik, pp. 236-239.

23. In Canada, women did not obtain the right to vote in federal elections until 1918. The provincial franchise was extended to Manitoba women in 1916 and to women in British Columbia in 1917. All other provinces except Quebec granted the franchise to women in the period 1916-1922. In Quebec, women did not obtain voting rights until 1940. See Terrance Qualter, *The Electoral Process in Canada* (Toronto: McGraw-Hill, 1970), p. 9. For data on the extension of the suffrage to women in several other Western political systems, see Stein Rokkan, *Citizens, Elections, Parties*, p. 33.

24. This is not to say that currently there is, in fact, an "iron law of andarchy" in political life. The past decade has witnesed a thoroughgoing reexamination of women's societal roles. A redefinition of these roles would seem to be a basic precondition for large scale increases in rates of female political participation. The extent to which such a redefinition will be achieved is difficult to forecast.

Chapter Nine

Citizens, Politicians, and Parties:
Retrospect and Prospect

The political elite in Canada is not representative of the population which it leads.

John Porter, *The Vertical Mosaic,* p. 388.

A political party is constantly plagued by the need to reconcile two divergent essentials: group solidarity and broad social representation.

Samuel Eldersveld, *Political Parties,* p. 47.

WE have tried to answer two questions. What factors induce a small proportion of the people in a democratic political system to accept and retain positions in local party organizations? Under what conditions will a fraction of this already small minority come to hold influential positions within these organizations or become contenders for public office? The questions are straightforward; however, they are not easily answered. A group of officials asked to explain why they joined their party may not wish to, or, indeed, may be unable to articulate some or all of their reasons. They may not even be aware of some of them. Political parties are such amorphous entities that mere entry into them, let alone progression through their hierarchy of positions, can be extremely difficult to describe systematically.

To acknowledge the difficulties involved is not to say they pose insurmountable obstacles. In dealing with them two complementary perspectives were utilized. The social structural perspective implies that a person's social and political statuses are affected strongly by the statuses, skills, and resources one is born with and acquires subsequently. The socialization perspective implies that a person who manifests attitudinal and behavioral patterns that are significantly different from those of other people was reared in a distinctive environment from which, over time, he or she acquired values, attitudes, and information that also differed. Informed by these perspectives, we hypothesized that party officials predominantly derive from a very small segment of middle and upper-middle class persons who have been reared, by average standards, in highly politicized milieux. The values, attitudes, and interests that members of this small segment of the population acquire as a consequence of the concatenation of social and political factors in their environments, if combined with a favorable set of contextual conditions, lead them to launch careers in political parties.

In trying to explain why and how a small portion of this already small group of people attain positions of prestige and influence within a political party, we suggested that although the magnitudes of the proportions of each type might vary by party and with local conditions, party organizations will be composed of three types of officials. Members of the first type, Stalwarts, occupy the lower and middle levels of the squat and truncated pyramidal structures into which Canadian parties are organized. The second type, Insiders, hold the highest level positions in local hierarchies and have considerable influence in party affairs ascribed to them by colleagues. The third type, Elites, not only can be distinguished by their possession of highest level organizational positions and substantial amounts of ascribed influence, but also by the fact that they most often are current holders or current or past contenders for a variety of appointive and elective public offices.

We further hypothesized that different clusters of attributes would distinguish each type of party official: Stalwarts would be men and women whose backgrounds and current social statuses were somewhat lower than those of their colleagues; a disporportionate number would be women; they would be less committed to party work than would Insiders and Elites. Elites would be people of high social statuses and backgrounds who were reared in especially politicized settings, and who had served their parties faithfully and effectively for long periods of time. Insiders would tend to occupy intermediate positions between the Stalwarts and the Elites on various social status, political socialization, and political career continua.

Retrospect

Chapters 2 and 3 largely were given over to testing our notions about the backgrounds and statuses of people who do and do not join political parties. Aggregate comparisons revealed that party officials more often are long time residents of their communities, native-born, middle-aged, Protestants, males, and of Anglo-Celtic ethnic origins. Moreover, as a group, party officials are drawn disproportionately from upper socioeconomic strata. Indeed, their mean occupational prestige scores are only marginally inferior to those of MPs in the 28th Parliament. Aggregate social and demographic differences between party officials and their nigh-dweller matches, as expected, are more modest. More important, however, is that despite discernible interparty differences, no party's cohort of officials approximates the socioeconomic composition of the general public. Middle and upper-middle class elements of the population always are overrepresented.

A systematic examination of several basic features of the political socialization of party officials, nigh-dwellers, and the general public revealed substantial aggregate differences among them. Party officials tend to report earlier initial ages of political awareness and psychological identification with a political party. Particularly impressive are differences in political interest development patterns. Regardless of the age period examined, party officials are much more likely to report increasing levels of interest than either nigh-dwellers or members of the general public. As a group, party officials also report having been reared in highly politicized milieux. By the same token, substantial minorities of the nigh-dwellers and general public also were reared in more or less similar political environments. Because they were, and because political activities are not carried out solely by party members, in Chapter 3 we examined the social and political backgrounds and current statuses of nigh-dwellers and members of the general public who report engaging in at least one electoral campaign activity going beyond voting.

We found, especially among the nigh-dwellers, that people who participate in such activities derive disproportionately from middle class backgrounds and have been reared in relatively more politicized environments. They currently are members of the middle and upper-middle classes and are psychologically implicated in the political process in ways that are not common to fellow citizens who confine their political participation to voting in periodic elections. Parties are fairly selective in their requests for the public's help. The parents of people approached by representatives of the parties more often are native born and of Anglo-Celtic origin. Those approached are more frequently high income earning members of a profession, or owners and executives of businesses. At various periods of their lives they also have been interested in and more informed about politics and public affairs than have people whose assistance the parties have never solicited. Particularly striking is the fact that all parties, including the NDP, frequently appeal for help to people who describe themselves as having only weak partisan attachments. In fact, approximately one-half of these nigh-dwellers and about forty percent of the general public claimed that at the time their help was solicited they were Independent Liberals, -Conservatives, and so forth.

The reasons people offer to explain why they would or would not engage in these activities appear partially to reflect, and, in fact, they well may be consequences of, the distinctive organizational features and electoral activities of the parties. For example, the majority of responses to a "why did you stop working" question are that they simply had "dropped out" or "had not been approached again" or had been asked at an "inopportune" time. These are responses that could be expected from people who had done something on behalf of an organization that did not compensate them financially and only asked for their help infrequently and at widely spaced intervals.

⁕ /In contrast to what might have been expected, responses reflecting negative attitudes toward political parties and politics as a process are offered with somewhat greater frequency by members of that segment of the public which had been reared in the most politicized environments. We inferred from this that although relatively extensive exposure to politics and political figures does generate affect, it can be negative as well as positive. People so exposed, however, are unlikely to be indifferent/Negative feelings may induce people who otherwise would be grist for the party organizational mills to be firmly resolved to have nothing to do with them. Moreover, when people who are sensitized to politics do become involved in some capacity during an electoral campaign, their experience may be such as to make them extremely chary of any repetition. Another reason people may not work for political parties is simply that *they are not asked*. Not only are nigh-dwellers asked for their help more frequently than members of the general public but also nigh-dwellers who are friends and acquaintances of party officials are more frequently solicited for assistance than are strangers. Others who *are asked* and who do respond positively may not mind being involved intermittently in electoral campaigns, but may be reluctant to establish a more permanent affiliation. Members of the general public may feel they lack the social status to be comfortable in organizations that predominantly are composed of upper-middle and middle class people. Nigh-dwellers may lack the motivation to affiliate which is presumably provided by a strong sense of partisanship.

Chapter 4 focused on those people who do join political parties. A case-by-case matching of party officials and nigh-dwellers was undertaken to pinpoint factors that could be pertinent in the former's affiliation. The party officials start with only minimal socioeconomic advantages over the nigh-dwellers, but at the time of joining the initial status differences between the two groups have widened considerably. An evaluation of the role that political socialization plays in explaining why people join parties reaffirmed the importance of spending one's childhood and adolescent years in a more politicized environment. Since the comparisons were between each party official and his or her matching nigh-dweller, the socialization factor may operate in addition to whatever special social and economic resources the party officials now have as members of an advantaged stratum of the population.

In one sense only the party officials themselves could explain how and why they joined a political party. Consequently, we examined their responses to a battery of questions on the "whys" and 'hows" of joining. As a group the party officials diverge considerably from a model of committed politicians consumed with politics, ideologies, and programs. Some obviously are. However, for many joining seems to be a response to a decision made by others that they are needed. And, for still others, it appears to be a personal act whose time has come, but by drift as much as by compulsion.

With regard to the how of joining, analyses indicate that some officials started in high organizational positions and performed exciting tasks that would seem interesting and attractive to most outsiders. The majority did neither. There are, nonetheless, notable interparty differences in the proportions of officials who initially attain high organizational positions and perform glamorous party tasks. Social Credit places the largest proportion of their officials in these positions; Liberals the smallest; Conservative and New Democratic placements are in between. A number of tests of the hypothesis that cronyism is an important mechanism resulting in the assignment of friends to high positions indicate this is not the case. If anything, the relationship between party recruiter and recruitee is exploitative rather than rewarding. More generally, the parties go about the business of acquiring new members much as do other voluntary organizations. People are sometimes co-opted, personal contacts are traded on, and, when these do not suffice, the prospect of holding a high party office or engaging in interesting work is held out as an inducement to join.

Since initial recruitment into party work is both a subtle and complex process, in Chapter 5 canonical correlation and regression analyses were used to comprehend it more fully and to ascertain the manner in which a variety of antecedent and proximate social and political variables affected joining. In addition to age of affiliation, canonical analyses identified three other components, self-motivation, expertise, and co-option. A causal model employing seventeen social structural and political socialization variables was used to explain the experiences of all officials and of those in each of the parties. Between 40% and 60% of each party's variation in joining was accounted for by the model.

Liberal officials from higher social class backgrounds are more likely to have affiliated initially at a somewhat later age than their lower status colleagues and they also are less likely than the latter to have been co-opted. Co-option is more adequately explained for Conservative party officials than for others, bringing into the party a number of people who are politically oriented but whose familial and occupational situations seemingly are not conducive to joining. Conservatives who join at earlier ages are more likely to have law degrees and to have come from families whose fathers enjoyed high status occupations. They tend to have been involved in other nonparty or paraparty political groups prior to affiliating with the organization proper. By and large, patterns for the NDP are much like those for the Liberals. And, despite the NDP's ideological appearance and appeal—and in accord with an earlier observation that it also makes use of the services of people who are political leaners—the network of paths suggests that the party recruits as experts a number of older persons who have been prevailed upon to switch allegiances. For the Social Credit party, recruitment in its most classic sense of a "recruitment officer" appears to be central. Primarily, party agents either recruit some politically interested younger people who affiliate to continue previous non- or paraparty political activities, or else they look to supporters of other parties who are recruited for some special talents they possess.

The outcomes of the analyses were particularly satisfactory in view of the constraints implicit in the procedures, measurement imprecision, and the sharp restrictions on the number of explanatory factors included in the model.[1] Variables at every stage of personal development contribute to explain separate components of the joining experience. Although they are not always direct in their effects, political socialization events and experiences are important. In fact, it appears that a politicized early life environment influences not only who becomes a party official, but also how initial affiliation occurs.

In Chapter 6 we operationalized our view that party organizations contain three types of officials, Stalwarts, Insiders, and Elites. The typology is based on three organizational properties of local parties: the influence dimension, the extraparliamentary or internal structure, and the public dimension of office-holders and candidates. In all parties there is a strong relationship among these dimensions; leaders who are current or former candidates for public office or who hold highest level organizational positions also are regarded as the most influential members of their respective parties. These relationships provide the empirical support on which the three-dimensional typology rests.

In Chapter 7 an attempt was made to account for which officials were in the Elite, Insider, and Stalwart categories. Elites start life with some status advantages which, together with certain favorable political socialization factors, seemingly lead to success in their party careers. Although there are minor exceptions, in each of the parties Elites have the longest careers, hold the most positions, and have worked hardest for their parties during and in the periods between electoral campaigns. Conversely, Stalwarts have the shortest careers, hold the fewest positions, and have given the least amount of time to their parties. As anticipated, the Insiders generally occupy intermediate positions. The overall power of several social structural, political socialization, and party career variables to distinguish among the three types was investigated by multiple discriminant analysis which indicated in each party that such variables correctly group from 60% to 70% of the Elites, Insiders, and Stalwarts.

Some 19% of the 625 officials were women. In Chapter 8 we focused on two questions: 1) how does one explain the fact that there are approximately four times as many men as women in the four parties? and 2) how is it that the already underrepresented women are further underrepresented in the Insider and Elite and relatively overrepresented in the Stalwart categories of the party hierarchies? Women bring to their parties certain attributes and resources that vary markedly from those of women in the nigh-dweller and general populations. Moreover, on virtually every indicator, the party women also are more of a socioeconomic elite than are men in the general public. Nonetheless, comparisons of the early socialization experiences of men and women in parties and in the nigh-dweller and general publics suggest that sex-related socialization differences begin relatively early in life. Comparisons also suggest that as a group higher status women either are not as available to parties as women of somewhat lesser status or do not comprise as attractive a recruitment pool as do higher status men. In part, this may account for the underrepresentation of such women in parties. In comparison to men and women nigh-dwellers and members of the general public, many women in parties experienced extraordinarily intense political socialization. Their presence in political parties also may be explained by the fact that, of those who had politically active parents, the majority of the latter both were supportive and served as positive role models.

One reason women were underrepresented among the Insiders and the Elites of their parties is that one in five was in a paraparty group rather than the party proper.[2] Although the establishment of "special" organizations and positions may bring women into parties, their frequent confinement to them may induce some to abandon their careers and thus reduce their number. Another reason for women's underrepresentation may be the idiosyncratic and chauvinistic preferences and practices of current party leaders, the great majority of whom are men. In the Liberal party not one woman is a public officeholder or a candidate for a federal or provincial elective office. In the Conservative party, women have held relatively few high level positions and not one of them is a member of the provincial or national executive committee. In the New Democratic and Social Credit organizations a similar picture is presented. More important than any particularistic practices within individual party units is the historic pattern of discrimination that has existed against women in politics. As a group, women are ascribed little influence in party affairs; they hold few high level positions in their party hierarchies; and only a mere handful ever have been contenders for even local public office, let alone those at provincial or federal levels.

Invariably, an exploratory investigation will raise questions as well as answer them. Some are obvious. They have to do with whether the results obtained would continue to hold in other times and places, or if different strata of the population were involved. Although our parallel data for American party officials and a number of other studies of political participation in democratic societies make us confident that our findings and conclusions are generalizable to other environments, more precise specification of their time and place relevance obviously would require replication of this study. However, rather than speculate about these matters, we should like to note here four issues that (if given further attention) could considerably enhance understanding of the recruitment, composition, and activities of party leadership.

Threading through the analyses are discussions conducted in terms of the *interplay* of both political and social factors. Thus, on the one hand we have considered the roles of components of social structure such as economic position and sex in some depth because public beliefs and prejudices about their relative importance can open or foreclose opportunities to occupy political positions. To an extent, such factors are part of a "power elite" explanation of participation in the leadership structures of parties. The argument is that the larger the number of statuses giving access to power that are held by a person, the greater the likelihood of holding another position of potential power and importance (i.e., a high party or public office). On the other hand we also have considered the impact of social networks of relationships—in the family as well as those with friends and peers—because these factors seem to be part of a "social" explanation of participation. Thus, we have observed that nigh-dwellers who are friends and acquaintances of party officials are more often recruited for part-time work in campaigns and that at times the officials are co-opted into holding party offices by good friends and close acquaintances. The frequent absence of ideological feelings among the party officials coupled with reports that many derive social and psychological gratification from their party work also lend force to this social explanation. They suggest that although the locus and consequences of most functionaries' activities are political, much of their meaning is social. Since only a minority of those who, on a status basis alone, are most likely to engage in party organizational activities actually do so, it would appear that greater understanding of both the tendency to join party organizations and the actual nature of party work can come from exploring both the social and political dynamics of key social relationships among networks of persons in, or likely to be in, parties.

A second matter that may be pursued profitably is the varying consequences that intensive political socialization can have for people. The analyses of joining and of nonjoining indicate that one consequence of being reared in a highly politicized environment is a strong motivation to become involved

in politics and to do whatever it takes to get involved. Alternatively, it
✓ simply may make one ready to become involved should circumstances present
the opportunity. For a much smaller group of people, intense political socialization can have an opposite effect: that of avoiding participation for what
seem to be good and sufficient reasons./A formidable but rewarding task in
some future analysis would be to predict and explain alternative outcomes for
people who had undergone similarly intense political socialization—but
before rather than after its effects had been revealed by their behavior.

Growing up in a highly politicized environment may have different
outcomes because that experience is embedded in wider social contexts. Also,
these contexts can vary markedly in character over time. In Canada, the
1920s were marked by unstable economic growth and social change. Many
people immigrated to the country, while almost as many left for the United
States. The 30s were the period of the Depression; the 40s of World War II;
and the 50s a period of substantial economic growth and widespread pros-
perity. It is quite possible, despite any apparent similarity in developmental
experiences, that the character of the times interacts with the immediate
personal experiences of the developing child to produce different orientations
to party participation. This possibility is difficult to explore because the data
analyzed here provide only small numbers of cases for dealing with such
possible age-time combinations.

One further issue arises from constraints imposed by the strategy adopted
to conduct this investigation. We did not secure information on those who
might be termed "dropouts": people who had entered and participated in
party organizations, as did our respondents, but who had terminated their
involvement with them. A number of unrelated issues might have been
clarified with such material. By way of illustration, the significance of the
small number of Liberal women officials who entered their party in high level
positions might be clearer if we knew more about the entry points of women
who had dropped out of that organization.[3] More generally, career development might be better understood if there were data on dropouts. They are
difficult to obtain for two reasons: the loose and flexible structure of the
organizations themselves (and, hence, of record keeping) and the concept of
party organizational membership. People who may not have been active in an
organization for a number of years still may continue to think of themselves
or to be thought of by others as "party members." However, if such data
were obtainable, the analyst would be able to determine, at a particular point
in time, who actually is in each level of a party organization; who comes and
goes as time passes; how long people in different strata generally remain
active; and, finally, for what reasons people terminate their affiliation.

Evaluation

We now would like to stand back from our data and assess their relevance for a fuller understanding of political parties and their place in a democratic political system and society. A number of times we have observed that the /recruitment of officials and their subsequent activity can be comprehended in terms of explanations that apply to other voluntary organizations/ However, it labors the obvious to note that political parties also differ in a variety of significant ways from local Red Cross chapters, Chambers of Commerce, or Rotary Clubs. The most important difference is that political parties, unlike the latter kinds of voluntary associations, exercise substantial control over the pathways to political power; in Canada these pathways lead to judgeships and other political appointments as well as to membership in a provincial legislature or the federal parliament.[4] A very high proportion of contenders for these positions are drawn from the ranks of local party officials such as those who are the subjects of this volume, and virtually all successful candidates for elective offices are nominated by local parties.[5] Since activity on behalf of a political party can lead in some instances to highly visible, prestigious, not to mention politically powerful offices, one might asume that thousands of people figuratively would be knocking down doors of party organizations in their efforts to gain entrance. Obviously, this is not the case. At any given time only a small fraction of the population of Canada or of other Western democracies avail themselves of the opportunity to work for these organizations. Our study suggests three fundamental interacting factors that help explain why more people do not become party officials.

First,/the political socialization process in Canada does not encourage extensive involvement in party affairs. It is no great exaggeration to assert that ⁄the only participatory norm to which Canadians are urged to adhere is to "vote for a candidate of your choice." At best the kind of political socialization experiences to which the great majority are exposed help generate ambivalent attitudes toward political parties and activities. Second, party leaders use a variety of subtle and not so subtle techniques to constrain and channel public participation in their organizations. Third, the structural peculiarities of parties and their goals as organizations limit opportunities to enjoy careers within them and thus further inhibit and restrain political participation beyond voting/ Let us consider each of these factors in detail.

/In contrast to authoritarian and totalitarian systems,/Canada and other democratic societies ostensibly provide their citizens with virtually unlimited opportunities to participate in their political systems/ In addition to voting in elections, citizens can try, either as individuals or as members of organized groups, to influence both the content of policy decisions and the manner of their implementation. Ordinary citizens, if they choose, can offer themselves as candidates in elections or they can join and participate in the efforts of parties to elect candidates. However, with respect to politicization, democracies tend to be politically "cool." Unlike the situation in totalitarian systems, most citizens are not being continually mobilized to support the regime./People are not constantly bombarded by political stimuli emanating from a variety of official organs of the state. There are no equivalents to the "Octoberists" or "Young Pioneers." There are no arms of the state through which even preschool age children are exposed to political symbols, myths, highly favorable information about the state and its current leaders and policies, as well as interpretations of history in which both the country and political system are invariably cast as the "good guys."[6] There is no official party which ambitious people must join, and whose frequent meetings and indoctrination sessions they must attend if they are to obtain or retain desirable occupational positions. In Canada there are not even the kinds of parties found in some Western European countries that provide their members with recreational and cultural opportunities, together with large dollops of ideology.[7]

Of course, Canadian public schools are organs of the state and they are involved in the political socialization of citizens in the sense that they provide politically relevant information about the society and its key institutions and processes. All primary school children are given courses in Canadian history and many high schools currently offer one or more "civics" courses. Largely because of their sensitivity to possible charges of partisanship and political bias, however, school teachers and administrators take care to insure that the orientations of such courses are both nonpartisan and apolitical.[8] For example, stress is placed on the necessity of filling political offices with the "best man for the job, regardless of party." One report of a nationwide study of the effects similar courses have on high school students in the United States concluded that "there is a lack of evidence that the civics curriculum has a significant effect on the political orientations of the majority of American high school students."[9] In our view, however, the effects of such courses may be threefold.

By concentrating on descriptions of the *status quo* these courses may contribute to acceptance of the notion that politics, political activity, and public offices are reserved for men rather than for women. In so doing, they help discourage and exclude approximately one-half of the population from political activity other than voting. They in effect perpetuate cultural stereotypes regarding the impropriety of women holding political offices. By treating partisan controversy as a forbidden topic they may inadvertently develop ambivalent feelings toward politics as a process and toward political parties and their officials. On the one hand they may help instill a feeling that political parties may be instrumentally valuable for the functioning of a democratic political system. On the other hand they may contribute to the view that there is something not quite respectable, indeed, there is something a little shady about party politics as a process. By couching discussions of government largely in the guise of administrative processes, they may develop simplistic and stereotyped notions about how the political system really works.[10] It might be argued that the social science courses that are taught in Canadian universities help rectify at least the latter two conditions. If so, their ameliorative impact extends only to that very small segment of the population which enrolls in these courses.[11] For the great majority of Canadians exposure to formal political socialization by an instrument of the state is confined largely to elementary and high school.

Nevertheless, a variety of agents of socialization other than schools operate in democratic societies. Among the most important of these suggested by our material in Chapter 2 is the family. Most Canadian families, however, are not consciously involved in politically socializing their members. If we can extrapolate from a comment made by Pat Robertson to the effect that "politics were not the kind of stuff you discussed over the dinner table," even upper-middle class families are not overly interested in or concerned with discussing the conduct of public affairs or the fortunes of political parties with their children. Since people frequently do not receive the kind of compensatory political stimulation from their families/that might make up for the lack of direct political socialization from formal agents—stimulation which might encourage their interest and facilitate an intensive subsequent involvement in politics— there is a sense of inevitability in the fact that political participation usually is limited to voting. The minority who do receive such stimulation, however, have a very substantial head start in a journey along the path that ultimately can lead to positions of political power.

By way of illustrating the ambivalent attitudes most members of the public have toward political parties and politics fully 90% of both the nigh-dwellers and general public said, in assessing the role political parties play in keeping the system of government going, that parties either are "absolutely essential" (50%) or that they "help" (40%). Similarly, over one-half of both groups ascribed the commendable motive of trying to "improve government" to people who are active in political parties. Nonetheless, both considered political parties the least important of nine institutions and activities central to their personal lives. Moreover, well over 40% said they would not work for a party if asked, and gave as their reasons that they "disliked politics and politicians."

Further depicting the ambivalent feelings of many citizens for politics generally and parties in particular is the fact that although both nigh-dwellers and members of the general public ascribe altruistic reasons to people who work in parties, approximately 40% also say that these people do so for "personal material gains" and 10% because they are "pressured" to do so, the implication of the latter response being that party work is not something a normal person would engage in of his or her own volition. The very limited number of responses given to questions on: a) why people work in political parties; b) whether they themselves would work if asked; and c) why those who had worked in the past had stopped, illustrate the relatively shallow and unsophisticated perceptions most people have of parties. The stereotypic nature of these perceptions is reflected in the fact that very similar proportions of both the nigh-dwellers and the general public gave the same kinds of responses to these questions. As for the prevailing norm that politics are a man's game and that women should confine their activities outside the home to more appropriate forms of association, there is no need to recapitulate the material presented in the last chapter.

Instead, we will elaborate on some of the consequences that relatively intensive political socialization can have for people in a politically cool society. These are probably best illustrated in Chapter 3. Those who came from highly ✳ politicized backgrounds were more likely to have been asked to do something for a party by one of its representatives. They also were more likely to have responded positively to this request, and to say that they would be similarly positive if their assistance should be solicited again. Comparisons of the political socialization experiences of party officials, nigh-dwellers, and members of the general public, and in case-by-case matching of the officials with nigh-dwellers also illustrate the significance of early life political socialization. These comparisons make three things clear. The officials were reared in far more politicized environments than were members of the control groups and appear to have been sensitive to a variety of socializing agents such as school and peer groups. The more politicized environments in which the party officials had been reared seemed to have stimulated their earlier political development. They report earlier ages of political awareness and initial psychological identification with a political party, more durable partisan attachments, and the development of an early and sustained high level of interest in politics. Officials reared in politicized environments also responded to their experiences more positively than did members of the public reared in relatively similar settings. Indeed, the more politicized segments of the public are also more likely to have referred negatively to political parties and politics in explaining why they would not work for a party if asked.

Another illustration of the importance of intense early political socialization is afforded by women party officials. Although both the nigh-dweller and general public women tend to have been reared in the same sorts of less politicized milieux as were the men, not only were the women party officials ultimately more politicized than the nonparty women, but the effects of these experiences seemingly are greater for them than for the men in the control samples. Especially important for the party women is the fact that their families more frequently appeared to support and encourage their interest in politics. It seems reasonable to infer that this support inculcated in them a belief that political participation, even for women, was both natural and desirable.

The presence of four times as many men as women in the parties is one pertinent illustration of our observation that party officials channel and limit the public's participation. There are numerous other illustrations. Our material, for example, indicates that the parties tend more often to ask upper-middle class people for their assistance. Party officials also more often sought the assistance of people brought up in politicized environments. Since the kind of political environment in which a person was reared is hardly visible to the naked eye, we may infer that this is a rather specialized selective process in which officials frequently look to friends and draw on personal information about those whose help they solicit. [12]

Why should parties which seemingly are in immediate need of as much help as possible at election time be so selective? There are a number of possible reasons, three of which strike us as especially important. First, party officials, like members of other voluntary associations, like to associate and work with individuals who are likely to share their values, interests, and perspectives: people, in short, who are like themselves and who, therefore, are likely to respond positively to their solicitations. Second, there is an association in Western societies between the social status of individuals and judgments regarding their competence; the assumption is that individuals of high status almost by definition also are competent. A major exception to this presumptive relationship is the group that comprises some 50% of the population, women. Third, in historical perspective, parties are institutions of relatively recent origin. [13] Even in Western democracies, the feeling persists that parties divide a society. (In the words of Lord Halifax, "the best party is but a king of a conspiracy against the rest of the nation." [14]) They represent and articulate particularistic as opposed to national interests, and at least some of their officials use the political process to feather their own financial nests.

One way of trying to overcome these lingering attitudes is to involve the very "best" people in party activities. Relatedly, their desire for respectability and acceptance also may explain why, with the exception of Communist parties in Western Europe, party officials who most frequently become electoral candidates are overwhelmingly well-educated, middle-aged, male professionals and businessmen.[15] It will be recalled that in every party the Elites and Insiders who make up the candidate "pool" are much better educated and more frequently high income earning members of the professional and business communities than are Stalwarts. In short, from their perspectives current party officials may be acting quite rationally when they limit their requests for even temporary assistance, not to mention full-time help, to individuals whom they feel are most likely to share their attitudes and values.

The unique structural features of parties, some of which were commented on in the first chapter, act as additional constraints on the public's participation. Most of the tasks pertinent to the goal of electing candidates to public office are routine and often boring; they require little, if any, intellectual effort. Certainly, most of these tasks would neither fire the imaginations of prospective joiners nor would their repeated performance be likely to maintain the enthusiasm for organizational work of many officials, especially those at or near the bottom of a party hierarchy.

The squat and truncated pyramidal form of local organizations is a handicap to upward mobility in party careers. Frequently there are no distinct federal and provincial party organizations. When coupled with the fact that involvement in federal politics does not bestow markedly greater prestige on people than does participation in provincial politics, these factors combine to restrict significantly opportunities to enjoy careers in Canadian party organizations. It is difficult and in some areas impossible to begin party work in positions or in an organization primarily concerned with electing party candidates to municipal offices. One cannot use these as springboards to positions concerned with electing provincial legislators, and, then, "graduate" to positions or to a separate organization where efforts focus on parliamentary elections.[16] But it is precisely the possibility of a systematic and relatively continuous upward movement through a hierarchy of positions that attracts many people to, and keeps them in, complex organizations. Deprived, more or less, of this possibility, people may be less eager to engage in routine, uninteresting work for which they almost never receive immediate tangible compensation. More important, at least in a political party, people may be far less willing to adopt a long-term perspective and to defer immediate gratification in hope of later rewards. Such a perspective is vital because there can be only one winner in any electoral contest and hence only one set of officials who can enjoy the immediate gratification of being a part of a successful group effort.

At an individual level, the major future-oriented rewards a party has to offer are candidacy or appointment to public office or perhaps the proffering of a government contract. However, since these are only intermittently available to a relatively few officials, parties must rely heavily on purposive and solidary incentives to motivate their functionaries to continue their careers.[17] It has been argued that these incentives are less effective than are material rewards.[18] Thus, it is hardly surprising that scholars have reported that contemporary party organizations are characterized by substantial turnover of personnel, frequent interruptions of party careers, and sharp variations in the levels of personnel commitment and effectiveness.[19] Our own investigation is in agreement. Even though ours is a group of active party officials, the great majority of whom hold middle and top level positions in their organizations, a substantial proportion had interrupted their careers for varying periods of time and they differed sharply in their commitment of effort to party work. The great majority cited purposive reasons for both joining and staying in politics; substantial numbers also mentioned solidary and political incentives. Again, however, it is important to remember that we were studying active officials. Had we been able to extend our investigation to ex-officials, we might have found that purposive and solidary types of incentives did not provide sufficient motivation for them to continue their party careers.

Although the distinctive structural characteristics of local parties and the frequently mundane nature of most of the required tasks combine to limit and discourage many people from joining or staying in parties, these same factors can be used to motivate and encourage the participation of a smaller group whom we have labeled Insiders and Elites. The organizational amorphousness of parties such as these and the fact that statutory laws take no official notice of them provide the flexibility and latitude that permit a variety of *ad hoc* special arrangements. Leaders are free to place new, particularly desirable recruits at any level of the hierarchy. They can create new or parallel organizational positions and they can reassign functions from one position to another. Our study has shown that many of the future Insiders and Elites were part and parcel of the same social and political networks as current high ranking party officials. They knew and were known to them. They more often were placed initially in higher level organizational positions and given interesting tasks to perform, and they more often enjoyed successful careers. Since success helps generate feelings of gratification and expectations of future success, after entry Insiders and Elites commit substantial time and effort to their party work. They stay in their parties and alternate between holding a variety of high party officers and being their parties' standard bearers in elections.

They help decide the candidacies of colleagues and hold a virtual monopoly on intraparty influence. Because they do, they ultimately decide who their successors will be, thereby perpetuating the character of their organizations.

This is not to say that local parties are closed shops. Democratic norms and conventions prescribe openness of entry and bring, unbid, a certain number of politically interested, talented, and ambitious individuals. Many of those who are willing to work and who are effective will rise to Insider and Elite status because all voluntary associations, political parties included, need the services of able and committed people if they are to survive, let alone achieve their goals. It is clear that strong commitment is rewarded in all parties, even though the relative importance of specific indicators of commitment may vary.[20] Organizational needs notwithstanding, current party officials still can and do act as gatekeepers, normally determining who gets in, who moves up, and who moves out.

The low level of politicization—the political coolness of Canadian society—greatly facilitates the ability of party elites to serve as personnel gatekeepers. Given the relative absence of any sustained and intensive politicization, other than in the exceptional family, and the disinterest or, at best, ambivalent feelings many people have about political parties, politicians, and politics as a process, even those in the upper-middle class often have not the slightest desire to do anything political other than vote. Thus, more than half of the general public and four out of every ten nigh-dwellers either already had refused to work for a party or said they would have refused if their assistance had been solicited. More important, perhaps, is that most people are never asked to participate. Additionally, those people who did do anything more than vote for a party when their help was *not requested* may be discouraged either by party officials or by the experience itself from doing so again. That party officials may not roll out a red carpet to welcome unsolicited part-time helpers is suggested by the fact that only about a third of the general public and less than a fifth of the nigh-dwellers who gave unsolicited help said they would do so again in the future. For most such people, then, one experience was enough!

Prospect

If the ways in which political institutions function affect the public's perceptions of and attitudes toward them, it could be argued that parties ought to work diligently to refurbish their images. This study has suggested that at best the public's attitudes are ambivalent. Other investigations are even more pessimistic; they have indicated that many of the public's members view parties, indeed, the whole political system, with remarkably jaundiced eyes.

Mildred Schwartz has noted that during the '60s Canadians seemed to be much more disillusioned with their government than Americans were with theirs, despite the dislocations that were being experienced in the United States.[21] A 1974 national election study has suggested that the attitudes of Canadians did not change much in the early '70s. By way of illustration, the score of an average Canadian on a 0-4 scale of political efficacy was only 2.1, with the average scores of people in five of the ten provinces being lower. In a concluding evaluation of Canadians' images of their country, the authors observe that, "Examples of Canadians' distaste for politics are numerous. . . . [T]he general comments on politics were 33% positive and 52% negative. The general comments on politicians were a staggering 78% negative in tone. Politicans are generally seen by Canadians as 'terrible,' as 'crooked,' as doing a 'bad job,' as 'out for themselves,' as 'wasting the money we pay in taxes,' as 'serving the big interests,' and as 'generally ineffectual.' Government has the same image; attitudes towards it are 75% negative. Similarly, the *general comments on parties are 78% negative.*"[22]

It is interesting to speculate on whether these attitudes might change for the better if Canadians were socialized by schools and the media to want to participate politically and if parties were required by law to accept anyone who wished to affiliate. With regard to the latter possibility, a half century of American experience with such laws suggests they make it more difficult for party leaders to act as gatekeepers.[23] However, these statutes neither insure that previously unrepresented or underrepresented groups will achieve "proportional representation," nor that they will be made welcome and permitted to share in a meaningful way in the conduct of party affairs.[24]

Assuming that party leaders voluntarily were to make the composition of their local party organizations reasonably representative of the distribution of major social groups in the population, that they were to facilitate the meaningful participation in party affairs of new officials who were members of previously underrepresented groups, and, of course, that significantly larger numbers of such people were to want to participate in party activities because they had been socialized to do so, some democratic theorists would argue that as a result Canadians would feel more politically efficacious, less politically alienated, and much more inclined to give the political system and its principal institutions and leaders good grades.[25] If their arguments are valid, then the level of the public's diffuse support for the political system would be considerably enhanced: a very good thing, one would think, in a country that has been bedevilled throughout its history by problems of national unity.[26] However, the fulfillment of conditions for greater meaningful participation in party activities could have other consequences, not all of which would be readily anticipated or desired.

One possible consequence is that local party units would come under considerable pressure to expand both their organizations and the scope of their activities. New offices, perhaps even whole tiers of new positions, would have to be created for aspiring officials. Party organizations also would come under pressure to generate activities that would give people in these new positions something to do in the periods between as well as during actual election campaigns. Some of the activities, of necessity, would have to be pertinent to the parties' historic mission of filling public offices with their candidates. Public offices currently filled by appointment might have to be converted to elected offices, and local politics down to the school board level might become much more partisan. Other activities, however, could be social, educational, and recreational. If these things were to transpire, Canadian parties might come to resemble the mass parties of Western Europe.[27]

Further, party officials such as those who are the subject of this study might be able to enjoy the kind of organizational careers that are possible in more structured hierarchies. If they could, there also might be less turnover in membership (especially at the lowest echelons), longer periods of continuous service, a higher level of commitment to party goals, and a more effective performance of tasks. However, if the membership of local parties did become relatively stable, the organization might come under further pressure to provide new positions for people seeking entry, and to increase the size of their professional bureaucracies to organize and supervise the activities of people in the substantially expanded local parties. At the very least, it could be anticipated that each local unit would have to adopt the practice of many British constituency parties of employing full-time salaried agents and small office staffs. Each party's provincial and national organization probably would experience a concomitant expansion of their professional staffs since there would be a need to coordinate and direct the expanded activities of their units. Enlargement of party bureaucracies would enable some Insiders and Elites to "turn professional" and to make party politics a vocation. If former amateurs and other party bureaucrats were content with supervising and coordinating the work of party amateurs, no major problems would be likely to arise. If, however, these new professionals wanted to do more than merely supervise and coordinate— for example, if they wanted to control decisions such as the selection of party candidates—then one could anticipate a substantial degree of intra-organizational tension and ultimately conflict between them and the amateur officials wanting to retain traditional prerogatives.[28]

The probability that intra-organizational conflict might occur would be increased if factional fights rooted in generational and ideological differences among new entrants and veteran party officials were to develop. Almost inevitably, these kinds of factional disputes would be exacerbated if and when constituency agents and provincial and national party professionals became embroiled in them.[29] The growth of a professional bureaucracy also might lead to another kind of factional conflict between a party's extraparliamentary and parliamentary wings. In Canada, MPs and MLAs historically have enjoyed a substantial degree of autonomy in their relations with their extraparliamentary organizations but that autonomy could be undermined by centralized, professionally led extraparliamentary organizations bent on exerting tighter control over party affairs.[30]

If factional disputes between: a) legislators and extraparliamentary organization officials; or b) amateur and professional officials; or c) cohorts of amateurs, divided by ideology or age, were to become sufficiently severe, it can be anticipated that new political parties would arise quite naturally and would not have to be "invented." The political importance of the provinces and traditionally strong regional feelings provide both a structural and a psychological basis for the development of new parties. Their appearance at either the provincial or national levels could place additional strain on an already fragile national unity and make it even more difficult for the British model parliamentary system to operate than is currently the case with four national parties.

In short, if democratic societies such as Canada were to become more politicized and party organizations were to expand to accommodate a much larger body of participants, the consequences that could ensue might not be immediately salutary even from the perspective of those opposed to the domination of politics by socioeconomic elites. The problem obviously would be to maximize any benefits of expanded participation in party organizations while avoiding internal dislocation and disruption as well as any additional public disaffection with the larger political system that might be associated with expansion.[31] However, if the experience of the Liberal party with the Action Trudeau Movement[32] following the 1968 Canadian election is a reliable indicator, this is no easy task. Two inferences can be drawn from its aftermath. First, party leaders find it very difficult to reconcile the expectations of new organizational affiliates that they will play meaningful roles in decision making with their own desire to retain control over the decision process. Second, if forced to choose between sharing control of significantly expanded organizations and maintaining their hegemony over current structures, party leaders can be expected to opt for the latter. Because they will, Canadian political parties and their counterparts elsewhere will continue to be dominated by the kinds of people who are the subjects of this book. The tripartite conceptualization of local party organizations as groups of Stalwarts, Insiders, and Elites will continue to be a useful tool for comprehending their reality.

NOTES

1. The percentage of variance explained is comparable to that in other studies using similar techniques. See, for example, Kornberg and Mishler, *Influence in Parliament*, chap. 9; and Samuel C. Patterson, Ronald D. Hedlund and G. Robert Boynton, *Representatives and Represented: Bases of Public Support for the American Legislatures* (New York: Wiley, 1975), chaps. 9 and 10.

2. In our two American research sites women comprised one-third of the Democratic and Republican organizations, largely because of a structural factor, the "50-50" electoral regulations that govern most states, including Washington and Minnesota. These regulations stem from a 1924 decision of both major parties to provide for equal representation of the sexes in their respective national committees. Subsequently they were extended by either state law or party regulations to district, county, and precinct committee levels. See Marguerite J. Fisher, "Women in Political Parties," *The Annals of the American Academy of Political and Social Science*, 251 (1947), p. 90.

3. This problem also arises with respect to the inclusion of lower echelon and marginal members of the organizations. For example, many women may have entered their parties in very low (or marginal) positions—so low, in fact, that the positions were not even identified by higher executives as positions or memberships in the organization. Hence, what might have been a subsequent rise in status for their occupants could not be recorded.

4. The extent to which parties are involved either overtly or covertly in the selection and support of candidates for local elective office varies from one locale to the next. In all provinces, however, parties traditionally have been intimately involved in dispensing political patronage in the form of appointments to the bench and to boards and commissions at all levels of government. On patronage in Canadian politics, see Noel, "Leadership and Clientelism," in Bellamy, *et al.*, eds., *The Provincial Political Systems, passim*. See also Jonathan Manthorpe, *The Power and the Tories* (Toronto: Macmilliam, 1974), chaps. 17, 18; David Smith, *Prairie Liberalism* (Toronto: University of Toronto Press, 1975), chap. 2; S.J.R. Noel, *Politics in Newfoundland* (Toronto: University of Toronto Press, 1971), pp. 283-284; P.J. Fitzpatrick, "New Brunswick: The Politics of Pragmatism" in Martin Robin, ed., *Canadian Provincial Politics* (Scarborough, Ont.: Prentice-Hall, 1971), pp. 119-120; J. Murray Beck, "The Party System in Nova Scotia: Tradition and Conservatism," *Canadian Provincial Politics*, p. 174; Vincent Lemieux, "Quebec: Heaven Is Blue and Hell Is Red," *Canadian Provincial Politics*, pp. 273-274.

5. Kornberg and Mishler, for example, report that in the 28th Parliament 80% or more of the MPs of each party had been active party workers when they were first nominated for public office. Kornberg and Mishler, *Influence in Parliament*, p. 71. Similarly, 88% of the provincial MLAs studied by Clarke, Price, and Krause in 1972 had been party activists prior to election to provincial legislatures, "Backbenchers," in Bellamy, *et al. The Provincial Political Systems*, p. 219. On the decline of "Independents" in the House of Commons see Roman March, *The Myth of Parliament* (Scarborough, Ont.: Prentice-Hall, 1974), pp. 14-21.

6. The objectives of the kind of political socialization citizens of authoritarian and totalitarian political systems undergo are obvious: to make explicit that the political institutions and processes of the state and the party (or, in rare instances, parties) are legitimate in their origins and highly efficacious and beneficent in their operation.

7. Epstein, *Political Parties in Western Democracies*, pp. 85-92, 111-121, 130-187.

8. Jon H. Pammett and Michael S. Whittington, "Introduction: Political Culture and Political Socialization," in Pammett and Whittington, eds., *Foundations of Political Culture*, p. 23. Additional studies of the impact of formal education on political socialization in Canada are contained in Elia Zureik and Robert Pike, eds., *Socialization and Values in Canadian Society*, 2 Volumes (Toronto: McCelland and Stewart, 1975).

9. Kenneth Langton and Kent Jennings, "Political Socialization and the High School Civics Curriculum in the United States," *American Political Science Review*, 63 (1969): 866.

10. Pammett and Whittington, *Foundations of Political Culture*, p. 26. See also A.B. Hodgetts, *What Culture? What Heritage?* (Toronto: Ontario Institute for Studies in Education, 1968).

11. This lack of emphasis on Canadian government and politics in school curricula is underlined in the report by the Commission on Canadian Studies: "Most students graduating from high school today lack basic knowledge about Canadian political matters. Moreover, unless they go on to major in political studies at a university, their knowledge of political institutions and public affairs of this country [Canada] will not likely have expanded appreciably by the time they complete an undergraduate degree." T.H.B. Symons, *To Know Ourselves: The Report of the Commission on Canadian Studies* (Ottawa: Association of Universities and Colleges of Canada, 1975), p. 65.

12. It could be argued that even if parties played only a passive role in the recruitment of new workers, socioeconomic forces, political socialization and societal norms regarding the inappropriateness of political activity probably would interact to yield cadres of party officials similar to those studied here. That parties *do* actively "pick and choose" new officials, however, is abundantly clear in the data presented in Chapters 3 and 4.

13. For a review of the intellectual and institutional history of parties see Giovanni Sartori, *Parties and Party Systems* (London: Cambridge University Press, 1976), chaps. 1 and 2. See also Austin Ranney and Willmoore Kendall, *Democracy and the American Party System*, chaps. 5 and 6; Joseph LaPalombara and Myron Weiner, "The Origin and Development of Political Parties," in LaPalombara and Weiner, eds., *Political Parties and Political Development* (Princeton: Princeton University Press, 1966), pp. 3-42.

14. "*Of* Parties," in J.P. Kenyon, ed., *Halifax: Complete Works* (Harmondsworth, Middlesex: Penguin Books Ltd., 1969), p. 209.

15. For data on Western political parties generally see Epstein, *Political Parties in Western Democracies*, chaps. 7 and 8, pp. 167-232, and Putnam, *The Comparative Study of Political Elites*, chap. 3. Data contrasting the occupations of Communist, Socialist, and other MPs in France are presented in Mattei Dogan, "Political Ascent in a Class Society: French Deputies, 1870-1958," in Dwaine Marvick, ed., *Political Decision-Makers*, p. 67. The increasing tendency for MPs in the British Labour Party to be drawn from the ranks of the middle class is reported in Richard Rose, *The Problem of Party Government*, (Harmondsworth, Middlesex: Penguin, 1976), pp. 50-54. On Canada see Allan Kornberg and Hal H. Winsborough, "The Recruitment of Canadian Members of Parliament"; Kornberg, *et al.*, "Toward a Model of Parliamentary Recruitment in Canada," in Kornberg, ed., *Legislatures in Comparative Perspective*, pp. 250-281.

16. That there is no local-provincial-federal level political career line in Canada is supported by research on the candidate recruitment process. Surich and Williams argue that there are separate federal and provincial recruitment streams. See Joachim Surich and Robert J. Williams, "Some Characteristics of Candidates in the 1972 Canadian Federal Election," paper delivered at the Annual Meeting of the Canadian Political Science Association, Toronto, June 1974. For additional data on this point see March, *The Myth of Parliament*, p. 31.

17. Lesser forms of patronage such as jobs with provincial highway repair crews and licensing favoritism are still widely utilized as material incentives, particularly in the Atlantic provinces. Even here, however, such traditional types of minor patronage appear to be in decline. See S.J.R. Noel, "Leadership and Clientelism," p. 209.

18. Schlesinger, "Political Party Organization," in March, *Handbook of Organizations*, p. 768.

19. See, for example, Eldersveld, *Political Parties*, p. 167.

20. As noted in Chapter 7, the direction of causality in these relationships is not always clear. In some instances levels of commitment to party work may be a function of perceptions of the role requirements of holding party office. Even so, it is reasonable to assume that a high level of commitment enhances one's political career prospects.

21. Mildred Schwartz, "The Political Outlook of Canadian Voters in the November, 1965 Election," unpublished paper delivered at the Annual Meeting of the Canadian Political Science Association, June 1967. See also Mildred Schwartz, *Politics and Territory* (Montreal: McGill-Queen's University Press, 1974), pp. 196-214; and Richard Simeon and David J. Elkins, "Regional Political Cultures in Canada," 404-412.

22. Clarke, *et al.*, *Political Choice in Canada*, chap. 1. Emphasis added.

23. Frank J. Sorauf, *Party Politics in America*, 3rd ed. (Boston: Little, Brown, 1976), pp. 229-233.

24. Of course, parties themselves set rules regarding who shall be eligible to play a role in the candidate selection process. Perhaps the most noteworthy recent example of substantial rule changes of this type are the reforms instituted by the McGovern-Fraser commission in the Democratic party's representational formula for its 1972 presidential nominating convention. See William Cavala, "Changing the Rules Changes the Game: Party Reform and the 1972 California Delegation to the Democratic National Convention," *American Political Science Review*, 68 (1974): 27-42; and Joseph H. Boyett, "Background Characteristics of Delegates to the 1972 Convention: A Summary Report of Findings from a National Sample," *Western Political Quarterly*, 27 (1974): 469-478.

25. For a convenient summary of these themes in the participatory democracy literature see Carole Pateman, *Participation and Democratic Theory* (London: Cambridge University Press, 1970), chap. 2; and Peter Bachrach, *The Theory of Democratic Elitism: A Critique* (Boston: Little, Brown, 1967), *passim*.

26. Preliminary evidence showing a positive relationship between political participation and regime support is contained in Allan Kornberg, Harold D. Clarke, and Lawrence LeDuc, "Some Correlates of Regime Support in Canada," *British Journal of Political Science*, 8 (1978): 199-216.

27. Maurice Duverger, *Political Parties*, pp. 106-108.

28. Regarding the conflict between "amateurs" and "professionals" in party organizations in the United States see Wilson, *The Amateur Democrat*, chap. 10. On intraparty conflict in Great Britain see Richard Rose, "The Political Ideas of English

Party Activists," *American Political Science Review*, 56 (1962): 360-371, and "Parties, Factions and Tendencies in Britain," *Political Studies*, 12 (1964): 33-46; and Allan Kornberg and Robert C. Frasure, "Policy Differences in British Parliamentary Parties," *American Political Science Review*, 65 (1971): 693-703. Rose points out that intraparty conflict does not necessarily pit extraparliamentary activists against parliamentary leaders, but rather that conflicts can divide entire party organizations vertically, "Political Ideas," p. 371. In Canada the most salient recent example of intraparty conflict has concerned the activities of the "Waffle" group within the NDP. In the late 1960s and early 1970s the Waffle attempted simultaneously to move the NDP in a more socialist direction and to espouse a strongly anti-American form of Canadian nationalism. See William Christian and Colin Campbell, *Political Parties and Ideologies in Canada*, pp. 150-155. Walter Young argues that party recruitment conflicts within the NDP's predecessor, the CCF, are best explained in terms of the conflict between an ideological movement and an electorally-oriented party. See Young, *The Anatomy of a Party, passim*. See also Leo Zakuta, *A Protest Movement Becalmed* (Toronto: University of Toronto Press, 1964). On intraparty conflict within the Social Credit party see Stein, *The Dynamics of Right-Wing Protest*, chaps. 4-9.

29. On the tendency of constituency agents in British parties to become involved in factional disputes and for a review of other problems with the use of party agents see Allan Kornberg and Robert C. Frasure, "Constituency Agents and British Party Politics," *The British Journal of Political Science* 5 (1975): 459-476.

30. Roberto Michels promulgated his famous iron law of oligarchy as a consequence of his observation of and personal involvement in a political party undergoing bureaucratization. See *Political Parties, passim*.

31. The proposition that there is an inverse relationship between the extent of citizen participation in political life and regime stability has been a major issue in recent disputes over the normative adequacy of the "empirical democratic theory" literature. A representative selection of the most important arguments in this debate is summarized in Henry S. Kariel, ed., *Frontiers of Democratic Theory* (New York: Random House, 1970).

32. For a study of members of the Action-Trudeau movement see Jon H. Pammett, "Adolescent Political Activity as a Learning Experience: The Action-Trudeau Campaign of 1968," in Pammett and Whittington, eds., *Foundations of Political Culture*, pp. 160-194. The Action-Trudeau movement which the Liberals established to channel the enthusiasm of young Canadians for Mr. Trudeau's candidacy during the 1968 election campaign disbanded quickly after the election. Calls for participatory democracy sounded by the Liberals during the campaign notwithstanding, it became obvious to would-be participants in the Liberal party that its leadership had no desire to open party decision-making processes. Although data on the point are unavailable, impressionistically it seems that many of the younger people who were mobilized to support the Liberals in 1968 and who tried to remain active in the party after the election were disillusioned by the fact that party leaders appeared no more receptive to their attempts to influence the direction of party policy than in the pre-Trudeau era.

Index

AP